Rebound 2003

P9-ARX-144

1986

University of St. Francis
GEN 780.903 M922
Moulton, Carroll.
Music in time :

3 0301 00083418 0

MUSIC IN TIME:
A SURVEY OF WESTERN MUSIC

ISBN 0-89113-427-1

Copyright©1983, Films for the Humanities, Inc.

CARROLL MOULTON

Music in Time:

A Survey of Western Music

LIBRARY
College of St. Francis
JOLIET, ILL.

FFH PUBLICATIONS • PRINCETON, NEW JERSEY

780.903
M922

This book has been conceived as a supporting text for the superb video series, *James Galway: Music in Time*.

During the Cultural Revolution, Chinese musicians who were prohibited from practicing and even from hearing music maintained their art by replaying music in their memories, by fingering their imagined instruments inside the pockets of their Mao jackets. This is perhaps the most graphic illustration that music is not something that can always be conjured up, but a gift.

Music is to be heard, first of all. And to be heard fully, it has to be understood. The objective of the video series is to present the best possible performances of the landmarks in the history of Western music, and to film them in the places to which they belong—to show the medieval monasteries in which Gregorian chant flourished, the instruments of the early Renaissance, the piano in Chopin's house, the landscapes and cityscapes from which composers have drawn their inspiration.

But a true appreciation of music rests on understanding, not just perceiving. And that is the objective of this book: to provide the background information, the analysis of form, the comparisons, and the vocabulary to enable students to articulate what they sense.

The chapters follow the videocassettes exactly with the exception of Chapter 1, which has been conceived as an Introduction to provide the overview the editors believe a necessary prerequisite to beginning a survey of music.

119,018

Table of Contents

Chapter 1

Introduction

Introduction

What *is* music?

It is easy to assert that "everybody knows what music is," but that simply acknowledges the fact that music is easier to recognize than to define. During this course you will undoubtedly experience varieties of music which you have never heard before—you may even be reluctant to admit that some of them *are* music. We all know that music speaks differently to different people. The music that is natural to one age or culture often seems strange to another. But the need for music in some form seems to be an innate human characteristic.

From the earliest times, no civilization seems to have been without music in some form. Some cultures failed to develop pictorial art, and many have been without written language; but music, the universal form of communication, can be documented in virtually every society. Man has always had a need for music, whether it be the rhythmical beating of drums, the amusement of blowing through a hollow reed by the river, the summons of the war trumpet, or the formal music of the concert hall. In many cultures, such as that of ancient Greece, music was integrally related to singing and dancing; this seems natural, since man could explore melody through the instrument of his own voice, and he could experiment with rhythm through the movements of his body. Whether in primitive or in modern times, music has served some of mankind's basic needs: music calls dogs and hunters to the hunt, expresses the lover's thoughts, glorifies more than words alone and unites a congregation in worship, rouses to war, magnifies pomp and celebration. Across time and national boundaries, without regard to social class or political ideology, music speaks directly to the heart and to the emotions; it is truly the universal language.

What constitutes music, as opposed to mere sound? What are the principal instruments for making music? And what are the characteristics of the leading styles in the history of Western music, in which the major musical forms have developed? Before we begin the more detailed discussion of music in time, we will attempt to answer these questions with a preliminary survey of the elements of music.

Like a language, music functions on at least two levels: an immediate surface level, and a deeper structural one. Language has a surface meaning which is controlled by a deeper structural grammar. In the same way, music has a surface *texture* which is controlled by a deeper structural *form*.

In everyday speech, we are usually concerned mostly with the surface meaning of language; hence, we are often quite careless about grammatical structure. In highly formal speech—poetry, for example—the grammatical structure is more important; it is a well-known fact that shades of meaning are often conveyed by the interplay of surface and structure in a poem. Music is like this sort of language: we are interested in the surface texture to be sure, but music is most meaningful when we understand the relationship between the surface texture and the structure.

Consider another analogy: architecture is sometimes spoken of as "frozen music". That is, architecture achieves in space what music achieves in time. The brick wall on the front of a building has a very specific local texture which depends on the precise manner in which the individual bricks are laid. At the same time, the wall has a more important function in the overall structure of the building. We may be able to see and understand this function only if we stand far enough away from the wall so that we can see the whole building at once. It is also possible that, if we stand so far away, we may no longer be able to see clearly the texture formed by the individual bricks. True appreciation of the relationship between the pattern of bricks forming the texture and the function of the wall itself may depend on our memory—that is, we may be required to remember the pattern of the bricks when we stand far enough away to see the whole building; we may be required to remember the whole building when we are close enough to see the pattern of the bricks. This is precisely how music works.

Often we experience the particular texture of a passage of music in a certain way. Our perception of it depends on the precise manner in which the composer has written the individual notes (to continue our analogy to bricks). We can also learn to stand far enough away from the immediate musical experience so that we can see something of the structure which the notes reveal. This is what becoming an educated listener is all about.

So the two most basic elements of music are *texture* and *form*—the first is small-scale and local, the latter is larger and universal.

Texture is always spoken of in qualitative terms. We speak of a "thick" or a "thin" texture; a "bright" or a "dark" texture. It makes no sense to speak of "a lot" or "only a little" texture: what we hear is 100% of what there is to be heard. There are several common kinds of musical textures which have their own names (and a great many uncommon ones for which you are free to invent your own descriptive terms). We shall consider three of the most important.

1. **Monophonic Texture.** If you sing a tune by yourself, that's monophonic texture. The word comes from two Greek roots: *mono*, meaning "one", and *phonos*, meaning "sound". One sound—at a time, that is. If you get a group of your friends together and you all sing the same tune together, that's still monophonic texture (if everybody sings it correctly!) because there is only one musical line, though it is shared by many different performers. We call such a single musical line a *melody*. Nowadays, this kind of texture is quite rare in "art music", although in the Middle Ages it was common.

2. **Homophonic Texture.** Suppose you have a friend who plays the guitar. If you sing a tune and your friend accompanies you with chords on the guitar, that is called *homophonic* texture. Again the derivation is from the Greek: *homo*, meaning "the same"; and our old friend *phonos*, "sound". So homophonic means "the same sound". Now you may argue that a voice and a guitar are not "the same", and you are right. But the word works the same way as "homogenized milk": there, two different elements (milk and cream) have been blended together in such a way that they cannot be separated. So it is with homophonic texture: two different elements (in our example, voice and guitar) have been blended together in such a way that they cannot be separated musically; the result is perceived as a single musical idea.

3. **Polyphonic Texture.** There is a third common kind of musical texture which is a little bit like both of the other two. If you sing a tune by yourself while a friend sings another tune, that is called *polyphonic* texture. Again, Greek origin: *poly* means "many"; and *phonos* again. More than one sound at a time, in the sense of more than one musical line at a time. Two or more melodies combined. These melodies are usually related in some way (though they do not have to be). You can experience the pleasures of polyphonic texture if you sing *Row, Row, Row Your Boat* at exactly the same time (and

starting on the same note) that a friend sings *Frère Jacques*. The two melodies are independent of each other, yet they seem to "go together". The reason is *harmony*.

It is very rare for music to employ only one kind of texture for very long and there are infinite varieties of each different kind. Here is an example: if your guitar-playing friend simply strums chords while you sing a tune, that is a very unsophisticated kind of homophonic texture. If that friend "picks" the notes of the same chords one at a time, that is a lot more interesting. The texture is still basically homophonic, but the better a "picker" your friend is, the more interesting the accompaniment will be. As it becomes more interesting, it begins to take on the quality of another melodic part (or perhaps several) and the texture shifts towards polyphonic. There are no clear cut lines, and you learn to identify textures only through experience.

Before we go on to discuss form, we must pick up three other terms. Two of them we have already used: *melody*, *harmony*, and *rhythm*.

Rhythm is the most basic of all musical materials. Again, its derivation is from the Greek—*rhythmos* means "an ordered pattern". Unlike melody and harmony, rhythm exists independently of music: there is rhythm in the seasons and in the tides, in our breathing and heartbeat, in our running and walking. Rhythm is the term used to describe the way in which music moves through time, and in its most general sense it does not have any particular implications. The speed at which a piece of music moves is called the *tempo* (from Italian, "time"), and the tempo can be quick or slow. It is simple to change the tempo without changing the rhythm. Example: the "clip-clop" of a horse's hooves when the horse is walking has the same rhythm as the "clip-clop" of the horse's hooves when it's trotting, but the tempo is slower. When the horse gallops, however, the "Ba-da-DUM" is a different rhythm (and a different tempo).

There are many different types of rhythm. Just as certain kinds of melody are more appropriate for joyful or sad occasions, for war or for love, or for various emotions, we have long connected different sorts of rhythms with various musical purposes and occasions. Marches have a 4-beat rhythm in order to encourage marchers to use both feet regularly and at the proper speed; some dances are solemn, others lilting or bouncing. A rhythm natural to the dance may be impossible for marching, and unsuitable for a lament for the dead.

In the standard notation of music, rhythm is expressed in measures or bars; they measure the time between stresses. Such divisions are shown by bar lines. (A bar is equal to one measure.) Just as there are stresses or accents within words and within sentences, so there are stresses in music; the stresses in music are like the stresses in poetry, recurring on a regular basis. Within each musical measure, there is a fixed number of beats; the most common numbers are two, three, four, and six. In every measure, we expect that the first beat will carry the major emphasis, or accent. The regular return of the accent at the beginning of every measure results in musical meter. Some patterns of rhythm, especially those with four and six beats to the measure, include a subsidiary accent; the major emphasis still falls on the first beat, but it is followed by a minor accent on one of the following beats. If a composer chooses to alter this pattern for a special effect, by placing an accent on an unexpected beat of the measure, we speak of syncopated rhythm.

Rhythmical patterns with two, three, and four beats to the measure are the most common of all. For example, let us assume a series of four notes, each with the time value of a quarter-note. If only two of these notes are used in each measure, we have a bar in two-four time (or duple meter), as in many songs, marches, and lullabies (ONE-two, ONE-two, etc.). If three notes are used for each measure, we have a pattern in three-four time (or triple meter). This is the meter used by many dances, including the waltz (ONE-two-three, ONE-two-three). Notice that in each case there is normally only one accent per measure; the emphasis falls on the first beat.

At the introduction of a composition or a section with a different rhythm, the composer indicates the time signature: at the bottom is the kind of note which will be the unit of measurement (usually half, quarter, or eight-notes), and at the top, the number of such notes which will constitute one measure. If the unit is the quarter-note and four quarter-notes are used, we have the pattern of 4/4 time (or quadruple meter): ONE-two-three-four. In this case, an auxiliary accent normally falls on the third note (much lighter than the accent on ONE, but still perceptible). 4/4 time often produces a spacious, dignified effect, as in *The Battle Hymn of the Republic*.

One more rhythmical pattern should be mentioned: 6/8 time. The lilting effect of this rhythm results because the major accent (which falls on the first note of each measure) is followed by an auxiliary accent on the fourth. (ONE-two-three-foúr-five-six.)

To determine the meter of a piece of music to which you are listening, count with the rhythm of the musical beat. Try it with *America*; see if you can count out a beat of four:

1. MY	2. coun	3. try	4. 'tis
1. OF	2. thee	3. I	4. sing…

It will not work. If you try marching to it—you can always march to a 4/4 beat—you will be hopping from foot to foot. Now try a beat of three:

1. MY	2. coun	3. try
1. 'TIS	2. of	3. thee
1. SWEET	2. land	3. of

and so on. (One beat may consist of one or of many notes.) You can always tell whether the rhythm is three or four, although it is sometimes difficult to distinguish between 4/4 and 6/8 time (you may confuse three eighth-notes for one beat of a quarter note); and in contemporary music, with very complicated and frequently changing time signatures, this simple counting system does not work.

By themselves, rhythm and meter do not indicate how slowly or how rapidly a piece of music moves through time (i.e. the speed at which the beats are to be felt). This rate is set by the *tempo* (the Italian word for "time"). Just as melodies and rhythms suggest various occasions and emotions in everyday life, we instinctively link the tempo of music to clusters of human feelings: gaiety, surprise, melancholy, boldness, etc. Musical tempo (the plural is tempi) is customarily marked by the composer on the score, with a set of Italian terms that derive from the eighteenth and nineteenth centuries. Some of the principal terms in use are:

largo	very slow
adagio	slow
andante	fairly slow, at a walking pace
moderato	moderate
allegro	brisk, happy, cheerful
presto	rapid
prestissimo	as fast as possible

All these terms are subjective: after all, what one person thinks of as allegro may be another person's andante. In order to standardize these directions, a mechanical device called the metronome was invented about 1700. The metronome measures, by means of a pendulum, an adjustable number of beats every minute. Various ranges of beats have been agreed upon for the tempi listed above.

Of course, a musical composition can include a number of different tempi. And sometimes, even within the same tempo, a composer can achieve special effects by speeding up or slowing down the rate of the music. Such effects, also marked in scores, are signified by Italian terms: *accelerando* (getting faster) and *ritardando* (or ritard: getting slower). For example, the finale of Beethoven's Symphony No. 9 (*Choral*) displays a dizzying *accelerando*: the orchestra progresses from *allegro* to *prestissimo* after the climax of the choral *Hymn to Joy*.

Melody derives from the Greek work *melos* (meaning "song"); a "tune" is a melody. A melody is a series of sounds that we perceive as a single, unified musical idea; these ideas combine pitch and rhythm. Melodies in songs are generally obvious: they are fashioned to correspond with the most important phrases of the sung text. The principal melody of a song normally introduces the entire composition, as in the patriotic songs *America* and *The Star Spangled Banner*. In orchestral pieces, the principal melody (sometimes called the primary theme) may or may not stand first. But it is always recognizable because of its unusual coherence and "singing" character.

Melodies may be slow or fast, relatively long or relatively short. The famous four-note theme which begins Beethoven's Symphony No. 5 is an example of a very brief melody; this theme recurs again and again in each of the symphony's four movements, interwoven with a series of remarkably ingenious variations, yet, in the hands of such a master as Beethoven, we feel pleasure and comfort each time at meeting an old friend. On the other hand, some of the later nineteenth-century composers, such as Johannes Brahms and Antonín Dvořák, fashioned melodies which are sustained like great arcs; sometimes, they are even interrupted, only to coalesce later in the work.

The number of *possible* melodies is limited only by the number of notes that the human voice can sing or a particular instrument can play; the number of *musically desirable* or artistically perceived or technically performable melodies is limited by the tastes of a particular period—in our own, we have a greater tolerance than earlier ages for experimentation and a greater willingness to accept irregular, even cacophonous passages as melody. But whether the melody is short or long, sweet or jarring, whether it moves upward or downward on the scale, is soft or loud, smooth (*legato*) or choppy (*staccato*), whether it moves through adjacent notes on the scale or with wide or narrow skips, whether it occupies a wide or relatively narrow range in pitch—whatever the variations, there is but one requirement for melody: that the listener perceive the notes as a single, coherent statement.

To unify the different portions of a melody, a composer normally constructs it in segments, which are called phrases. Each phrase ends in a cadence (from the Latin *cadere*, "to fall"). At a cadence, the listener experiences a brief "falling" sensation, a signal that a major portion of the melody has been completed. In songs, such cadences correspond to the natural divisions of the text into syntactical units; they are also a help to the singer, who can pause to take a breath. If the cadence is incomplete, only a portion of the melody is over; if it is complete, the entire melody is finished. Take, for example, the first four lines of the *Star Spangled Banner*:

Oh, say can you see
By the dawn's early light,
What so proudly we hailed
At the twilight's last gleaming?

At the word "light" there is an incomplete cadence; a singer pauses to take a breath (corresponding to the pause at the comma in the text). At the word "gleaming", as the melody returns to the tonic note of the key (see under harmony, below), there is a complete cadence. This cadence represents a long point of musical stability, preceding the next portion of the song, which repeats the same melody.

A good melody has always played a leading part in making music popular. For example, the heartfelt melodies of the Romantic composers of the nineteenth century—Franz Schubert, Giuseppe Verdi, and Peter Ilyich Tchaikovsky—sing to us so expressively that it is not surprising that these composers' works are staples of today's repertory. What may not be so obvious is that humble melodies (from folk songs and dances, children's songs, and work songs) have found their way into the works of the greatest composers since virtually the start of Western music: Bach, Mozart, Haydn, and Beethoven are only a few of the composers who made rich use of native melodic materials. Most of these melodies cannot now be credited to their original composers. But the genius of the musicians who assimilated them in operas, chorales, symphonies, and quartets has made them part of our musical heritage.

The third basic element of music, in addition to melody and rhythm, is **harmony** (from Greek *harmonia*, or "fitting together"). Whenever two or more different musical tones are sounded simultaneously, we have a form of harmony. Whereas melody and rhythm, in some form, can be traced comparatively far back in time, what we usually think of as harmony in music—based on the chords of our major and minor scales—is relatively modern. Chordal harmony only begins in the music of the Renaissance, and becomes firmly established in the seventeenth century. Of course, harmonies of other types existed before this. But just as we are accustomed to certain shapes of melody and to certain types of rhythm in music, we have come to expect certain patterns in the simultaneous sounding of notes. Some of these patterns are inherently satisfying to our ears: they are based on chords which resolve the elements of other chords, which have left us with a feeling of suspension, or irresolution. Such resolving harmonies (which often occur at cadences) are called consonant: they relax tension. Other harmonies create tension, because they suggest clash, irresolution, or surprise; these are called dissonant harmonies. The interplay of consonance and dissonance is a basic feature of musical harmony.

Harmony functions in many pieces to support the melody. Thus, if a song is performed to instrumental accompaniment, the singer's part normally carries the melody. The instrument may play exactly the same notes, or it may play different combinations of notes and chords which pleasingly accompany the principal tune. In the latter case, we speak of harmony. Likewise, in a purely instrumental piece, as on the piano, the right hand may play the melody and the left hand supply the accompanying harmony. Or in orchestral composition for many instruments, one group of players (for example the violinists) may carry the melody; the other instruments provide harmonic accompaniment.

Harmony has varied significantly in the successive ages of Western music. In the earliest music we have, the Gregorian chant of medieval monks, there was no harmony: only the voices of the choir, chanting in unison the specified tunes for liturgical services. Such chant is an example of monophonic texture. In the late twelfth cen-

18

tury, monophonic chant gradually began to be supplemented by polyphony. Freely rhythmical parts were added in the upper register, to be sung simultaneously with the chant. But polyphonic writing, which continued through the Renaissance, was still not harmony, properly speaking: the different parts of polyphony were thought of, and heard as, several horizontal lines, rather than as vertical, simultaneously sounded chords. And the medieval system of modes [see Chapter 2] was not equivalent to our system of scales and keys, since major and minor keys had not yet clearly emerged.

The clear definition of major and minor, and the vertical conception of simultaneously sounded tones, dominate music from about 1600 to 1900; this is the traditional harmonic system which we will summarize below. But it is important to recognize that this system has been only one of many in the history of music. Numerous composers of the twentieth century, for example, have abandoned the traditional "rules" of harmony, and experimented with new scales and chords, in their efforts to enlarge the fundamental elements of music.

In traditional harmony, scales and chords combine to form the major and minor keys. The major scale is formed by a series of eight tones, beginning on the first (or "tonic") note of the key. These tones ascend mostly in whole-tone steps, with half-tones (or semitones) between the third and fourth steps, and again between the seventh and eighth. In the minor scale, there are semitones between the second and third steps, the fifth and sixth steps, and the seventh and eighth. Thus the key of C major is defined by this scale:

(The top note C repeats the first note, at the interval defined as an octave.) C minor is represented thus:

The intervals of the third and the fifth appear in chords based on the tonic note of each key. The basic C major chord (in so-called "root position") is thus the notes C, E, and G sounded together. The corresponding chord for C minor is C, E-flat, and G. When the scale begins on notes other than C, the same principles for major and minor are harmonically rotated. Thus, in the key of D Major, in order for the scale to ascend in the proper sequence of whole tones and semitones, two "sharped" (or raised) notes are necessary: F-sharp and C-sharp.

Keys are related to one another in two ways. The intervals of the fourth and the fifth are especially important in harmony. The ancient Greek philosopher Pythagoras, in the sixth century B.C., discovered that their naturally pleasing sounds accorded with fundamental ratios in mathematics [see Chapter 2]. In each key, the first note of the scale is called the tonic. The fifth note is termed the dominant, and the fourth is the sub-dominant (the tone "below the dominant"). Thus, in the key of C Major, the dominant is G and the sub-dominant is F. Chords built on the dominant and the sub-dominant are primary chords in the progression of harmonies in any particular key. If a piece should employ modulation between keys (a shift from one basic key to another), such modulation is often to the dominant or sub-dominant. Thus, a Mozart minuet (short dance) may start in D Major, modulate to the dominant key of A Major in the middle section, and revert at the end to the tonic key of D Major.

In addition, keys are related to one another by virtue of the number of sharps or flats they require (or their "key signatures"). For example, both D Major and B Minor have key signatures with two sharps; we therefore speak of B Minor as the "relative minor" of D Major. Such relationships (which may be extended to include the related majors or minors of the dominant and sub-dominant) are also a prominent feature of modulation.

In diatonic harmony (harmony "through the tones"), chordal progressions involve only the tones of the particular key in which the piece is written. The principal cadences of the work often employ chords of the tonic, dominant, and sub-dominant, with a reversion to the tonic in the final cadence. This type of harmony is typical of the music of the Baroque, Classical, and Romantic periods.

Because of the importance of diatonic harmony in the development of Western music, we are often tempted to make the mistaken assumption that it is the only possible harmony. However, since the late nineteenth century, the most significant European and American composers have experimented with quite different types of harmony, based on modifications of the major and minor scales, and also on radically different scale systems. Here we can mention only a few of the principal departures. The chromatic scale consists of all twelve tones of an octave, in an ascending or descending order of semitone steps. Such notes were occasionally used, of course, by traditional composers for special harmonic effects (hence, the term "chromaticism", which literally refers to the notes of the diatonic scale being "colored" by extra tones). Another variation from diatonic harmony is based on the whole-tone scale, which consists entirely of whole tones (six notes). Finally, an extremely common scale in Oriental music is the five-tone (or pentatonic) scale, which has been assimilated by some modern Western composers. Rising from C, the pentatonic scale would run:

Some modern composers have abandoned the principle of tonality altogether. In the works of Arnold Schoenberg and his followers [see Chapter 14], we speak of atonality: no fixed key dominates the music. In Schoenberg's music, all twelve notes of the chromatic scale are treated as equally important through the regular, systematic employment of each note. Thus, traditional diatonic harmony, which emerged in Western music after the Renaissance, held sway for roughly three centuries. In contemporary music, the principles of traditional harmony are seldom strictly observed. Indeed, it is arguable that the dissolution of harmonic "rules" has been underway for over a century. Some historians of music would date the origins of this tendency to Richard Wagner's opera, *Tristan und Isolde*, first performed in 1865.

Now we have some of the concepts required to consider musical *form*. Let us continue the architectural analogy. What is a house? It can be anything from a mud hut to the most radically new geodesic house. Yet, all human dwellings have certain features in common, though those features may actually be built out of different materials, finished in different ways, or painted different colors. So it is with musical compositions: though they come in an enormous number of different varieties and though each individual piece has its own surface, all music shares a number of common features.

The most basic element of musical structure is *contrast*—change. A musical work is made up of a number of sound events, each of which is different in some way from the ones which preceded it. Sometimes the differences are very large: a composer may write a passage for full orchestra playing very loudly immediately after a very soft passage for a single solo violin. Sometimes the differences are very subtle: a composer may change only a single note of a melody in such a way that it gives the whole melody an entirely new aspect. Even if a composer does "exactly the same thing" twice, the second "thing" is different because the first has preceded it. Change—the sequential change of sound events in time—is the very substance of music.

The elements of rhythm, melody and harmony are the materials which a composer uses to create a larger structure. They are the "bricks" which he uses to build first a wall, then a whole building in sound.

There are many different levels of musical structure. Individual pitches are put together in conjunction with rhythmic elements to create a motive—the smallest coherent unit of musical thought. A motive (the classic example is the first four notes of Beethoven's Fifth Symphony) is, in some ways, the musical equivalent of a word. Like a word, it is made out of smaller component parts (notes = letters), and like words, motives are the basic building blocks of larger structures. Motives are put together to form phrases, phrases are put together to form periods or sections. The language analogy is applicable here, too: words form clauses, clauses form sentences. In fact, the name of the punctuation mark "period" has precisely the same meaning as a musical period: it marks the end of a complete unit of thought.

Form is the term which is used to denote the largest level of musical structure. We say that individual pieces or movements have "such-and-such" sort of form. What we mean is that there are a number of typical patterns of musical structure that occur over and over again. In order to see those patterns (or more accurately, to hear them) it is necessary to identify musical events (so that we can recognize them), to label them (so that we can keep track of them), and to be on the lookout for them (so that we can recognize the musical form which they reveal). As we observed above, this requires training the memory in such a way that we can keep track of both the small-scale events and the larger-scale ones—the bricks and the wall, if you prefer.

This process is made easier by understanding precisely what a composer does. First, let us consider the derivation of the word itself. It comes from two Latin words, *con*, meaning "with" in the sense of "together with"; *ponere*, meaning "to place". A composer is someone who "puts together" elements to create a larger piece of music. If we understand that the composer's task consists of creating relatively small amounts of material and then finding ways to combine that material to create a unified whole, our task of "understanding" what he has done is much simpler. In a sense, the task of the listener is to "de-compose" the music—to take it apart mentally and understand what makes it work.

An aside: sometimes people feel disturbed by this idea. They prefer to "just listen to" the music; to let it touch their emotions without making demands on their intellect. This is, of course, a perfectly acceptable way to listen to music. We can like the looks of a fine building without knowing anything about the way it is constructed. Yet, full enjoyment seems to depend on a combination of these two ways of listening—many people discover that their emotional response to music is actually heightened by their intellectual understanding.

Suppose a composer has created a musical idea—a whole phrase, let us say. It is made up of the three elements we have already discussed: melody, rhythm, and harmony. This is one point at which the concept "inspiration" is relevant: nobody knows just where such musical ideas come from. But now the composer is faced with a somewhat different task. He must take that idea and make it into an entire piece of music. Here the concept of "craftsmanship" is relevant: from his experience, the composer must judge how best to deal with his "inspired idea". Basically, he has three choices: he can repeat the idea exactly; he can modify it to a greater or lesser degree; or he can create a wholly new idea. Here is where judgment comes in. If a composer repeats the same idea too many times without change—or without enough change—the music becomes boring to the listener. If, on the other hand, he write a continual series of new ideas each of which has no relation to the preceding ones, the music becomes confusing to the listener. Some change is always necesary; some continuity is equally essential.

Musical Instruments

The instruments of the modern symphony orchestra have remained basically the same for nearly two hundred years; their ancestors, in one form or another, have been recognizable since the Renaissance. We may divide most of the instruments into four families: strings, woodwinds, brass, and percussion. Three instruments (piano, organ, and harp) have special characteristics; we will discuss them at the end of this section.

The **string instruments** of today's orchestra include the violin, the viola, the violoncello (usually simply called "cello"), and the double bass. These four instruments constitute a definite family—similar, although not directly related, to the Renaissance instruments called viols. Each has four strings (the double bass occasionally has five); the strings of each instrument are made to vibrate by a bow which is drawn across them. The player handles the bow in the right hand, and with the left hand manipulates the finger-board, thus altering the length of each string which is left free to vibrate. The pitch is thus controlled: longer lengths produce lower pitches, and shorter lengths higher ones. The range of each instrument averages three octaves. The violin possesses the highest range of pitch, and the double bass the lowest.

The violin is, of course, the most famous solo instrument of this family. It was originally perfected by Andrea Amati (c.1520–1611), who lived and worked in the Italian city of Cremona, near Venice. From Amati, there was a direct line of influence in the making of violins to the two most celebrated members of the "Cremona school": Antonio Stradivari (1644–1737) and Giuseppe Antonio Guarneri (1687–1745). Our earliest printed music for violins is a set of French dances, published in 1581. The sweetly singing tone of the instrument and its range in the upper register have made it a favorite of composers ever since. Perhaps the most famous violin virtuoso (or star performer) of all time was Niccolò Paganini (1782–1840), who did more than anyone to pioneer new styles in bowing and effects of staccato and pizzicato (sharp plucking of the strings).

The **woodwind** family includes eight instruments in the typical symphony orchestra: piccolo, flute, oboe, English horn, clarinet, bass clarinet, bassoon, and contrabassoon (or double bassoon). These are listed in the descending order of their range: the piccolo produces the highest tones, the contrabassoon the lowest. The woodwinds all have a range of between two-and-a-half and three-and-a-half octaves. They all depend on the principle of the ancient woodpipe: a column of air is set into vibration by the player, and the vibrations are altered by means of various holes or stops (operated by keys on modern instruments), so that the pitch may be changed.

The piccolo and the flute are both side-blown instruments: they are held horizontally and the air column is set into vibration by a stream of air directed at the mouthpiece by the player's lips. The tone of the piccolo is piercingly sharp: it can be heard over a full orchestra or band. The flute produces a silvery tone, almost velvet-like in its smooth sweetness, an octave below the range of the piccolo. Originally, the flute was made of wood; the present-day instrument is constructed of metal.

The oboe and the English horn are double-reed instruments. As a mouthpiece, they have two small pieces of cane inserted in the mouthpiece, placed so that there is a narrow passage for air. The oboe possesses a sharp, melancholy sound; its cousin, the English horn, is pitched a fifth below the oboe, and has a more mellow, darker tone.

The clarinet and the bass clarinet are each equipped with a single reed. The clarinet is one of the most agile and versatile instruments in the orchestra. It has a particularly wide range of pitch (three-and-a-half octaves), and an impressive dynamic range (from extremely soft to very loud). Mozart was the first composer to employ clarinets in the symphony, although the instrument was developed toward the end of the seventeenth century. Clarinets (together with double bass, piano, drums, and saxophone) are extremely common in jazz bands and combos.

The bassoon, like the oboe, is a double reed instrument. Its range corresponds almost exactly to the cello among the strings. But whereas the cello produces a warmly lyrical tone, there is an almost humorous quality to the sound of the bassoon, and the instrument

119,018

LIBRARY
College of St. Francis
JOLIET, ILL.

25

has been used by many composers to suggest prankishness or pomposity. The contrabassoon (which is also called the double bassoon) produces some of the lowest notes in the orchestra: its range takes it just past the C which is three octaves below middle C. To produce these low notes, over sixteen feet of tubing is required; it is wound around four times to make the instrument less cumbersome.

The woodwinds of the orchestra often supply coloristic effects when the principal melody is carried by the strings or brass. But some symphonic composers (e.g. Mozart, Vivaldi, and Haydn) have excelled in passages for solo woodwinds; and woodwind instruments are often added to the basic instruments of the string quartet (violins, viola, and cello) for quintets, sextets, etc. The woodwinds are especially useful in programmatic music (music which represents a specific place or story) for suggesting a pastoral setting (birdsong, shepherds' pipes, the rustling of leaves, etc.).

Along with the standard woodwind instruments of the symphony orchestra, we should mention the saxophone. The saxophone (invented around 1840), although it is made of metal, is properly speaking a wind instrument: like the clarinet, it contains a single reed. The saxophone is an uncommonly versatile instrument, capable of both stridency and lyrical sweetness. Although many associate it with jazz bands, it is occasionally used in symphonic compositions, especially in Romantic and modern music.

The third great family of instruments is the **brass**. Brass instruments include: trumpet, trombone, tuba, French horn, and cornet. The first four of these are regularly found in the symphony orchestra; the cornet is now largely confined to military and brass bands (although it was more popular than the trumpet in orchestras of the nineteenth century).

The trumpet's ancestry can be traced as far back as ancient Rome. This instrument produces the most boldly brilliant tone in the orchestra. Long associated with war and military pomp, it is also capable of beautifully rounded and resonant sounds when it is played softly or with a mute. The trumpet, like the other brass instruments, produces tones through the vibrations of a column of air, which the player sends through a system of metal tubing. The modern trumpet, unlike its predecessors in ancient and medieval times, is equipped with three valves, which allow the player to change the pitch easily. Its range is roughly that of the English horn among the

LIBRARY
College of St. Francis
JOLIET, ILL.

wind instruments; it can extend from the F-Sharp below middle C to an octave above high C (roughly two-and-a-half octaves).

The French horn, with a range somewhat lower and broader than that of the trumpet, is so called because the modern instrument was developed in France; however, it is the direct descendant of very ancient horns, used in hunting. The brass tubing is coiled in a circular fashion (rather than in the generally elliptical shape of the trumpet, cornet, and tuba); it widens at the end of a bell shape, roughly twelve inches in diameter. The sound of the French horn is the most appealing of the brass instruments; the instrument is capable of strikingly lyrical effects.

The trombone serves as the baritone voice of the brass section. In the Renaissance, this instrument was called the sackbut; it was used in sacred music and in brass ensembles in the Baroque period, and then gradually was incorporated into the scores of more varied forms. The first composer to employ the trombone in a symphony was Beethoven (in his Symphony No. 5). Larger than the trumpet, the trombone is equipped with a slide; by altering the slide's position, the player can extend the tubing and thus control the pitch. The tone of this instrument is both stirring and majestic; it produces a darker, richer, and brassier sound than either the trumpet or the French horn. It is a staple of brass and military bands.

The tuba is the bass instrument of the brass family. It is so large that it must played in the vertical position (as opposed to the trumpet and the trombone, which are held horizontally). The tuba's metal tubing is coiled several times around, and ends in an imposing bell shape. Like the contrabassoon, it is seldom employed for solo passages; rather, it supplies bass accents and occasional special effects.

The fourth family of the symphony orchestra is the **percussion** instruments: drums, cymbals, glockenspiel, chimes, triangles, xylophone, tambourine, and castanets. The name "percussion" refers to the fact that all these instruments are struck in playing, either with the hand or with sticks or hammers of various types. Some of the percussion instruments produce tones of indefinite pitch (e.g. triangle, cymbals, and certain types of drum); others produce a range of tones, just like the instruments of the string, woodwind, and brass families.

Drums, which can be traced back to the most ancient civilizations, consist of a frame enclosing a hollow space of various shapes; dried skin is stretched over the frame. The sound of the drum varies according to the size and shape of the cavity, the type of skin used on the "head", the tension, and the manner of striking. There are numerous types of drum in use throughout the world, but three are especially important for concert music. The kettledrums (sometimes called by their Italian name, timpani) are played in sets of two or three, each "tuned" to a different pitch by means of knobs which control the tautness of the head. The kettledrum consists of a large, bowl-shaped metal frame, with a circular head covered by calfskin. The player strikes the drums with sticks that are equipped with padded, ball-shaped ends. The drum family also includes the snare drum, a much smaller instrument with two parchment heads, and the bass drum. Both of these are of indefinite pitch; the sound of the bass drum, however, is significantly lower and more muffled than that of the snare drum.

The cymbals consist of two large plates of brass that are struck together to produce a shimmering crash; the plates are equal in size. Cymbals are often co-ordinated with drums in jazz bands, and drumsticks are used to strike them; here, the sound produced is more bell-like and mysterious. The glockenspiel is a set of horizontal steel plates of various sizes, inserted within a metal frame. When the plates are struck with a small hammer, brightly tinkling sounds are produced. Similar to the glockenspiel, but more bell-like in tone, are the chimes; in this instrument, metal cylinders of various lengths are suspended within a frame. The triangle (a metal instrument of triangular shape, struck with a steel stick) produces an indefinitely pitched, metallic tinkle.

The xylophone (whose name is Greek for "wood sound") consists of a series of wooden blocks of varying length, mounted on a frame. The wooden blocks are tuned, rather like the strings of a piano, and are struck with small hammers. The xylophone is found in much music of Africa and the Far East; it was first used in the symphony orchestra in 1874 by the French composer Camille Saint-Saëns. The tambourine and castanets are both hand-operated percussion instruments. The tambourine consists of a small drum, encircled by a series of little bells or jingles. It is shaken or struck. The castanets, popular in Spain, are small wooden clappers.

Three important instruments remain to be discussed: the piano, the organ, and the harp. The piano is a descendant of the older clavichord and harpsichord; it attained something like its modern form by the early eighteenth century, but did not become a powerful virtuoso instrument for soloists until the age of Beethoven and Franz Liszt. The piano (from Italian *pianoforte*, literally "soft-loud") is part-string, part-percussion. Its strings are extended either in front of or above a sound-board (depending on whether the piano is a grand or an upright); the keys on the keyboard are connected to small hammers, which strike the strings to produce the notes. Two pedals affect the length and quality of the tones: the sustaining pedal permits the player to extend the duration of notes, even after removing the fingers from the keys that have played them, and the soft pedal alters the impact of the hammers, resulting in a quieter sound. (A third pedal on some pianos, the *sostenuto*, permits the pianist to sustain certain notes but not others.) The piano has an advantage over many other instruments, in that the player can regularly provide both melody and harmony.

The piano has been the focal instrument in some of the most popular orchestral and solo forms in music. Mozart invented the modern form of the piano concerto, in which the piano and the orchestra have approximately equal roles. Beethoven developed the dynamic range of the piano in his sonatas; the Romantic composers Schumann, Chopin, Mendelssohn, and Liszt experimented with a variety of short solo forms (including Preludes, Impromptus, Nocturnes, and Études, or studies—devoted to honing one particular aspect of the player's technique). The piano is also regularly used in chamber music and the art song (or *Lied*). As Paganini was to the violin, Franz Liszt (1811–1886) was to the piano in the nineteenth century. Liszt's supreme technique, complemented by his teaching and composing skills, led to full realization of the instrument's potential [see Chapter 11].

The organ, superficially similar to the piano because of its keyboard, relies on an entirely different mechanism. On the organ, the keys are connected to rods (called trackers) which open and close the valves controlling a large number of pipes. Air is forced through the pipes, which are of different sizes and placed on a windchest. The playing action thus differs from the piano in two significant ways. A note may be sustained with the same tone-quality for as long as the player depresses a key (in contrast to the piano, where once the hammer strikes the string, the note begins to diminish in loudness); on the other hand, as soon as the player releases the keys of an organ, the notes cease (although they may continue to echo in a large, enclosed space, such as a church).

The sound of the organ is extraordinarily rich and varied. Many of the pipes are constructed to imitate the tones of various instruments in the orchestra, e.g. flute, trumpet, clarinet, etc. The late medieval composer Guillaume de Machaut (c.1300–1377) is reputed to have called the organ "the king of instruments" in tribute to its versatility and powerful sound. Organs have a long history: water was used to produce and sustain wind pressure in an organ-like instrument called the hydraulis, built in the third century B.C. in Alexandria by a Greek engineer. The great church organs began to be constructed in Germany in the middle of the fourteenth century. By 1550, many of the features of the modern organ had become standard: the registration "stops" belonging to each keyboard (and to the keyboard for the feet, known as the pedalboard), and the system of couplers, which could join the registration of manual keyboards together, or to the pedalboard.

Finally, we come to the harp—a descendant of the ancient Greek lyre. The modern harp is a series of strings of different lengths, set in a large, standing frame. The strings are vibrated by plucking, and their pitches can be altered by either a semitone or a whole tone with the use of seven pedals. The harp has a range nearly as large as the piano's. The tone of the harp is shimmering and warm; like the piano, it can provide both melody and harmony, and is capable of a sweeping sound when a number of strings are struck in rapid succession. The use of the harp in symphony orchestras did not become commonplace until after 1800; modern orchestras normally employ two harps.

Until roughly the middle of the eighteenth century, orchestras were small, in keeping with the domestic surroundings in which they performed. But with the activities of the "Mannheim school" of composers and musicians in Germany, orchestras expanded to include forty or fifty players [see Chapter 7]. Beethoven further enlarged the orchestra; the Romantic composers of the nineteenth century doubled and re-doubled instrumental parts, and the example of Richard Wagner's scores led to increased use of brass and percussion. The modern symphony orchestra normally employs ninety to one hundred players, distributed as follows:

Strings	Woodwinds	Brass	Percussion	Other
Violins: 34	Flutes: 2 or 3	French horns: 4	Drums	Harps: 2
Violas: 12	Piccolo: 1	Trumpets: 4	Cymbals	Piano *or*
Cellos: 10	Oboes: 3	Trombones: 4	Chimes, etc.:	Organ, *if*
Double basses: 10	English horn: 1	Tuba: 1	*3 or 4*	*required.*
	Clarinets: 3		*players alter-*	
	Bass clarinet: 1		*nating among*	
	Bassoons: 3		*instruments.*	
	Contrabassoon: 1			

The senior violinist serves as an assistant to the conductor, and is called the concertmaster. Before the start of a symphony concert, players normally tune their instruments to the pitch of A above middle C, traditionally given out by the oboe.

The placing of the instruments in modern symphony orchestras is variable, but one general rule controls the various seating plans: the louder instruments (brass and percussion) are positioned toward the rear of the concert platform, and the softer ones (strings and woodwinds) toward the front. In operatic orchestras, the players are normally seated in a pit below the level of the front of the stage. All orchestras are arranged in a wide semi-circle, so that each player has an unobstructed view of the conductor. Players of the same instrument (e.g. cello, or trumpet) are always positioned together.

The conductor has the primary responsibility for insuring that the orchestra plays as a smoothly functioning team. Many people assume that the conductor's only duty is to give the tempo (or beat time); but this is a misconception. The role of the conductor extends to giving important cues to solo instruments or groups; to insuring the proper balance and proportions in the sound of the ensemble; and to shaping the performance of a work in a coherent interpretation. Thus, modern conductors must combine rhythmical precision with musical scholarship, a detailed knowledge of all the orchestra's varied instruments, and imaginative flair. Since the nineteenth century, conductors have emerged as virtuosi in their own right.

The Principal Periods and Styles

As we trace the development of music in time, we can distinguish six major periods and styles. They are: Medieval music (c. 900–1450), music of the Renaissance (1450–1600), Baroque music (1600–1750), Classicism (1750–1820), Romanticism (1820–1900), and Twentieth-Century music. It should be emphasized at the outset that these descriptive labels are only a shorthand, and that the reality of musical development is far more complex than the period titles and dates imply. In every era, some artists have been more "traditional" or more "progressive" than others. Musical styles, like styles in literature and painting, seldom progress in neatly defined waves. Some composers (for example Ludwig van Beethoven at the turn of the nineteenth century, or Claude Debussy at the beginning of the twentieth) resist categorization, even as transitional figures; their genius is too varied to be summed up by any one style. Nevertheless, before we study the significant composers and works of Western music in detail, some acquaintance with the general characteristics of the major periods will be useful.

Medieval Music (c.900–1450). The influence of the Church penetrated almost all facets of life in medieval Europe. As in many subsequent periods, religion was one of the primary inspirational forces in music, and the services of the Church provided the chief musical outlet. Our earliest extant music is Gregorian chant, a complex repertory of melodies devised for the monastic Divine Office and for the various parts of the Mass. We assume that the chant developed from disparate sources (Greco-Roman music, Jewish chants from the Synagogue, and Eastern elements) during the first six centuries of Christianity's existence. Pope Gregory the Great, around the year 600, is credited with the refinement and condification of the chants. The first chants were not written down in a wholly decipherable musical notation until about the year 1000; but it is relatively certain that this music closely resembled the chant of Pope Gregory's era, since the Church's insistence on the stability of the faith led to a conservative attitude towards both the texts and the music of services.

Gregorian chant, and much other medieval music, is likely to sound strange to our ears. There was no harmony in chant: only the voices of the choir, singing the melodies in unison. The melodies do not employ our system of major and minor scales, but rather the medieval modes [see Chapter 2], and the rhythm of medieval sacred music may strike us as comparatively monotonous.

Secular music of the Middle Ages displays more rhythmic and

melodic variety. The songs of traveling minstrels (variously called *troubadours*, *jongleurs*, and *Minnesinger*), have survived in significant numbers; frequent motifs were war and chivalric love. We also have the explicitly profane songs of wandering students, called the Goliard poets. In time, sacred music began to borrow secular elements, e.g. increased rhythmic variety and the incorporation of two or more vocal lines in the same work (polyphony).

The purpose and occasions of music, which had been strictly sacred or strictly secular, were gradually broadened. Music and its leading composers received powerful patronage at the courts of England and France, as well as the center of Church authority, Rome. The leading figure of the late Middle Ages is Guillaume de Machaut (c.1300–1377). Machaut was the first composer to bridge the sacred and the secular; he wrote the first setting of the Mass as an integrated unit, and composed numerous *ballades* and *rondeaux* (settings for secular songs).

Renaissance Music (1450–1600). Renaissance means re-birth. The term is used to characterize the dynamic re-awakening of art and culture in Europe which began in Italy in the fourteenth century. The Renaissance spread North and West from Italy in the course of the next two hundred years; in England, the flowering of the Renaissance coincides with the reign of Queen Elizabeth I (1558–1603).

The Renaissance world-view, as opposed to the outlook of the Middle Ages, celebrated the varied potential of earthly man; the glorification of mankind and of the natural world was now fully reconcilable with the glorification of God. The arts generally sought a simpler and purer style; for example, the complexity of medieval Gothic cathedrals yielded to the simpler majesty of Renaissance basilicas, inspired by the models of classical Greece and Rome. The severity and other-wordliness of medieval painting were replaced by humaneness and warmth; and the discovery of perspective in painting of the Italian Renaissance radically altered representation of shape and form.

In music, certain tendencies of the late Middle Ages continued unabated. Powerful courts patronized the leading musicians, and the principal forms of composition (Masses and motets in sacred music, madrigals and ballads in secular music) were further developed. At the same time, important new trends can be discerned. First, the Church acted to reform polyphonic sacred music in the mid-sixteenth century, largely as a response to the Protestant schisms of Martin Luther, John Calvin, and King Henry VIII. Sacred music was now to be written in a simpler style, and purged of confusing or distractingly secular elements. As a result, sacred and secular forms became more sharply distinguished. We can also trace the rise of purely instrumental music to the Renaissance. Prior to this period, music had been written almost entirely for solo voices, or for voice with instrumental accompaniment.

The leading composers of the Renaissance are Guillaume Dufay (c1400–1474), Johannes Ockeghem (c.1430–1497), Josquin dez Préz (c.1450–1517), and Roland de Lassus (1532–1594) of the Netherlands; Andrea Gabrieli (c.1510–1586), Giovanni Palestrina (c.1525–1594), and Giovanni Gabrieli (1557–1612) in Italy; and William Byrd (1542–1623) and John Dowland (1563–1626) in England. Dufay represents the new quality and cosmpolitanism of music in the fifteenth century. He assimilated French, Italian, and English elements in his sacred motets (polyphonic compositions for unaccompanied voices) and in his charming songs. In the music of Dufay, we see the first musical manifestation of the Renaissance in Europe. Ockeghem is notable for the broader range and richer sound of his polyphony; Josquin for the development in his music from polyphony to harmony. Roland de Lassus and William Byrd were as adept at secular music as at sacred works. Dowland, England's greatest song-writer and lutenist of the Elizabethan age, brought a new mastery of the nuances of the text to the composition of his songs. And with the organ and brass works of Andrea Gabrieli and his nephew Giovanni (both were organists at St. Mark's Cathedral in Venice), purely instrumental music—grand and almost orchestral—had its origins. At the end of the Renaissance, the European center of music shifted to Italy, and the stage was set for the development of larger forms: notably the opera and the ballet.

Baroque Music (1600–1750). The term baroque is probably derived from a Portuguese word, meaning "rough" or "irregular". The etymology is somewhat misleading, since music of the Baroque period is the first music to exhibit consistently the ordered notions of harmony which we take for granted. Yet in all the arts of this period, there exist a restless energy and a dynamic preoccupation with complexity that may justify the original meaning of "baroque".

The chief Baroque composers are Johann Sebastian Bach (1685–

1750) and George Frideric Handel (1685–1759). The careers of Bach and Handel reflect quite different approaches to music, and display contrasting relationships between the composer and society. Bach derived his musical inspiration almost totally from his Lutheran, Protestant heritage; although he wrote for secular patrons, most of his music was composed for religious services in the churches which employed him.

Handel, on the other hand, was a master of public spectacle and showmanship. His creative energies were long focused on Italian opera, a form inaugurated at the beginning of the Baroque era by Claudio Monteverdi (1567–1643) in Venice. Only when opera failed to please the public in his adopted country (England), did Handel devote his genius to developing a new, larger form of sacred music: the oratorio.

In Baroque music, the major and minor keys (and the diatonic harmony which is built on them) are clearly and consistently recognizable. The Baroque era witnessed the development of important new forms in music: opera, oratorio, suite, concerto grosso, and fugue [see Section D, below]. Baroque style in music exploits marked contrasts. For example, Baroque concerti feature opposing groups of instruments: a smaller group of soloists is answered and complemented by a larger group of instruments (as in Bach's *Brandenburg Concerti* and in Vivaldi's *The Four Seasons*). The use of "terraced dynamics" (alternating loud and soft passages, involving the same thematic material) is a marked characteristic of the period. In opera, arias of the soloists are contrasted with freer passages of declamation (or recitative). Much Baroque music pointedly contrasts the upper melodic line with a "continuous bass" (or *basso continuo*), which provides harmony by doubling the lowest vocal or instrumental part.

Melody and rhythm tend to be continuous in Baroque music, as opposed to the discrete, elegant phrasing of Classicism. In harmony, perhaps the most important structural feature of the Baroque is the full development of polyphony. Polyphony of this period, which is remarkably sophisticated and complex, is called counterpoint. In counterpoint, two or more melodic strands are simultaneously interwoven; the technique is fundamental in many of the works of Bach and Handel. Perhaps the most important contrapuntal form is the fugue, in which two or more instrumental voices successively introduce a main theme (called the subject) and an answering theme.

The voices (whether on the same instrument, as on the organ, or on different instruments) then develop the themes, in both the tonic and dominant keys. Skillful harmony may produce much tension and grandeur in the fugue, as it builds from a single melodic line to a massive intermingling of voices, and then is resolved in the finale.

The Baroque period also witnessed the invention of ballet, brought to full maturity by Jean-Baptiste Lully (1632–1687), who was born in Italy but who worked at the splendid court of King Louis XIV at Versailles. In England, the greatest master of the Baroque was Henry Purcell (1659–1695); he composed sacred music, opera, instrumental pieces, and a magnificent collection of choral works. The last great Baroque composer was Antonio Vivaldi (1678–1741), who introduced the notion of "picturesque" music; some of Vivaldi's works (such as the concerti for violin named *The Four Seasons*) depart from the concept of music as an absolute art, and furnish a descriptive "program". Program music, in which the composer deliberately suggests a geographical place, a literary work, or a set of experiences, was to become highly popular in the Romantic era [see below].

Classicism (1750–1820). The use of the word "Classical" to describe music of this period harks back to the term's original sense of "normative" or "standard". In music of the classical style, the forms of the Baroque were modified and further refined. Composers substituted polished phrasing for the driving, rhythmical energy that was common in the Baroque age. The Church was no longer the principal center of musical activity; it was rather the fashionable eighteenth-century salon which attracted the most talented musicians and composers. Music of the classical style was written for the entertainment of aristocratic patrons; such nobles could well afford to engage composers (and whole orchestras) as part of their permanent household staff.

Classicism prized order, symmetry, and elegance in music. The great composers in this style include Christoph Willibald von Gluck (1714–1787), Franz Joseph Haydn (1732–1809), and Wolfgang Amadeus Mozart (1756–1791). Much of their music was written to divert audiences who were lending only one ear; it possesses a generally witty, charming sound, in which deep emotion is subdued or restrained. Music had yet to be treated as an art which was worthy of the undivided attention of its audience, or as an expression of profound, universal feelings; public concert halls, for example, did not become popular until the early nineteenth century. In music of the classical style, form and content conform to the function of occasional entertainment.

But the great classical composers are far from superficial. Indeed, this period lays the foundations for Romanticism in the transformation of old forms and the development of new ones. Gluck and Mozart revolutionized Italian opera; Mozart invented the form of the piano concerto as we know it; Haydn was the father of the symphony and the string quartet, which have continued to challenge composers as the premier forms of orchestral and chamber music.

Some historians would also include Ludwig van Beethoven (1770–1827) in the classical group. The shaping influences on Beethoven's early work were indisputably Haydn and Mozart. But his influence was so keenly felt by the Romantic composers that he almost seems one of them. Beethoven revolutionized every form in which he worked: symphony, opera, string quartet, and piano sonata. His principal innovations are discussed in detail in Chapter 9. Beethoven was the first composer who successfully challenged the patronage system in music; he was able to live comfortably from the sale of his works for publication. More importantly, his conception of music as the universal language of the common man, and as a profoundly liberating force, radically changed the ways in which audiences listened to musical works.

Romanticism (1820–1900). The keynote of Romanticism in music is the spontaneous expression of powerful emotions. Whereas the eighteenth-century composers restrained their personal feelings, the Romantics of the nineteenth century enthusiastically embraced them. This was an era of revolutions in Europe, and also an age of nationalism; many composers identified with revolutionary and national ideals, and followed Beethoven in the conviction that music could powerfully express the brotherhood of man.

We may divide the principal Romantic composers into three groups. The first group consists of Frédéric Chopin (1810–1849), a brilliant pianist who significantly enlarged the range of forms for short piano solo compositions; his commemoration of his native Poland in his piano works was prophetic, in that later Romantic composers would be largely inspired by nationalist traditions. Franz Schubert (1797–1828) created early Romantic symphonies but is chiefly remembered for his cultivation of the *Lied*, or art-song. Schumann (1810–1856) is important as composer and critic; he did much to encourage the talented composers of his generation, through his writing in the *Neue Zeitschrift für Musik*, one of the first musical journals. Mendelssohn (1809–1847) enlarged the scope of program music, even as he played a leading role in reviving the works of Bach. Brahms (1833–1897) is the most important direct successor of Beethoven; although his symphonies seemed conservative to some of the more radical Romantics (e.g. Liszt and Wagner), he demonstrated that the classical roots of Beethoven's genius could successfully be transplanted to a Romantic idiom.

The second group of Romantic composers consists of the giants of nineteenth-century opera: Giuseppe Verdi (1813–1901) and Richard Wagner (1813–1883). Verdi's melodic gift and his unwavering sense of the dramatic make his works the culmination of Italian grand opera. Wagner, absorbed by the possibilities of a total union of the arts in this form, composed all his own verse libretti, and lavished boundless energy on the realization of his "music-dramas" for the stage. Just as Verdi was able to transcend the Italian tradition of *bel canto* in a great series of popular works (e.g. *Rigoletto, Aida,* and *Otello*), Wagner was able to unite the disparate elements of earlier German Romantic opera, and to infuse them with compelling power. Wagner's experiments with chromatic harmony (especially in *Tristan und Isolde,* 1865) foreshadow some of the distinctively modernist techniques in music.

The third group of Romantics is dominated by the "nationalist" composers. Many of these musicians turned to native folk melodies and instruments (e.g. the balalaika in Russia) to express the spirit of their country in music. The most important of these composers are Antonín Dvořák (1841–1904) in Czechoslovakia, Jean Sibelius (1865–1957) in Finland, and the two towering figures of Russian Romantic music: Modest Mussorgsky (1839–1881) and Peter Ilyich Tchaikovsky (1840–1893). Others include the Norwegian Edvard Grieg (1843–1907) and the Spaniard Manuel de Falla (1876–1946).

Although the date 1900 is often selected as a boundary for the Romantic era in music, several composers at the turn of the century are especially hard to classify. Their work contains numerous Romantic elements, but also exhibits an unusual degree of experimentation which anticipates modernist techniques. This group of composers includes Claude Debussy (1862–1918) and Maurice Ravel (1875–1937) in France, Giacomo Puccini (1858–1924) in Italy, and Gustav Mahler (1860–1911) in Austria. Debussy and Ravel experimented with unusual harmonies and structures; the term "Impressionism" (originally applied to French painting of the late nineteenth century) is often used to characterize their work. The Impressionists (including Claude Monet, Jean Renoir, and Camille Pissarro) employed color and form in painting in a wholly new way: to suggest, rather than to state. Similarly, in the music of Debussy and Ravel, the fundamental elements of melody, rhythm, and harmony are used to create a cluster of suggestions, rather than a clear-cut statement. The operas of Giacomo Puccini experimented with exotic settings, untraditional harmonies, and the rhythms of actual speech. Gustav Mahler, having assimilated the doctrines of Sigmund Freud about the human unconscious mind, brought to his symphonies a profoundly psychological approach, sharply juxtaposing disparate forms in the way that dreams contain superficially irreconcilable elements.

Modern Music (1900–present). Modern music resists classification. Without the benfit of historical perspective, it is difficult to identify the innovations which will prove to have been most influential when the next century of composers looks back on contemporary music as a thing of the past.

But certain very general threads run through the fabric of modern music. The most important tendency has been the rejection of the tuneful melody and expressive emotionalism of Romantic music. The leading composers since 1900 have been, on the whole, more intellectual than their immediate predecessors; their music has been written at least as much for the head as for the heart. Secondly, modern composers have sought to revive in Western music some older forms, and have imported other, unfamiliar elements from traditions that have hitherto been considered quite separate, e.g. from jazz, Oriental music, the medieval modes, and electronic instruments. Finally, some of the most important modern composers have attacked in their works the notion that music must be composed with irreducible, fundamental elements (melody, harmony, and rhythm); rather like the scientists who split the atom, these writers have sought to explore new possibilities in sound.

The leading modern composers include: Igor Stravinsky (1882–

1971), Arnold Schoenberg (1874–1954), Olivier Messiaen (1908–), and György Ligeti (1923–). The significant concepts of these composers' works are polytonality (composition of music in more than one key), atonality (the deliberate avoidance of any fixed key, and use of the twelve-tone scale), polyrhythm (use of several different rhythms simultaneously), and serialism (in which a specific series of notes governs the development of an entire composition). The jagged rhythms and seeming avoidance of melody in modern music parallel the rejection of conventional styles in much modern painting and literature; in many works, the listener is called upon to make far more effort than has traditionally been required to perceive the structural outlines. But such effort is often amply repaid. The greatest modern composers, like their counterparts in previous ages, have succeeded in ingeniously, provocatively blending the old with the new.

The Major Musical Genres

In this section, we offer a survey of the major musical genres, both vocal and instrumental. Brief definitions of each form are followed by a representative list of outstanding exponents and works; for more detailed critical description and historical background, the reader is referred to the sections of individual chapters which discuss the composers who are listed.

Ballet: a stage spectacle with musical accompaniment, in which dancers convey a mood or tell a story through the use of expressive movements, gestures, and mime. The form dates to the seventeenth century in France, where Jean-Baptiste Lully devised elaborate spectacles for the court of King Louis XIV at Versailles. Ballet was also an integral part of opera for a long period; operatic ballets reached the height of their popularity in the early nineteenth century. Besides the works of Lully, notable ballets include: Adam, *Giselle* (1841); Delibes, *Coppélia* (1870); Tchaikovsky, *Swan Lake* (1876), *The Sleeping Beauty* (1890), and *The Nutcracker* (1892); Stravinsky, *The Firebird* (1910) and *The Rite of Spring* (1913); de Falla, *The Three-Cornered Hat* (1919).

Cantata: a vocal composition for solo and/or choir, either sacred or secular. Early cantatas were accompanied by a solo instrument or continuo; later cantatas tend to use a larger accompaniment. Notable exponents of the form were Alessandro Scarlatti, Heinrich Schütz, Johann Sebastian Bach, and George Frideric Handel in the Baroque era, and William Walton, Ralph Vaughan Williams, and Igor Stravinsky in the twentieth century. The cantata gradually evolved until it became an alternate term for a short oratorio.

Concerto: a work in which one or more solo instruments is contrasted with the rest of the orchestra. The concerto has origins in the early Baroque period (Giuseppe Torelli and Claudio Monteverdi). It was expanded to a longer form in the *concerto grosso* (as practiced by Handel and by Bach in the *Brandenburg Concerti*). But the modern form of the concerto, a large-scale composition in which a solo instrument is placed on an equal footing with the orchestra, was established in Mozart's 27 piano concerti toward the end of the eighteenth century. The standard concerto is in three movements, the second being a slow movement. Beethoven's piano concerti established the third movement (finale) as the equal of the first in importance. Leading exponents of the piano concerto (besides Mozart and Beethoven) have been Schumann, Grieg, Brahms, Chopin, Liszt, and Tchaikovsky (all in the Romantic period). Modern composers (notably Poulenc and Shostakovitch) have continued to compose in this form, which is one of the most popular in the concert repertory. Notable concerti for violin and orchestra have been composed by Beethoven, Brahms, Dvořák, and Tchaikovsky. Almost every instrument in the orchestra has been exploited in concerto form by composers since 1700.

Fugue: a complex form of contrapuntal composition, which reached its fullest development in the Baroque era. Two or more instrumental voices (often on the organ) successively introduce a main theme (the subject) and an answering theme. These are then developed in both the tonic and the dominant keys. The indisputable master of the fugue was Johann Sebastian Bach, although many composers practiced in the form. Fugal principles have often been used in secular compositions; they have been adapted to opera by Wagner (in *Die Meistersinger*) and Verdi (in the finale of *Falstaff*).

Lied (art-song): a short composition for solo voice, usually with piano accompaniment, popular in the Romantic era. The piano shares equally with the vocal line in creating a mood, and in conveying a dramatic vignette. The art-song differs from the folk song in its greater complexity of phrasing; in following an extended verse, it is said to be through-composed (not, like folk song, consisting of short and frequently repeated verses). Notable exponents of the *Lied* have been Franz Schubert (who invented the modern form), Robert Schumann, Johannes Brahms, and Richard Strauss.

Madrigal: a short song for four or five voices, often unaccompanied, sung in the vernacular, often on pastoral and amorous themes. Although of Italian origin, the madrigal is most familiar in English songs of the Elizabethan age. Leading composers of the madrigal include: Giovanni Palestrina, Roland de Lassus, Thomas Morley, Thomas Weelkes, William Byrd, and Orlando Gibbons.

Mass: a musical setting for the five principal parts of the Ordinary (invariable sections) of the Christian service commemorating the sacrifice and death of Christ. These sections are: *Kyrie* ("Lord have mercy"), *Gloria* ("Glory to God in the highest"), *Credo* ("I believe in one God"), *Sanctus* ("Holy, holy, holy"), and *Agnus Dei* ("Lamb of God"). The first integrated musical setting of the Mass is credited to Guillaume de Machaut (c.1300–1377). A special type of Mass is the Requiem, based on the liturgy for the dead, with the *Gloria* and *Credo* omitted, and the medieval sequence *Dies Irae* added. Notable composers of Masses and Requiems are the following: Ockeghem, Palestrina, Byrd, Bach, Mozart, Beethoven, Berlioz, Verdi, Dvorák, and Benjamin Britten. (Although Brahms composed a work which he called *A German Requiem*, its text is not that of the Roman Catholic service, but rather a series of Biblical passages of a consoling nature.)

Motet: a sacred work for unaccompanied chorus, popular in the late Middle Ages and the Renaissance. The texts were usually drawn from Scripture. Notable polyphonic motets were written by Machaut, Dufay, Ockeghem, des Prés, Victoria, Palestrina, and Byrd.

Opera: a shortened form of *opera in musica*, Italian for "a work in music", a drama that is sung to musical accompaniment, and staged with costumes, sets, etc. Opera originated in the experiments of the Florentine *Camerata* toward the end of the sixteenth century, and was evidently inspired by the Renaissance concept of ancient Greek drama, where there was a union of the arts in performance. Claudio Monteverdi's *Orfeo* (1607) is commonly designated the first opera; it employed a large instrumental ensemble (by the standards of the time: about thirty players). Opera is the most ambitious form in music, involving the most diverse composition for orchestra and soloists, a lengthy libretto, and attention to production values. The most successful operas have been those in which the composer has suggested a keen psychological perception of character through the music. From 1750 to 1900, opera's development exhibits a gradually increasing continuity within the acts, so that the different elements (overture, solo aria, recitative, ensemble numbers, ballet, etc.) become less and less separate; there is also a growth of psychological and dramatic realism. The following is a short list of outstanding operas, notable either because of their innovations in form or for their inherent excellence: Gluck, *Orfeo ed Euridice* (1762); Mozart, *Don Giovanni* (1787), *The Magic Flute* (1791); Beethoven, *Fidelio* (1805); Rossini, *The Barber of Seville* (1816); Wagner, *Tannhäuser* (1845), *Tristan und Isolde* (1865), and *Die Meistersinger* (1868); Verdi, *Rigoletto* (1851), *Aida* (1871), and *Otello* (1887); Mussorgsky, *Boris Godounov* (1874); Puccini, *La Bohème*(1896) and *Madama Butterfly* (1904); Richard Strauss, *Salome* (1905) and *Der Rosenkavalier* (1911); Poulenc, *The Dialogues of the Carmelites*(1956); Stravinsky, *The Rake's Progress*(1951).

Oratorio: a musical setting of a religious libretto for chorus, orchestra, and soloists; usually performed without costumes or scenery, and suitable for either the concert hall or the church. The term (derived from Italian for a "place of prayer") may also be used to refer to Passions, i.e. musical settings of the Passion of Jesus Christ as recounted in the Gospels. The first oratorios were written around the year 1600. The best-known exponents of the form are Alessandro Scarlatti, Schütz, Handel, Haydn, Beethoven, and Mendelssohn. Handel was the undisputed master of the form, turning to the oratorio after Italian operas failed to please his English audiences and became too expensive to produce. The best-known of his many oratorios is the *Messiah* (1742). Outstanding settings of the Passion were composed by Schütz and Bach; the latter's *St. Matthew Passion* (1729) is sometimes called his masterpiece.

Quartet: a variety of chamber music, composed in several movements. The string quartet, inaugurated by Haydn, conventionally features two violins, viola, and cello; the instruments are all roughly equal in importance, and Haydn's quartets have been called witty four-way conversations. After Haydn, the quartet became established as the premier form of chamber music. Variations are possible in the type of instrument (e.g. sometimes the piano or oboe replaces one of the strings) and in the number of players. With five performers, such a work is called a quintet, with six a sextet, etc. Notable composers of quartets and related forms have included Mozart, Schubert, Beethoven, Schumann, Mendelssohn, Dvorák, Brahms, and Bartók.

Sonata: a composition for a solo instrument (most often the piano), or for an instrument (or several instruments) with keyboard accompaniment. The word (from Italian *suonare*, "to sound") originated in the sixteenth century, as a general term for instrumental (as opposed to vocal) music. In the seventeenth century, the sonata was constructed like a suite which contained three to six movements. In the Baroque era, the modern form of the sonata was developed by Domenico Scarlatti and C.P.E. Bach: a composition, usually for a solo keyboard instrument, of three movements. Haydn, Mozart, and Beethoven all played an important role in developing the form yet further.

Sonata-allegro form: a type of musical construction that takes its name from the typical first movement (allegro) of the classical sonata. Sonata-allegro form is one of the most basic musical structures, common in symphonies, quartets, trios, and many other types of work. (It is sometimes called first movement form, or compound binary form.) The form comprises two sections. In the first, a theme is introduced in the tonic key, followed by a second, contrasting theme in the dominant key. This section is called the *exposition*. The second segment involves the *development* and the *recapitulation*. The former features a freer working out of the exposition's thematic material; the latter repeats both original themes, this time in the tonic key. The recapitulation may end the movement, or it may be followed by a short coda.

Suite: a common form of instrumental work in the Baroque and Classical periods, consisting of several movements based on dance rhythms (e.g. the Minuet, the Gigue, the Sarabande, etc.).

Symphony: the premier, large-scale form for orchestral composition. Derived from the *sinfonia*, or short orchestral overture that was popular in the early eighteenth century, the symphony is usually in four movements (but occasionally in three, five, or even two). A slow movement is often placed second in the order; but Beethoven and other composers departed occasionally from this practice. The enlargement of the orchestra and the experiments with dynamics of the Mannheim school of composers in Germany (mid-eighteenth century) were significant for the development of the form, but Haydn is now generally credited as the "father of the symphony". The form has continued to challenge composers for two hundred years, and has been the vehicle for many of the most innovative effects in music. The following is but a selection from the ranks of distinguished composers of symphonies: Mozart, Beethoven, Schubert, Schumann, Mendelssohn, Brahms, Berlioz, Bruckner, Mahler, Tchaikovsky, Ives, Sibelius, Vaughan Williams, and Shostakovich.

Tone poem: sometimes called the symphonic poem, this form is a descriptive orchestral work (often in a single movement), usually based on a specific landscape, literary work, or imaginative fantasy. The tone poem is the most ambitious form of orchestral "program music", and has engaged the effort of a number of great composers since its invention in the nineteenth century by Franz Liszt. A number of musicians have used it as the vehicle for national feelings (as in Smetana's *Má Vlast* and Sibelius' *Finlandia*). Other notable composers in the form include Richard Strauss and Ralph Vaughan Williams.

Chapter 2

The Truth from Above

The Truth from Above

Music has always played an important part in the life of mankind. Records from numerous ancient civilizations, thousands of years before the Christian era, reflect the existence of vital traditions in music for almost every aspect of human existence: religious music, lullabies, work songs, love songs, dances, and war songs. Possibly the most ancient record of music for the entertainment of society comes from Sumeria in the Middle East: a cuneiform inscription of about 2400 B.C. refers to the capacity of music to calm the passions, to chase away tears, and to fill the temple courts with joy. Evidence from Sumeria, Egypt, and China indicates that the earliest musical instruments included—in addition, of course, to the human voice—the drum, various percussion instruments such as the tambourine and the rattle, and reed instruments of the wind family (possibly resembling in sound our oboe and clarinet).

The word "music" itself comes from Greek, *mousikē* (pronounced moo-zee-kay), which literally means "the art related to the Muse". In Greek mythology, the nine Muses (sometimes referred to collectively in the singular as "the Muse") were the daughters of Zeus, god of the sky and the weather; their mother was Mnemosyne, the personified goddess of memory. The Greek Muses were thought of as patrons for a wide variety of what we should now call arts and sciences: among their provinces were poetry, music, dance, astronomy, history, and philosophy. In fact, the verb related to "Muse" in ancient Greek simply meant "to be educated".

Music thus occupied a special place in Greek culture. The Greeks employed three principal instruments for music, in the narrower sense of formal composition and performance of ordered sounds. These were the voice, the stringed instrument called the lyre, and the *aulos*—a pair of pipes, each with a double reed and with holes stopped by the fingers. (The *aulos* is often termed a flute, but this is misleading: it probably had a far shriller tone than our modern flute, and sounded more like a bagpipe.) These instruments were prominent at religious observances, since music-making was associated with the cult worship of two of the most important gods in the Greek pantheon: Apollo (connected with the lyre), and Dionysus (linked with the *aulos*). Both gods were sons of Zeus: Apollo was linked with brightness, order, and harmony; Dionysus, with passionate emotional release. Dionysus was also the patron god of the theater, both tragedy and comedy. The great Greek dramas of the fifth century B.C. were presented in honor of the god; and music was an integral part of dramatic production. Some theories of the origins of Greek drama suppose that the literary form emerged from choral songs (dithyrambs) that were performed with music and dance to celebrate the power of Dionysus.

Besides Greek drama, most of the other forms of ancient Greek literature were intimately connected with music—a fact which was later to have a profound impression on many European composers, after the re-discovery of ancient classical culture during the Renaissance. Epic poetry, odes, hymns, marriage-songs, and elegies (laments) all had their appropriate music. Just as in modern times, music also had its more informal genres: drinking-songs at dinner parties, folk songs, love songs, and songs of war. Unfortunately, whereas numerous literary texts and a fair selection of occasional poems have survived, only half a dozen scraps of Greek music are extant. They are so fragmentary, and in such enigmatic notation, that we cannot conclude with any certainty how ancient Greek music sounded.

We do know a considerable amount, however, about ancient Greek theories of music. Some of these are important for the later development of Western music, since musicians of the Middle Ages studied and commented on Greek theory and what they believed to be its practice. From early times, the Greeks made philosophical connections between musical intervals and important mathematical ratios. Especially significant were the discoveries of Pythagoras in the late sixth century B.C. Pythagoras is credited with identifying the octave, the perfect fifth, and the perfect fourth; he matched these intervals with precise mathematical proportions on the string of a lyre (2:1, 3:2, and 4:3 respectively). The Pythagoreans believed that mathematics and music were intimately connected, and that the study of both was the foundation of true philosophy.

The later theorist Aristoxenus (fourth century B.C.) informs us in more detail about the basic elements of Greek music. In his book the

Harmonics, Aristoxenus discusses a system based on the interval of the fourth, or tetrachord (literally "four strings" on the lyre). Something like our modern system of scales was constructed by linking tetrachords together; but for the Greeks, the inside notes of the interval were variable rather than fixed, and involved the use of small intervals which we no longer distinguish as individual pitches. Various systems of tetrachords were linked together to make up the various *modes* (the nearest equivalent modern term is "scales"). Each mode—there were eight—was named after the geographical area of the Greek world in which it was thought to have originated: Dorian, Phrygian, Lydian, etc. Just as we associate certain musical keys with specific moods (C minor with melancholy, D major with cheerful energy, for example), the Greeks systematically associated the different modes, not only with emotional states but character traits as well.

The philosopher Plato (429–347 B.C.) believed that music actually induced character traits, and could therefore influence people for good or ill. In a number of his works, Plato discussed the different modes of Greek music and prescribed those which encourage courage, nobility and endurance, and urged avoiding those which lead to idleness, debauchery, and cowardice. Plato's pupil Aristotle (388–322 B.C.) expanded his teacher's theories on the ethical power of music. Where Plato had rejected purely instrumental music, Aristotle accepted it as legitimate expression; he recognized that the power of music is independent of words, and is somehow inherent in the music itself. Such Greek notions of the power of music were to be influential on Church teaching during the Middle Ages, although the Church modified the ancient emphasis on the shaping ethical power of music by insisting that the fundamental purpose of music was to glorify God.

Greek theories of music were handed down and elaborated by the Romans. The Romans conquered Greece and annexed it as a province in 146 B.C.; their dominance in the Mediterranean led to mastery of the known world, from Spain to Syria, in the next two centuries. That the Romans used music for a wide variety of occasions is indisputable; but not a single trace of their music has come down to us. In 476 A.D., the Roman Empire in the West collapsed, the victim of internal corruption and numerous barbarian invasions. Yet within the Roman world, an enduring seed had been planted: the new faith of Christianity. For the next five hundred years, the transmitters of ancient Greco-Roman culture were to be the Christian monasteries throughout Europe. These foundations were established for contemplative prayer and for the missionary purpose of spreading the faith. The monasteries were also notable as the isolated centers of learning during the Dark Ages. In the monasteries, the art of writing was preserved, and the ancient texts—of pagan Greece and Rome, as well as of the early Church Fathers—were copied by hand and often provided with commentaries. It was also in the monasteries that a variety of ancient musical traditions—Greco-Roman, Jewish, and Byzantine—coalesced to form the first Western music for which written notation survives.

Religion has always played an integral part in musical inspiration—from the Gregorian chant of medieval times, through the great chorales ("church songs") of the Reformation, the Mass settings of Mozart, Beethoven, and Brahms, and into our own century. From the hymns of Ralph Vaughan Williams [see Chapter 12] to spirituals and Gospel-music, from the intricate counterpoint of Bach to the free improvisation of evangelical services, religion has inspired much of the world's most compelling music.

The earliest and most complete written musical sources to survive from the Middle Ages are almost all of sacred music. There was no lack of secular (literally, "worldly") music at this time: love songs, war songs, and both court and folk dances were composed or improvised and performed. But because the Church was the center of learning in medieval Europe, because the clergy monopolized the art of writing for many centuries, and because the Church had both the economic base to sponsor music and the social stability to preserve it, it is about sacred music that we are most fully informed. Such music was composed with one clear purpose: to glorify God, to recognize and witness the truth from above.

The earliest such music is liturgical chant. Sometimes called *plainsong*, it consists of a single vocal line sung in unison (without any harmony) by a choir of monks or nuns. For musical variety (and also for practical reasons), two distinct methods of performing the chant came into common use: *antiphonal* style, in which two choirs seated across the church from each other alternately sing separate phrases of the text; and *responsorial* style, in which a single soloist, or cantor, intones the initial phrase of text, which is then taken up by the entire choir. The latter style was probably borrowed from the music of the Jewish synagogue of the pre-Christian era.

Chant sounds quite strange to modern ears. It is a highly refined and formal music, purified over the course of centuries until it was totally unlike secular music, and sounded almost unearthly. This was intentional; the Church maintained an ambivalent attitude towards musical innovation throughout the Middle Ages and well into the Renaissance.

The strange quality can also be explained through the actual musical techniques which chant employs. First, its melodies are quite different from the types of melody with which we are familiar. Chant does not employ modern major and minor scales, but is built on a system of modes (varieties of scales). We do not know whether these modes were descended directly from the ancient Greek modes discussed above, or whether they were imported from the Byzantine Church chant during the eighth century; they do sometimes seem to evoke an Oriental flavor.

Second, chant does not seem to have had a strong metrical rhythm (there are still large gaps in our knowledge of this aspect of chant performance). Rather than having a fixed rhythm of their own, chant melodies seem to have followed the natural emphases and accents of the Latin texts which they served. Each note in a chant melody appears to have had approximately the same time-value. Some melodies provided one note for each syllable of text—a style which is consequently known as *syllabic*. Another, more elaborate style, provides many notes for a single syllable, particularly ones with important meaning; this style is called *melismatic*, and the long pattern of notes for the single syllable is called a *melisma*. As might be expected, this particularly ornate style was employed to adorn the texts for the great feast days in the Church calendar (especially Christmas and Easter), though it is a feature of almost every chant to some extent. The melismatic style in particular had important implications for the future development of music.

In summation, chant sounds strange to us because it is so different from what we are accustomed to in the three most basic elements of music: melody, harmony, and rhythm. Nevertheless, chant is the cornerstone upon which all subsequent Western music rests; we shall soon see how it was enlarged upon, ornamented, and transformed.

Around the year 600, St. Gregory the Great (Pope from 590 to 604) initiated the refinement, expansion, and codification of early chant; the repertory is often called *Gregorian Chant* in his honor. It is a reasonable guess that the music notated in the earliest surviving manuscripts (from around 900 A.D.) is very similar to the music of Pope Gregory's time, for the Church regarded music, like the Latin texts themselves, as emblematic of the stability and timelessness of faith itself, and chant therefore changed only very slowly over the succeeding centuries.

We cannot read this early notation precisely. It does not consist of musical notes on a staff, like our own familiar musical notation. Rather, it is a system of markings called *neumes* written over the syllables of the texts to be sung. These neumes, which look rather like modern French accent marks, indicate whether the melody rises or falls; so they tell us the direction, but not the distance. We must therefore deduce that the early musical manuscripts must have served only as a kind of reminder for singers who already knew the chant melodies by heart.

More precise musical notation was not developed until after the year 1000 A.D., when scribes began to add horizontal lines on which the neumes were written. This allowed precise measurement of the pitch intervals which formed the melody, and allowed someone who did not previously know a melody to sing it from notation. Early examples of such notation have only one line, though additional lines were soon added; a number of modifications were made before the five-line staff which we use today was universally accepted. Though the problem of pitch notation was solved early, precise rhythmic notation was not developed until considerably later.

Chants were associated with the two basic types of service of the Catholic Church. The first was called the Divine Office—the relatively private, contemplative observances of the monks at various times throughout the day known as the *canonical hours*: Matins and Lauds (before dawn and at sunrise, respectively), Prime and Terce (in the morning), Sext and None (at noon and mid-afternoon), Vespers (at sunset), and Compline (at dusk). At these regularly appointed times, the monks would assemble in choir and sing as a community: Latin psalms and *antiphons*—short refrains from Biblical texts—appropriate to the time of year, as well as *canticles*—particularly important texts like the *Te Deum* (We praise thee, O God) and *Magnificat*

(My soul magnifies the Lord) which were sung every day.

The second type of service was more public: the commemoration of Christ's Last Supper and sacrifice on the Cross—the Mass. Both the monastic community and the congregation of the faithful were present at Mass; and the different parts of the service, recited or sung in Latin, required more elaborate forms of chant. Some of the Mass texts were variable, according to the ecclesiastical calendar (the succession of seasons, saints' days, and other holy days). These texts were collectively called the "Proper of the Mass". Others were standard and unchanging; these were the "Ordinary of the Mass". The sections of the Ordinary are named from their first word or phrase:

> Kyrie ("Kyrie eleison": "Lord have mercy")
> Gloria ("Gloria in excelsis Deo": "Glory to God in the highest")
> Credo ("Credo in unum Deum": "I believe in one God")
> Sanctus ("Sanctus, sanctus, sanctus": "Holy, holy, holy")
> Agnus Dei ("Agnus Dei qui tollis peccata mundi", "Lamb of God that takes away the sins of the world")

Because congregations were thoroughly familiar with the words of these texts from countless repetitions, it was the texts of the Ordinary of the Mass that were most commonly set to music by composers of later times. Beginning with the *Notre Dame Mass* of the fourteenth-century composer Guillaume de Machaut—the first extant musical setting of the Ordinary of the Mass as an integrated unit [see below]—these five sections have served as the nucleus for all subsequent musical settings of the Mass.

Parisian Polyphony in the Twelfth Century

As we have observed, Gregorian chant was exclusively monophonic: formal, elegant, but also somewhat austere. But gradually, the center of sacred music shifted from Rome to Paris; and music became subject to the same artistic trends and strivings as other medieval art. By the twelfth century, cathedrals were encrusted with ornate carvings, their windows ablaze with vibrantly stained glass; manuscripts of ancient texts were adorned with miniature paintings and elaborated with commentaries. In each case, the procedure was the same: a fresh layer of ornament was applied to a pre-existing structure.

Music was subject to the same process of elaboration, carried out in the same manner. A new layer of ornament was superimposed on the pre-existing chant, and the two were sung simultaneously. This added part was called *organum*, and the resulting two-voice texture is the earliest example of *polyphony* (literally, "many sounds") in the West.

At first, organum was probably improvised by skillful monastic singers; only fragmentary written sources of such music have survived. Around the year 1160, however, in a church which was the predecessor of the present Cathedral of Notre Dame in Paris, we know that organum began to be composed. The first composer whose name has been preserved along with his music is **Leonin**, choirmaster of the church; the music style which he is credited with inventing is called "Notre Dame organum". A complete set of Leonin's compositions in organum style survives, which covers the entire Church calendar.

Leonin found an early solution to a very difficult musical problem: the notation of rhythm. Rhythm had not been a problem in chant, since everyone sang the same melody and all the notes were (probably) of equal time-value [see above]. In polyphony, however, two—and later, more—singers performed different melodies simultaneously; some way had to be found to keep them together. Leonin's solution required the singers to memorize six rhythmic patterns. These patterns were derived from the rhythms of poetry, and you can get some idea of how they worked by comparing the first pattern:

DUM—dee—DUM—dee—DUM

with the second:

DEE—dum—DEE—dum—DEE—dum.

Leonin indicated which pattern was to be used in a given place, by means of the shape of the first few notes of a passage. (Remember that the problem of pitch notation had been solved by writing the notes on a staff.) Though this solution seems clumsy to us, it made possible everything that followed, and was revolutionary in its own time.

In precisely the same manner in which Leonin had elaborated already-existing Gregorian chant, his successor elaborated on Leonin's works. **Perotin** became chief musician of the same church in Paris around 1180. Perotin rewrote a number of Leonin's compositions in a rhythmically more sophisticated style, and added as many as three upper parts to the chant. Two complete examples of Perotin's work survive, one for Christmas and another for Easter; they are the first known examples of four-part polyphony.

Whereas the sound of the ancient chant suggested the uniform, rounded lines and dark, enclosed spaces of Romanesque architecture (employed in European church buildings c.900–1150 A.D.), the newer, more complex polyphony may be compared to the more elaborate lines of Gothic architecture. The Gothic style, in which many of Europe's greatest cathedrals were built from the twelfth to the fifteenth centuries, welded almost innumerable details into a complex, flowing harmony. The organum of Leonin and Perotin, singing a descant above the chant melody, was similar to the lofty triforium and clerestory of the Gothic cathedrals; it is perhaps not coincidental that the career of Perotin overlaps with the beginnings of the great Gothic cathedral of Notre Dame.

Although we are most fully informed about the development of sacred music, we should not overlook the many secular forms that flourished. Across Europe there was a vital tradition of traveling minstrels. In France, they were called *troubadours* and *trouvères* (literally, "inventors" in the sense of composers); they were often members of the nobility—Richard the Lionhearted (King Richard I of England) is perhaps the most famous. In Germany, they were called *Minnesingers* (literally, "singers of Minne", an old term for courtly love); the most famous of these was **Walther von der Vogelweide** (c.1170–1240), who, like Richard Lionheart, travelled to the Holy Land on one of the Crusades—musical evidence of his journey survives in his quasi-religious song of war, the *Palestinalied (Song of Palestine)*.

More than a thousand songs of the *troubadours, trouvères*, and *Minnesinger* have been preserved. Their topics are typically courtly love (often extolling the virtues of a high-born and unattainable lady, or the suffering of the singer in the absence of his beloved) and the heroics and suffering of war. Musically, these songs are monophonic. Though contemporary manuscript illustrations often depict the singers accompanying themselves on the harp, vielle, lute or other instruments, we have no idea what they played because no notation for such instrumental accompaniment has survived.

In addition to exalted themes of love and war sung by the educated aristocracy, there were songs on less elevated themes. In France, a class of "professional" musicians called *jongleurs*—who often doubled as acrobats and jugglers—performed at public fairs and other gatherings of the common folk. A number of wandering students and young clerics, known collectively as the Goliards (from an Old French word for "glutton") travelled Europe begging for food and lodging; in return, they entertained audiences with songs of drunkenness, gambling, and love of a less than courtly nature. These songs, often witty and irreverent, were composed in Latin. The most famous collection of these goliardic songs is the so-called *Carmina Burana*, named for the Benedictine monastery of Beuren in which the manuscript containing them was discovered; these are explicitly "profane" songs of student debauchery, of wine, women, and love.

So far in this chapter we have discussed music in which the distinction between sacred and secular was clearly maintained. But it must not be supposed that either type of music existed in total isolation from the other. The influence of sacred music—especially chant—was clearly the more powerful. The songs of the *troubadours* and *trouvères* borrowed many features from chant, not least the basic principles of its notation. At the same time, sacred music was not immune from the influnece of secular styles: some scholars have seen the origins of the vigorous rhythms of organum in the dance music of the period.

During the thirteenth century, composers continued to elaborate and adorn existing music; by now, organum—which had itself originated as an elaboration of earlier music—was being elaborated. The ornate melodies added by Leonin (and later by Perotin) had no words of their own; the singer merely vocalized the vowel of the original chant melody. Early in the thirteenth century, words were added to these melodies; the resulting new genre was called *motet*, from the French "mot", meaning "word". The motet soon became the most important type of composition, and received the attention of composers throughout this century.

Motets were originally concerned exclusively with sacred subjects, but it was not long before secular texts were set as well. Though the motet had begun with the addition of words to pre-existing organum, composers soon began to compose fresh upper parts which were independent of organum. The medieval emphasis on tradition was so strong, however, that—instead of writing wholly independent new pieces—composers used fragments of chant as the lowest of the (usually) three voices. This voice was called the *tenor*, from Latin "tenere", to hold. This method was applied to motets with both sacred and secular texts.

By the end of the thirteenth century, the link with chant weakened and, in place of chant melodies, composers began to use secular songs, dances, even the upper parts of other motets, as the tenor. Nevertheless, the practice of basing each new composition on some portion of an earlier one continued for a long time.

Perhaps the most important thirteenth-century development was the invention and refinement of a system of notation which allowed the performer to read the rhythmic structure of the music directly from the page. This system, first described by the theorist **Franco of Cologne** (fl. 1250–80) accounts for the enormous freedom and diversity of music in this period.

Early in the fourteenth century, another theorist and composer, the Frenchman Philippe de Vitry (1291–1361), proclaimed an *ars nova* ("new art") in music. De Vitry recognized and codified the expanded rhythmic possibilities of Franco's notation, and encouraged composers (himself included) to practice an art utterly different from the *ars antiqua* of the thirteenth century. This new art flourished in both France and Italy.

In France, the greatest composer of the century was **Guillaume de Machaut** (c.1300–1377), a cleric, diplomat and poet as well as composer. Among his patrons were the Kings of Bohemia and Navarrre, Jean the Duke of Berry, and King Charles V of France.

Machaut wrote both sacred and secular music. We have previously spoken of the importance of his *Notre Dame Mass*, the earliest polyphonic setting of the complete Ordinary. In addition, he wrote a number of secular motets. But he is best known for his secular songs—he wrote both the poems and the music—in the three standard forms (called *formes fixes*) of medieval French poetry: *ballade*, *rondeau*, and *virelai* Each of these forms had its own very concisely prescribed structure, rhyme scheme, and refrain pattern.

These works are the clearest examples of the *ars nova* style. Machaut's polyphonic writing demonstrates a new sense of direction and mastery. Machaut also effectively solved the chief problem presented by the *formes fixes* in coordinating the musical and poetic structures. A great deal of his music survives, some in manuscripts whose preparation he is known to have supervised personally.

Italian composers of the thirteenth century did not take to polyphony with the same enthusiasm as their French counterparts; for reasons which we do not fully understand, Italian music of this period seems to have remained exclusively monophonic. After about 1330, however, a group of composers working at the courts of northern Italy began to cultivate secular polyphony. One of these, the blind organist **Francesco Landini** (1325–1397), made significant contributions to the field. Unlike his French contemporary Machaut, Landini wrote no music for the church—at least, none survives. But like Machaut, Landini composed a large number of secular songs in the three genres which were the Italian equivalents of the French *formes fixes*: the *ballata, madrigal*, and *caccia*.

Landini wrote about 150 ballate for two and three voices, notable for the fact that their chief interest appears almost exclusively in the top voice. Examples like *Questa fanciulla amor (This Maiden Love)* and *L'alma mia piange (My Soul Weeps)* demonstrate why his contemporaries considered Landini the finest composer of the age.

Only about a dozen of Landini's madrigals survive. Though they bear the same name, these pieces are quite unlike the madrigals composed in sixteenth-century Italy or Elizabethan England [see Chapter3].

The caccia (literally, "hunt" or "chase") was a particularly light-hearted sort of composition. Its name is a play on words: the caccia was written for two voices constructed in *canon* [see Glossary], a kind of polyphony in which both voices sing the same melody but start at different times. Thus, they "chase" each other through the song. These two upper voices were usually supported by an independent third part performed instrumentally. The subjects of these songs are topics of everyday human interest: descriptions of the hunt, market and battle scenes. The songs typically include "sound effects": horn calls, shouts, bird imitations and other such details.

Like Landini, the English composer **John Dunstable** (c. 1385–1453) explored the relatively new technique of emphasizing the melody in the top line of a polyphonic composition. Dunstable was widely traveled and broadly influential on the Continent, at a time when the court in England was still much influenced by French culture. He was attached to the court of the Duke of Bedford, the younger brother of the English King Henry V. The Duke became Regent of France in 1422, following Henry's victory at the Battle of Agincourt and his reclaiming of his French possessions. The following year, the Duke married the sister of the Duke of Burgundy, thus allying himself with one of the most powerful (and musical) centers of the day. Dunstable wrote both Mass settings and secular songs for the court; of his sixty surviving compositions, perhaps the most famous is the motet for the Feast of Pentecost entitled *Veni sancte Spiritus (Come, Holy Spirit)*.

Dunstable's motets represent a considerable advance over earlier examples of the genre [see above]: the music is more naturally fitted to the words, and the polyphonic parts flow smoothly. Dunstable's prominent use of the interval of the major third gives his music a remarkably modern sound—one which was perceived in fifteenth-century France and Italy as uncommonly "sweet".

John Dunstable's connections with the court of Burgundy—which was, as we shall see in Chapter 3, one of the most important musical centers of Europe—make make him especially important in the transition into the fifteenth century, when Europe was on the brink of the Renaissance. When the scourge of the Hundred Years' War (1337–1453) had passed, the vital artistic re-birth which had begun in Italy during the time of Landini was to spread across the Continent and into the British Isles. During this period, every aspect of medieval civilization—government, philosophy, and all the arts (and music not the least of them)—were to be profoundly transformed.

Questions for Review

1. What is the origin of the word "music"?

2. What did Plato and Aristotle believe about the power of music? How was their philosophy modified by the medieval Christian Church?

3. What is the difference between sacred and secular music?

4. Why is the earliest music preserved in the West almost all sacred?

5. In what ways does Gregorian Chant differ from music of later periods?

6. What is the difference between monophonic and polyphonic music?

7. How did Leonin transform the chant? How did Perotin transform Leonin's compositions?

8. What were the usual topics of songs composed by the *troubadours, trouvères* and *Minnesingers*?

9. Identify briefly the following:

    a) goliard

    b) Franco of Cologne

    b) *ars nova*

    b) *formes fixes*

10. What was the most important musical genre of the thirteenth century? How was it derived from Notre Dame organum?

11. What is the difference between the Ordinary and the Proper of the Mass?

12. Who wrote the first complete polyphonic setting of the Mass Ordinary? What else did he compose?

13. Describe the musical and textual characteristics of the *caccia*.

14. Why was John Dunstable's music perceived as "sweet" by the French and Italians?

Answers

1. "Music" comes from the Greek *mousike*, meaning an art related to the Muse or Muses.

2. Plato and Aristotle both believed that music had the power to shape human character for good or ill. The medieval Church insisted that the fundamental purpose of music was the glorification of God.

3. Sacred music is composed for religious texts or religious purposes; secular (literally, "worldly") is composed for such purposes as entertainment, dancing, amusement of the performers—in short, any non-religious purpose.

4. The earliest music preserved in the West is almost entirely sacred because the Church was the center of learning during the Middle Ages, because the clergy monopolized the art of writing, and because religious institutions had both the economic wherewithall and the continuity to be able to foster and preserve music.

5. A complete answer includes the following: it is exclusively sacred; it is very formal music, totally removed from any secular association; it is

monophonic; it has no strong metrical rhythm; it was originally written with a system of symbols called *neumes*.

6. Monophonic music consists of a single melodic line. Polyphonic music consists of two or more melodic lines sung and/or played simultaneously.

7. Leonin added a layer of elaborate ornamentation sung by a second voice to the pre-existing layer of chant; the two parts were sung simultaneously. Perotin rewrote Léonin's compositions and added one or two more voice-parts.

8. Typical topics were courtly love and the heroics and suffering of war.

9. a) Goliards were wandering students and young clerics who composed secular songs of a witty and irreverent nature.
b) Franco of Cologne was a thirteenth-century theorist who first described a system of rhythmic notation which allowed the performer to read the rhythmic structure of music directly from the page.
c) *Ars nova* literally means "new art". It refers to the new style of music composed in France and Italy during the fourteenth century. The name was coined by Philippe de Vitry, a French composer and theorist.
d) *Formes fixes* is the term which refers to the standard forms of medieval French poetry: *ballade, rondeau* and *virelai*. Each has its own specific and strictly determined structure, rhyme scheme and refrain pattern.

10. The motet was the most important musical genre of the thirteenth century. It is derived from the Notre Dame organum by adding words (*mots* in French) to the textless upper part(s).

11. The Ordinary consists of the texts that are included in every celebration of the Mass: Kyrie, Gloria, Credo, Sanctus, Agnus Dei. The Proper consists of texts that are changeable, depending on the Church calendar of seasons, saints' days and other holy days.

12. The first complete polyphonic setting of the Mass Ordinary was written by the fourteenth-century French composer Guillaume de Machaut, and is called the *Notre-Dame Mass*. Machaut also composed a large body of secular music, including motets; he is particularly known for writing both the words and music to a large number of secular songs in the *formes fixes*: *ballade, rondeau*, and *virelai*.

13. The *caccia* is a fourteenth-century Italian secular song with a light-hearted text which often depicts a realistic subject. It is written for two voices in canon which chase each other through the song, and a supporting instrumental part. It often includes such sound effects as horn calls, bird songs, shouts, etc.

14. It was perceived as "sweet" because of Dunstable's frequent use of the interval of the major third.

Chapter 3

Patronage and Renaissance

Patronage and Renaissance

In the last chapter, we saw the dominant influence of the Church in the development of medieval music. Alongside the polyphonic elaboration of chant, Masses, and motets, secular songs and dances flourished; even composers of sacred music borrowed some secular elements. But whether sacred or secular, music was written primarily for voice. Instrumental accompaniment was secondary, and purely instrumental music was only very rarely written down during the Middle Ages. Rather, medieval instrumentalists were skilled improvisers (like twentieth-century jazz musicians), making up accompaniments to their tunes as they went along.

The polyphonic style [see Chapters 1 and 2] continued to predominate. Notes that were sounded together were still perceived as elements of horizontal melodic lines, not as parts of harmonically combined sounds (chords). The modes continued to regulate the interaction of the several melodic strands; as a consequence, many compositions from the period have an exotic tonality that does not correspond to the sound of our modern major and minor keys.

We come now to the dynamic rebirth of European culture called the Renaissance. Renaissance literally means "re-birth" and specifically refers to the rediscovery of the classical cultures of ancient Greece and Rome by a group of Italian intellectuals during the fourteenth century. These men combined a willingness to break away from the rigid orthodoxies of their medieval predecessors with a fresh, dynamic assimilation of ancient literature and art. Because of their insistence on the greater importance of human beings in relationship to God, these intellectuals are called "humanists" and their philosophy "humanism". It was a movement which made itself felt in all areas of life, but especially in the arts.

Over the course of the next two centuries, the humanistic movement spread to France, Germany, the Low Countries (now Belgium and the Netherlands), Spain, and England . Politically, it coincided with the birth of nationalism and the final collapse of the medieval system of feudalism. Artistically, the Renaissance generally encouraged a new simplicity. Renaissance masters broke away from the complexity of the Gothic style; they sought a simpler and more human style of expression. The rediscovery of the classical master-pieces of ancient Greece and Rome was highly influential for sculpture, painting, and literature. The Renaissance broke radically with the most basic assumptions of medieval thought: that man's earthly life was poor and contemptible, merely a preparation for eternity in heaven or hell. For the first time in a thousand years, art-ists, writers, and musicians celebrated the variety and wonder of life on earth; they glorified man as well as God.

The new importance of human considerations resulted in the pro-lific composition of secular music, intended for entertainment. Music became an integral part, not only of church services, but of court life. In the late Middle Ages, the patronage of kings and princes had supported the traveling minstrels (*troubadours* and *Minnesin-gers*). Now, such patronage supported composers on a more perma-nent basis. It was in the early Renaissance that the patronage system, which was to endure until the time of Beethoven in the early nineteenth century, was firmly established. Every court needed composers and performers in its retinue, to provide entertainment and to celebrate the achievements and fair name of the ruler.

In the fifteenth century, some of the finest composers were to be found at the court of the Dukes of Burgundy, who ruled over what is now Eastern France, Luxembourg, and the Low Countries. The works of **Guillaume Dufay** (c.1400–1474), epitomize the new, cos-mopolitan quality of much fifteenth-century music. Born near the city of Cambrai (close to the modern nothern border of France), Dufay travelled widely in both France and Italy, and assimilated many elements of their differing musical styles. For a time he was a member of the choir of the Papal Chapel in Rome—an important musical center which drew upon the finest musical talent of all Europe.

It was probably during his Italian travels that Dufay became famil-iar with the music of English composers including John Dunstable [see Chapter 2], which was renowned for the "sweetness" deriving from its prominent use of the major third. Dufay made important contributions to both sacred and secular music. In the former cate-gory are several Masses, some of which are based not on the tradi-tional Gregorian chant melodies, but rather on popular songs of

Dufay's own time—a loud reminder that we are no longer in the Middle Ages. Dufay also composed a number of sacred motets: a particularly interesting example is the one he wrote to be sung at his own funeral, *Ave Regina Coelorum (Hail, Queen of Heaven)*. At the conclusion of this work, Dufay mentions himself by name in a sung prayer for divine mercy on his soul—something that would have been unthinkable in a medieval motet. Dufay's secular compositions include a special kind of motet composed expressly for public ceremonies of a political, rather than a religious, kind; a number of these also feature the names of the persons in whose honor they were written.

Dufay's most important secular works are his *chansons* (literally, "songs") with French rather than Latin texts. The themes of these songs are almost invariably concerned with courtly love, including the particularly charming *Ce mois de mai (This month of May)*. Many of Dufay's chansons are in the *formes fixes* first encountered in the works of Machaut [see Chapter 2], and most are for three voices; sometimes the two lower parts were performed on instruments.

Dufay is important for cultivating new genres, and also for drawing together the elements of several national styles, forging from them a more simple, direct, and mature musical language. Dufay's melodic writing is smooth and often rhythmically active, and approaches *cadences* (musical phrase endings) in ways that begin to sound familiar to modern ears.

Three other composers born in the Low Countries are particularly significant in the development of Renaissance music. The first is Dufay's friend and exact contemporary, **Gilles Binchois** (c.1400–1460). Binchois served Duke Philip the Good as chief composer at the Burgundian capital, Dijon. Although he was a cleric (as was Dufay), he is best known for his secular chansons; these show him to have been a somewhat more experimental—if less polished—composer than Dufay. These songs typically deal with courtly love, and often have a delicately mournful quality, as in his setting of *Deuil angoisseus (Anguished Mourning)*.

Johannes Ockeghem (c.1430–1497) composed in a style very similar to that of the Burgundians, though his own career led him elsewhere. He began as a singer in the choir of the cathedral at Antwerp, then a center of Burgundian power and wealth. He entered the service of the King of France in 1453, and remained as the principal composer at the court (then located at Tours) until his death. Ockeghem, like Dufay, composed both sacred and secular music; like his illustrious predecessor, he refined and rendered more subtle the musical expression of his time. Unlike Dufay, however, he is chiefly remembered for his contributions to the sacred repertory; ten of his Masses survive, one of them a very early setting of the *Requiem*, or Mass for the Dead, and twelve motets. Ockeghem's simplicity often conceals skillful, quasi-mathematical ingenuity.

Josquin Des Prez (c.1450–1517) was also born in the Low Countries (the exact place remains uncertain). He enjoyed an international career and reputation—both in his own time and for centuries afterward, Josquin was widely recognized as the greatest composer of his age.

Josquin's lament on the death of Ockeghem suggests a teacher-pupil relationship, though no other evidence is known to support the theory and the tribute may simply have been a token of respect for an eminent elder colleague.

Josquin's first mature works stem from his early twenties—years spent in Italy at Milan and Rome. For a period just after 1500, he spent time in France—perhaps at the court of Louis XII, though details are sketchy. A second sojourn to italy took him to Ferrara, a vital musical center. Fleeing an outbreak of plague in 1503, Josquin returned north to the city of Conde; there he served as provost of the cathedral until his death.

Like Dufay and Ockeghem, Josquin composed both sacred and secular music—nearly twenty Masses, some eighty motets, and about seventy secular works (both vocal and, notably, instrumental) are ascribed to him. While Josquin's sacred music reveals his debt to his great Northern predecessors, especially Ockeghem, his secular music clearly shows the influence of the popular styles of Italy as well as France. His own contributions include a more extensive use of imitation in his polyphonic writing, as well as a more systematic interplay of two- and three-voice textures to provide relief within the usual four-part framework.

In England, Josquin des Prez was much admired by Anne Boleyn, the unfortunate second wife of King Henry VIII (ruled 1509–1547). The King himself was a composer; he played the lute, the clavichord, and the virginals (a keyboard instrument with plucked strings that became popular in the time of Queen Elizabeth, toward the end of the sixteenth century). Henry VIII's break with the Church of Rome had important consequences for the development of English sacred music. **John Taverner** (c.1495–1545), appointed by Cardinal Wolsey as choirmaster at Christ Church, Oxford, composed eight Masses and several motets which are landmarks in English polyphonic music, not least because of their influence on later English composers, especially William Byrd [see Chapter 4]. Typical of Taverner's motet style is *O Wilhelme, pastor bone (O William, good shepherd)* in honor of St. William of York.

After the death of Josquin, the grip of the Netherlandish style was weakened, to be replaced by a number of musical styles which developed along national lines; composers of the important musical centers of Italy, France, England, Germany, and Spain each drew on aspects of the Netherlandish style, developing and altering them to suit their own local tastes and needs.

In Italy, the cities of Rome, Florence, and Venice were the musical and intellectual centers. Italian composers devoted themselves principally to three types of music: Mass, motet, and madrigal. Their developments in these genres were quickly imitated elsewhere, particularly in England and Germany. The spread of music from one area of Europe to another was simplified at the very start of the sixteenth century by the invention of a method for printing music.

The Venetian **Andrea Gabrieli** (c.1510–1586) made significant contributions to Italian music in the late Renaissance. The organist and music director of St. Mark's Cathedral, Gabrieli seized upon the architectural features of the building—it has many spacious galleries—as the inspiration for a new kind of music. Gabrieli's predecessor, **Adrian Willaert** (c.1485–1562) had composed a number of Psalm settings which called for two separate choirs—a reminder of the antiphonal style in Gregorian chant [see Chapter 2]. Gabrieli extended Willaert's concept; dividing his musicians into a number of separate vocal choirs, each with its own supporting group of instruments, he placed them here and there among the galleries of St. Mark's. Thus, contrast became one of the most important elements of this musical style.

Andrea Gabrieli also cultivated an instrumental genre known as the *ricercare* (from Italian " to seek out"). In this form, one instrumental voice plays a melody, which is then imitated polyphonically by each of the others in succession. When each instrumental voice has had its turn, the process begins again with a new melodic fragment. Sometimes the same melody is presented in different rhythmic variants, sometimes completely different material is introduced. The form had important implications for keyboard music: many ricercari were written for organ, and later examples are the clear forerunners of the Baroque *fugue* [see Chapter 5].

More conservative than Andrea Gabrieli, **Giovanni Pierluigi da Palestrina** (c.1525–1594) devoted his creative energies almost exclusively to the Church, especially the choir of the Sistine Chapel (in the Vatican, at Rome). Palestrina wrote nearly 100 Masses for four, five, six, and eight voices, and 150 motets, some for as many as twelve voices.

The Church had become sensitive to the criticisms of Martin Luther and other leaders of the Reformation [see Chapter 5] who complained that the excessively ornate style of late-Renaissance sacred music made it impossible for the congregation to participate in the Mass. The Council of Trent—convened by the Church (1545–1563) to reassert its authority in the face of Protestant schism—decreed that music should be used in such a way that "the words must be clearly understood by all." All secular elements which were not spiritually uplifting were to be purged; singers were enjoined to be modest and restrained.

In reponse, Palestrina created a style of polyphony known as *a cappella* ("in the style of the chapel"), which set the text so that the words are clearly audible, and eliminated the use of instruments (hence our modern use of the term *a cappella* to denote "unaccompanied choral music"). Palestrina's setting of Psalm 42, *Sicut cervus desiderat (As the hart panteth for water brooks)*, is a particularly well-known example of his style. The polyphonic lines have a breadth reminiscent of Gregorian chant, and the same timeless quality. Palestrina's particularly careful handling of dissonance has made his music a model for study to the present day.

Palestrina's revitalization of the Roman tradition of sacred music was particularly influential in Spain. The greatest Spanish composer of the time was **Tomás Luis de Victoria** (c.1549–1611). Born in the Spanish city of Avila (made famous by St. Teresa), Victoria came to Rome in 1565, where he remained for more than thirty years as composer and organist; he may also have studied with Palestrina. All of Victoria's works were intended for the Church: motets, hymns, Masses, antiphons, and settings for the Psalms. He returned to Spain in 1596, and became choirmaster of a convent in Madrid during the last years of his life. Victoria's severe sacred style reflects the Church's intense concern with religious orthodoxy early in the Counter-Reformation. Like his contemporary, the painter El Greco (c.1541–1614), Victoria was inspired by a passionate religious devotion.

Meanwhile, secular music continued to thrive. Slightly before the time of Victoria, an important school of instrumental music was beginning to develop. **Luis Milan** (c.1500–c.1561) focused his efforts on solo music for the *vilhuela*, a forerunner of the guitar. A number of Milan's songs were published in 1536; their distinctive Spanish sound reflects the origin of their rhythmic and melodic elements in folk music.

The development of secular music can be seen in other places as well. In Italy, a type of song called the *frottola* was the favorite genre for the first third of the sixteenth century. It was usually composed in four voice-parts; the top part was sung, and the lower three were performed on instruments. One of the earliest composers of frottole was **Bartolomeo Tromboncino** (c.1470–1535), who was attached to the court of Isabella d'Este at Mantua.

The simplicity of the frottola was a good foil to the complexities of sacred vocal polyphony, and the genre spread rapidly through the musical centers of northern Italy. Yet their very simplicity probably contributed to the shortness of the vogue for the frottola. By the year 1530, a fusion began to take place between the secular frottola and the polyphonic techniques of sacred music. The result was the *madrigal* (a new form unrelated to the fourteenth-century genre of the same name). The madrigal became the most important musical genre of the sixteenth century.

Although the madrigal originated in the four-voice frottola, five voice parts became the norm after 1550, and late sixteenth-century examples were composed for six, seven, and even eight voices. The increased number of parts allowed composers to create a richer harmonic language, and to vary the texture continually. Composers of madrigals became increasingly concerned with the relationship between the emotional sense of the text and its expression in the music. Thus, an important feature of madrigal composition—particularly toward the end of the century—is a process known as "word-painting" or "tone-painting", in which the composer deliberately mirrors the meaning of a word or phrase in his musical setting. Common examples include a rising melody at the mention of the rising sun, or the use of black notes (like modern quarter notes) to coincide with the word "death". Although this process was soon carried to extremes, it demonstrates a new concern with the relationship between music and words—a concern which also led, around 1600, to the new form which we call *opera* [see Chapter 4].

In France, the chief genre was the *chanson*, which had developed out of the early examples of Binchois and Dufay. Like the frottola, it was a simple four-part vocal piece, then was transformed into a more sophisticated genre which employed instruments for the lower parts. In the early sixteenth century, under the reign of François I (1515–1547), the chanson was a light, rhythmically vigorous composition dealing with French themes and easy to sing. The texts were often bawdy, and consisted of short sections repeated in simple patterns. The enormous popularity of the chanson in France is directly attributable to the more than fifty collections of such songs published by the Parisian Pierre Attaingnant (died c.1552), who invented the first practical method of printing music from movable type. Two of the best-known composers in these collections were Claudin de Sirmisy (c.1490–1562) and **Clement Jannequin** (c.1485–c.1560). The songs of Jannequin were especially remarkable for incorporating imitations of the sounds of everyday life—bird calls, street cries, the trumpets and drums of battle.

A final category of music which became important during the sixteenth century was dance music. Folk-dancing had always flourished, frequently to improvised accompaniment. The new popularity of dancing as a courtly pastime encouraged the composition of more elaborate pieces, which employed the techniques of other instrumental forms. Dances were often paired—that is, a slow dance was followed by a quick dance, sometimes based on the same melody. Such a pair was the *pavane* and the *galliard*. We can reconstruct the steps of such dances with considerable precision because they were elaborately described (with musical illustrations) in a treatise by the French cleric Thoinot Arbeau (1519–1595), entitled *Orchésographie* (*On the Dance*) (1589). Thus, we know that the pavane was a slow and stately processional with highly formalized walking steps and the added ornamentation of many bows and curtseys. It was usually followed by its opposite, the galliard: a hopping dance of very vigorous character in which the male of each couple leaped into the air; these leaps are often reflected in the music for this dance. The pavane was always in very slow duple meter [see Chapter 1], the galliard in quick triple meter.

To exploit the contrast in meter, tempo, and character provided by such pairings of dances, composers began to link pairs of dances together into larger groups which have come to be known as *suites* (from the French "follow"). In the sixteenth century, an enormous number of such dances were composed for groups of instruments. The suite became one of the most important forms of the Baroque period [see Chapters 4 and 5]; it lost its function as an accompaniment to dancing, but provided the model for a work of several contrasting movements. The *concerto grosso, sonata* and *symphony* can all be traced to the sixteenth-century suite.

The basic idea of contrast for its own sake was a central feature of music at the close of the sixteenth century, and became perhaps the most important concept of the Baroque period, after 1600.

Such contrast is particularly evident in the music of **Giovanni Gabrieli** (1557–1612), the nephew of Andrea [see above] and his successor at St. Mark's Cathedral in Venice. In the hands of Giovanni, the *polychoral* (literally, "many choirs") style reached full maturity. At the opening and closing of Gabrieli's compositions—whether for several vocal choirs or several instrumental ensembles—the forces are often united in massive blocks of sound. As the pieces proceed, however, short melodic fragments are typically tossed back and forth among the groups and (when they were performed in St. Mark's) tossed around the building itself. Gabrieli's experimentation with this sort of writing was to culminate in the typical structure of the Baroque *concerto grosso* [see Chapter 5], in which a small group of solo instruments alternates the same musical material with larger orchestral groups. Gabrieli's great motet *Omnes gentes (All the nations)* exemplifies this style in a composition for mixed forces of voices and instruments. Another of his works, the *Sonata pian' e forte* (literally, "soft and loud sounds") contrasts a group of loud instruments with a group of softer ones. In this case, contrast is evident not only in the placement of these two groups in different locations, but by a difference in their volume as well. This, too, was to have important implications for Baroque music.

The most varied and cosmopolitan composer of the late Renaissance was **Roland de Lassus** (1532–1594). Born in the Netherlands, Lassus traveled in the service of various aristocrats in his youth; he was thus exposed to Italian musical developments. In 1553, he was choirmaster at the Basilica of St. John Lateran in Rome. He returned to the Netherlands after visits to England and France, only to move again in 1556, when he entered the service of Duke Albrecht V of Bavaria, whose court was located at Munich. He was associated with Munich for the rest of his life, but made frequent journeys all over the Continent. His thorough acquaintance with European national styles in music was matched by the variety of forms in which he composed: Masses, motets, madrigals, German songs, and French chansons. De Lassus was so highly regarded in Italy that he is often known by the Italian version of his name: Orlando di Lasso. His work is so varied that no single style seems to characterize it: de Lassus was able to assimilate German dignity, French gaiety, and Italian sweetness of harmony. In his sacred music, de Lassus is generally more dynamic and emotional than Palestrina, exploiting to the fullest the dramatic possibilities of his motet-texts. Less inclined than Palestrina to heed the Church's call for music of sobriety and restraint, de Lassus' sacred compositions almost suggest the fullness and drama of the Baroque period. In his secular song *La Nuit froide et sombre (The Dark and Cold Night)*, Lassus exhibited an opulent harmony—reminiscent of the Venetian composers—combined with a typically French lyricism.

By the year 1600, Renaissance characteristics begin to fade in music as the Baroque style assumes dominance. Since the rise of humanism in the fifteenth century, music had developed from an adornment for religious ritual and become a sophisticated art form with many uses and purposes. It acquired powerful patrons at the courts of the Renaissance nobility, and became an imported and respected profession. The invention of printing meant that music no longer had to be copied laboriously by hand; technical innovations and new styles reached throughout Europe in a few years and not, as before, over a period of several generations. And the concern with the expression of emotion, which had begun with humanistic thought, would shortly become the central philosophical pivot on which music would turn until 1900 and beyond.

Questions for Review

1. Define the word Renaissance. Where and when did the Renaissance begin?

2. What is the name of the philosophy associated with the Renaissance? How did it differ from the philosophy of the Middle Ages?

3. What was the effect, in architecture and the other arts, of the rediscovery of the classical masterpieces of Greece and Rome during the Renaissance?

4. What do Guillaume Dufay, Gilles Binchois, Johannes Ockeghem and Josquin Dez Prez have in common?

5. Briefly identify the following:

    a) *chanson*

    b) John Taverner

    c) Ottaviano Petrucci

    d) *ricercare*

    e) *vihuela*.

6. How are Palestrina and Victoria associated? Where did each work? What religious influences affected their work?

7. What was the chief concern of madrigal composers?

8. How did the dance suite originate? Why was it important for later music?

9. Give some examples of contrast as a procedure for organizing music in the late Renaissance.

10. What is *polychoral* music? How is it related to the architecture of St. Mark's Cathedral in Venice?

Answers

1. Renaissance means "re-birth". The Renaissance began in fourteenth-century Italy among a group of intellectuals and artists willing to break away from the religious orthodoxy of their medieval predecessors, and to study and re-interpret Classical literature and art in terms of the Greek view that man is the measure of all things.

2. The name of the philosophy is Humanism. It differs from medieval thought in its insistence on the potential and glory of man on earth, rather

than, as in medieval times, deploring life on earth as contemptible and merely a preparation for the eternity of heaven or hell.

3. The rediscovery of the classical masterpieces of ancient Greece and Rome had a pronounced effect on the arts; the style of sculpture, painting, and architecture moved away from Gothic complexity to embrace a simpler, more harmonious mode of expression. Simultaneously, in music, composers worked in a purer and simpler style; the complexities of late medieval polyphony gradually were replaced by chordal harmonies.

4. Dufay, Binchois, Ockeghem and Josquin are all composers who were born in the Low Countries but who had international careers or influence throughout Europe.

5. a) *chanson*: From the French for "song"; refers to secular vocal compositions with French texts composed throughout the Renaissance. Dufay and Binchois were both noted for their *chansons*. Shortly after 1500, the term is used to refer to the relatively simple four-part vocal compositions of Claudin and Jannequin.

b) John Taverner: Choirmaster at Christ Church, Oxford. Taverner's Masses and motets are important landmarks in English polyphonic music, not least because of their influence on later English composers, especially William Byrd.

c) Ottaviano Petrucci: The first printer of music, who published a collection called *Odhecaton* in Venice in 1501.

d) *ricercare*: From the Italian "to seek", a secular instrumental composition cultivated by Andrea Gabrieli in which each instrument plays a melody successively in imitative counterpoint. The ricercare is an important forerunner of the Baroque fugue.

e) *vilhuela*: A Spanish plucked stringed instrument featured importantly in the works of Luis Milan. It was the forerunner of the guitar.

7. Madrigal composers were chiefly concerned with expressing the sense of the madrigal's words by musical means.

8. The dance suite originated when composers of the mid-sixteenth century, interested in the idea of musical contrast, linked together a number of dance pairs inherited from the traditions of folk music. This pairing is important in the history of music because it is one of the earliest examples of instrumental music consisting of a number of contrasting movements.

9. Contrast may be seen in: the dance suite, where meter, tempo, and character are varied from dance to dance; the polychoral works of the Gabrielis, where musical fragments are tossed from one group (instrumental or vocal) to another; madrigals, where constant variation in texture provides contrast.

10. "Polychoral" music is music written for more than one choir of voices or instruments. Chief proponents of this style were Adrian Willaert and Andrea and Giovanni Gabrieli, all of whom were the organists and choirmasters at St. Mark's Cathedral in Venice. (The cathedral has many galleries, which made it possible to place multiple choirs in different parts of the building.)

Chapter 4

The Golden Age

The Golden Age

Music, like the other arts—like life itself—became more secular in the Renaissance. Composers now wrote for a wider group of both performers and listeners, and for more varied occasions. Song forms were invented which were easy to remember; poems written in the vernacular (the local spoken language, not Latin) were set to music; instrumental accompaniment lent richness and body to the songs. Since this was also the age of great drama—Shakespeare and Jonson in England, then Corneille, Racine, and Moliére in France—we should not be surprised that the song was soon the vehicle for dramatic expression; and that before too long, drama and music would be combined into the form of opera.

The style of music changed, too. During this period, harmony becomes both very complex and very reassuring to the modern ear; the progression and resolution of chords are closer to what modern ears expect them to be, and so we feel at home. Rhythm, too, becomes more regular; you can tap your feet to much of this music, and not have to shuffle every now and then to regain the rhythm. Ironically, this is also the time when the conductor—the one who keeps time (among other things) for the musicians—makes his debut.

With the development of dramatic as well as metrically rhythmic music came the ballet, a form which flourished particularly at the court of Louis XIV in France; and with this courtly and opulent music, the Renaissance makes way to the next great period in musical style, the Baroque (approximately 1600–1750). [The general characteristics of the Baroque style in music are summarized in Chapter 1; for a more detailed discussion, see Chapter 5.]

The genre which reflects the transitional nature of this period is the *madrigal*: a short composition, usually for four or five voices. Its theme is usually secular—for example, love in a pastoral setting—and is always sung in the vernacular. (The word *madrigal*, from Italian "matricale", seems to mean "pastoral in the mother tongue".) One of the best madrigal writers in the latter half of the sixteenth century was Luca Marenzio (1553–1599), an Italian composer who came into the service of the Polish court toward the end of his life. Marenzio wrote over two hundred madrigals. The madrigal genre was extensively cultivated in both Italy and France.

In 1588, the year the English fleet defeated the Spanish Armada, a cleric of St. Paul's Cathedral in London, Nicholas Yonge, published a translation of Italian madrigals to English words. Many of the songs (as in *Dolorous Mournful Cares*) were translations of Marenzio's madrigals. Yonge's book was called *Musica Transalpina (Music from Beyond the Alps)*; it is a landmark in the development of English music, because the form was to become extraordinarily popular and to attract the talents of some of England's finest composers.

There were some important differences between the English and the Italian madrigals, even though Italian texts served as the models for the first madrigal-writers in England. First, the English composers tended to emphasize the music of madrigals, sometimes at the expense of the dramatic qualities of the words. In the English madrigal, the piece can be perceived more readily as a coherent, musical unity. Second, even though the Renaissance occurred late in England, the land of Queen Elizabeth was a unified nation—as opposed to the many independent city-states which comprised Italy during the Renaissance. A sense of national unity and pride underlies the English madrigals, many of which make elegant references to the sovereign, using a thinly disguised "code" of Greco-Roman allusions. For example, Queen Elizabeth herself is praised under the name Oriana (derived from ancient pastoral poetry) in the collection of madrigals by Thomas Weelkes [see below]. The English composers of this period brought to their music an intangible, but very real, sense of being English.

The notable composers of madrigals in the English Renaissance include **Thomas Morley** (1557–1602) and **Thomas Weelkes** (c. 1575–1623). Morley, who was probably a friend of Shakespeare's, was a pupil of William Byrd [see below]. In the late 1580s, he became the organist of St. Paul's Cathedral in London, and was associated with the Chapel Royal. He was so favored by the Queen that she granted him an exclusive license to print song-books and music paper in 1598. Thus, Morley occupied a remarkably important position in the musical life of his time—not only by virtue of his own works, but through the power to publish those of his contemporaries. It is likely that Morley composed the music for the songs in some of Shakespeare's comedies (e.g. *Twelfth Night*, first performed in 1600). In 1601, he published a book of 25 madrigals entitled *The Triumphs of Oriana*. Each madrigal ended with the phrase, "Long live fair Oriana", a more literary statement than "Long live the Queen." The songs, like the contemporary sonnets of such courtiers as Sir Philip Sidney, employed elegant allusions to classical mythology, and to a genre of classical literature which was extremely popular in the Renaissance: the pastoral. The pastoral dealt with lightly amorous affairs of shepherds and shepherdesses in an idealized, rural landscape. Some of the titles in Morley's collection included: *Bright Phoebus, Fair Oriana, The Nymphs and Shepherds Danced, Calm Was the Air*, and *Sing Shepherds All*.

An especially beautiful madrigal in Morley's collection is *As Venus Was from Latmos Hill Descending*. It was composed by Thomas Weelkes, the organist of Winchester College and Chichester Cathedral. Weelkes published several books of his own madrigals, as well as a collection of *Ayres or Phantasticke Spirites* for three voices: these latter songs show that Weelkes could be lightly satirical, as well as sweetly sentimental. When Thomas Morley died in 1602, Weelkes wrote a beautiful three-part song in lament, *Death Hath Deprived Me of My Dearest Friend*.

Alongside the madrigals, which were sung by both court aristocrats and commoners, other types of secular music were popular in Elizabethan England. The composer **Anthony Holborne** (died c. 1602) wrote instrumental pieces for wind and brass ensembles. He is reputed to have been the finest trumpeter in England; his book of short instrumental pieces, entitled *Pavans, Galliards, Almans, and other Short Aires*, was published in 1599. [The title refers to three types of dance; for Italian development of such dance forms, see Chapter 3.]

Also popular were short songs for solo voice and instrumental accompaniment, normally by the most favored instruments of the time, the lute and the viols. Such songs could be sung by ordinary folk for entertainment; they were generally less erudite in content than the madrigals, with fewer complex allusions to classical antiquity. The greatest composer of songs in this period was **John Dowland** (1563–1626). Dowland spent many years away from England in his youth; he worked in the diplomatic service in Paris, and then traveled to various European courts (Venice, Florence, Nuremberg, and Denmark). Because of his Catholic faith, he ran considerable risks at court, since the English sovereign was also the head of the Church of England and not famous for religious tolerance. Still, Dowland managed to become court musician to King James I (Queen Elizabeth's successor) in 1612.

Dowland is now recognized as one of England's most original composers. His books of songs are ancestors of the art song, or *Lied*, which we associate primarily with early German Romanticism [see Chapter 8 below, on Franz Schubert]. Dowland's songs differ from the contemporary English madrigals in that they are composed for a single voice with lute accompaniment. Such songs were commonly called airs, rather than madrigals, as in the titles of Dowland's songbooks: *Three Books of Songs or Ayres* (published in 1597, 1600, and 1603). Dowland acquired the reputation for melancholy in his songs: contemporary descriptions of the songs include the punning Latin "Semper Dowland, semper dolens." ("Whenever it's Dowland, it's always sad."). Such songs as *I Saw My Lady Weep* would seem to confirm this. But that he could write gay and lively pieces is shown by the songs *Sleep Wayward Thoughts* and *Fine Knacks for Ladies*. Dowland is commemorated as the "English Orpheus", an allusion to the singer of ancient Greek mythology, whose songs cast such a spell that they were said to charm even the spirits of the underworld.

The most versatile of the English composers, active in both secular and sacred forms, was **William Byrd** (1542–1623). Byrd has been called the greatest artist of the English Renaissance after Shakespeare. He was a pupil of the organist and composer, Thomas Tallis (c. 1505–1585), with whom he shared duties at the Chapel Royal. With Tallis, Byrd published a collection of motets, *Cantiones sacrae*, which were dedicated to Queen Elizabeth in 1575. Like Dowland, Byrd was a Roman Catholic; his fame as a composer (and some influential friends) protected him from official reprisals. Byrd composed church music for both Latin and Anglican liturgies; among his sacred works are three Masses, various motets, and the Protestant *Great Service*, in which various parts of the Catholic Mass were combined with Anglican *anthems* (the equivalent of motets) in English.

Byrd also wrote madrigals and songs for solo voice, as well as purely instrumental compositions. The latter were written in new forms for combinations of string instruments and also for a popular instrument, the virginals. The virginals featured one or two keyboards, with a set of strings parallel to the keyboard enclosed within a soundbox. Somewhat similar to the harpsichord in that the strings were plucked mechanically, the virginals were often mounted on a large table. This is the instrument which, it is said, was played by Queen Elizabeth.

Byrd's younger contemporary **John Bull** (c. 1562–1628) was a talented composer for the virginals; together with Byrd and Orlando Gibbons [see below], Bull published a book of twenty-one pieces for the instrument, entitled *Parthenia*, in 1611. The title, which is the Greek word for "maiden", is a play on the word "virginal".

The last of the great Elizabethan composers is **Orlando Gibbons** (1583–1625). Gibbons served as organist of the Chapel Royal (where he was appointed at the age of twenty-one), and of Westminster Abbey. Gibbons' output is similar to that of Byrd: motets, madrigals, anthems, and keyboard pieces. The anthems are particularly notable; they comprise some of the grandest and most dignified English sacred music. Gibbons' melancholy pessimism may be seen in such songs as *What Is Our Life*, set to a poem by Sir Walter Ralegh (who was executed in 1618). The madrigal entitled *The Silver Swan* is a particularly excellent example of the most refined English madrigal style.

We turn now to the late Renaissance in Italy. Around the year 1580, a group of poets and musicians in Florence founded a society called the *Camerata* ("association"). Count Giovanni Bardi (1534–1612) served as host; the group, which met at the Bardi Palace, included the composers **Jacopo Peri** (1561–1633) and **Giulio Caccini** (c. 1548–1618). The *Camerata* shared a fascination with ancient Greek drama, and with the combination of poetry, music, and dance that classical theater exemplified. Although the original circumstances of performance could not be re-created (since the details of Greek music and dance-steps were lost), the members of the *Camerata* were intrigued by the narrative and dramatic potential of words set to music. In contrast to the Elizabethans, who incorporated music into their plays for diversion and entertainment, these Italians strove to turn drama and dialogue into music. In 1597, Jacopo Peri composed such a musical drama, entitled *Dafne*; three years later, he adapted another classical legend in *Euridice* (1600). *Dafne* is now lost; *Euridice*, based on the legend of Orpheus, is historically important as foreshadowing the first, full-length opera.

Perhaps the most important result of the *Camerata* was its influence on the young **Claudio Monteverdi** (1567–1643), the greatest composer of the early Italian Baroque. Monteverdi was born in Cremona, near Venice. As a young man, he entered the service of the Duke of Mantua; he played the viols and composed madrigals for court entertainment. He seems to have heard Peri's *Euridice* soon after its first performance. In 1607, he produced *La Favola di Orfeo (The Fable of Orpheus)*, which is the earliest opera that is still now performed, and was the first to feature the accompaniment of a large instrumental ensemble. Based on the same legend of the classical musician Orpheus, who descended to the underworld to retrieve his wife Eurydice, Monteverdi's work represents a great turning point in the development of musical forms. Composed in a prologue and five acts, it features a stylized, Arcadian landscape, complete with nymphs and shepherds; the action is relatively wooden and unconvincing, and the opera is somewhat awkwardly divided into distinct "numbers": solo arias, ensembles, dances, etc. Yet we are likely, from the modern vantage point, to overlook the magnitude of Monteverdi's originality. He demonstrated that opera (from Italian *opera in musica*, a "work in music") was a viable musical form. Monteverdi's later operas, *Il Ritorno d'Ulisse in Patria* (The Return of Ulysses) and *L'incoronazione di Poppea* (1642) (*The Coronation of Poppaea*), display a further advance: for the first time in opera, characters are recognizably human, rather than idealized abstractions derived from classical myths and legends.

Opera was to become one of the most enduring large-scale musical forms. From its beginnings in Italy, it spread to France, England, and Germany in the later seventeenth and eighteenth centuries. It was to be some time before opera joined music and drama into a convincing unity, where the orchestra and the dramatic action exploited their potential to the fullest; the next important developments in the form had to await the genius of Christoph Willibald von Gluck and Wolfgang Amadeus Mozart. But the crucial first step had been taken by Monteverdi.

In 1613, Monteverdi succeeded Andrea and Giovanni Gabrieli as the chief musician of St. Mark's in Venice. He was active in a number of forms besides opera: Masses, motets, a variety of secular songs and madrigals, and a collection of sacred songs called the *Vespers of the Holy Virgin*, for varied numbers of voices and instrumental accompaniment. Monteverdi was also a distinguished teacher. One of his pupils was **Biagio Marini** (1597–1665). Marini was a violinist and composer; he was one of the first musicians to write difficult compositions for a solo instrument, thereby inaugurating the tradition of the virtuoso (or star performer). Marini's technical skill is showcased in his violin concerti and sonata for two violins.

Another Italian of the next generation, **Jean-Baptiste Lully** (1632–1687), is credited with inventing the form of the classical ballet. He was born Giovanni Batista Lulli in Florence, but travelled to France at the age of fourteen, became a French citizen, and remained in the service of Louis XIV at Versailles from 1653 until his death. King Louis XIV, *le roi soleil* (the Sun King), created at Versailles the most opulent court in Europe. Passionately devoted to music, dance, and court spectacles of every kind, the King often participated in the elaborate entertainments that Lully and others fashioned for the diversion of the nobility. Lully, as music master to the royal family, was Louis' favorite composer. He wrote some sacred music, but his major efforts involved opera and ballet. His opera combined Italian inspiration with French taste. Lully invented elaborate overtures, interspersed the action with ballets, and devised a form of *recitative* (or intoned narration) with instrumental accompaniment. Such operas as *Alceste* (1674) were based on classical mythology; but Lully seldom missed an opportunity to suggest flattering parallels between the ancient heroes and gods and the benevolent Sun King.

The ballet was at this time an equally stylized form, dominated by the characters and narrative of ancient myths. But Lully, in addition to making the form fashionably popular, is to be credited with some significant innovations. He brought female dancers into the professional company, and broadened the ballet's appeal by linking it, not only with opera, but with stage comedy. Here his collaborator was the greatest master of French comedy, Jean-Baptiste Poquelin, known as Molière (1622–1673). The genre in which the two worked together is known as comédie-ballet: two of the most notable examples are *George Dandin* (1668) and *Le Bourgeois Gentilhomme*, satirical plays which mocked the efforts of the middle class to imitate aristocratic fashion.

Lully also appears to have been one of the first conductors. As master of music at Versailles, his duties included composing, training the singers and dancers, and directing the musicians and ballet ensemble at performances. A story records that he used a long staff for beating time, rather than the modern conductor's stick, or baton. While conducting a *Te Deum*, or hymn of praise, to celebrate the recovery of his royal master from an illness, Lully accidentally struck his own foot in a particularly emphatic gesture; the resulting abscess developed into fatal gangrene.

During the 1650s, a frequent guest at Versailles was the English King Charles II, who had been forced into exile by the Civil War and the rebellion of Oliver Cromwell. Charles II was also a fervent devotee of music and drama (especially comedies). When he returned to England in the Restoration of 1660, he brought with him the popular styles of the French court. Music and drama had been severely suppressed by Cromwell's Puritan regime as frivolous, if not works of the devil. But after the Restoration, the theaters were re-opened, and there was a new surge of artistic activity. The comedy of manners, derived from Molière, flourished on the English stage. In music, the King encouraged both sacred and secular forms; he endowed a new concert hall, near Covent Garden in London, with royal patronage. The contemporary diarist Samuel Pepys records that he had heard that the King once requested "all the bawdy songs they could think of" from a group of folk musicians.

It was in this climate that the greatest composer of the English baroque, **Henry Purcell** (1659–1695), grew up. Purcell was the son of one of the King's musicians, and studied music as a chorister of the Chapel Royal. At the age of twenty, he succeeded John Blow (one of his teachers) as the organist of Westminster Abbey. An extremely versatile composer, he wrote for the royal band, composed incidental music for the Restoration plays of John Dryden and William Congreve, and imitated the Italian masters in suites for harpsichord and stringed instruments. Purcell is best remembered for his large-scale, ceremonial compositions. Many of these were choral works—anthems or odes, which were sung to the accompaniment of organ, brass, or a mixture of instruments. They were composed to celebrate birthdays, funerals, and other special occasions; and many were suitable either for church or concert performance. Among these works are *Come ye sons of art* (an Ode for the birthday of Queen Mary in 1694), and the *Ode on St. Cecilia's Day*(1692), a collection of four choral works which celebrate the traditional patron saint of music. Purcell also wrote one opera, *Dido and Aeneas* (1689). Based on the tragic encounter of the Roman hero Aeneas and the Carthaginian Queen Dido (Virgil's *Aeneid*, Book 4), this work is now frequently revived. It is the only English opera of stature before the twentieth century. (After Purcell, England fell under the sway of Continental influences in this form for two centuries.) Despite its trite, almost silly libretto by Nahum Tate, Purcell's *Dido and Aeneas* gathers considerable dramatic power from the superb psychological insight of the music.

The death of Purcell in 1695 marks the end of a vital tradition of English music. By this date, Italian and French styles were flourishing, and the influence of the German Baroque, which derived its inspiration from the Protestant Reformation, was being felt throughout Europe. English music suffered a long decline, from which it only recovered at the beginning of the twentieth century.

Questions for Review

1. What was the significance for English music of Nicholas Yonge's *Musica Transalpina*? When was this book published? What is the meaning of the title?

2. What were the most popular instruments in Elizabethan England?

3. Define the madrigal. Where did the form of the madrigal originate?

4. Name some of the distinguished composers of madrigals in Elizabethan England.

5. Briefly identify Anthony Holborne.

6. Who was John Dowland? What qualities distinguish his songs?

7. How did the circumstances of performance of Dowland's songs expand the role of music in society during this period?

8. Comment briefly on the significance of William Byrd and Orlando Gibbons in English music.

9. What was the *Camerata*? Where did it flourish? Identify the musical form whose origins are linked to the *Camerata*.

10. Define opera. When was the first opera performed? Who composed it? What was the subject of the first opera?

11. Characterize the purpose and style of Jean-Baptiste Lully's

music.

12. How did the style of Lully become popular in England in the second half of the seventeenth century?

13. What is a virtuoso? Who first composed for a virtuoso soloist? On what instrument?

14. With which celebrated French playwright did Lully collaborate at the court of Versailles?

15. Identify Henry Purcell, and name one of his major works.

16. Who was St. Cecilia?

Answers

1. Nicholas Yonge's *Musica Transalpina*, published in 1588, introduced the texts of Italian madrigals to England in translation. The title refers to "music beyond the Alps" (i.e. to Italy). Yonge's book was highly significant in the development of English music because the form of the madrigal soon engaged the attention of some of England's most talented composers.

2. The most popular instruments in Elizabethan England included: viols, lute, and virginals.

3. The madrigal is a short composition, usually for a number of voices (most often four or five), treating a secular theme (e.g. love in a pastoral setting). Madrigals were often sung without accompaniment, although instruments such as the lute could be employed in performance. The madrigal was always sung in the vernacular.

4. Some of the most distinguished composers of madrigals in Elizabethan England: Thomas Morley, Thomas Weelkes, William Byrd, and Orlando Gibbons.

5. Anthony Holborne, reputedly the greatest trumpeter in Elizabethan England, composed some of the first English works that were solely instrumental (usually for wind or brass ensembles).

6. John Dowland was England's greatest song-writer in the Elizabethan Age. His works gave equal attention to the music and the texts of the lyrics. They were performed to the accompaniment of the lute; Dowland himself was a superb lutenist. Many are distinguished by a mournful sound; but Dowland was capable of writing humorous and lively works as well. He was nicknamed the "English Orpheus" in an allusion to the musician of classical mythology whose songs charmed all living creatures and the spirits of the dead.

7. Dowland's songs could be performed by common folk for everyday entertainment; they reflect a gradual broadening in the purpose and circumstances of musical activity.

8. William Byrd is considered the most versatile composer of the English Re-

naissance. He composed a variety of church music (for both Latin and Anglican liturgies), as well as motets, madrigals, and keyboard works for the virginals. Orlando Gibbons, organist at Westminster Abbey, was similarly gifted; his work, somewhat darker and more harmonically developed than that of Byrd, evokes the Elizabethan Age. Gibbons was the last great composer of the English Renaissance.

9. The *Camerata* was a group of aristocrats, poets, and composers that formed a society in late sixteenth-century Florence. Fascinated by the Greco-Roman fusion of stage drama and music, these artists experimented with the narrative and dramatic possibilities of song. The *Camerata* is usually credited with being a formative influence in the development of opera.

10. Opera is sung drama to musical accompaniment. It incorporates setting, lighting, costumes, poetry, and music. The first opera, in a technical sense, was Peri's *Euridice* (1600). But the first opera which is still occasionally performed is *La favola di Orfeo* (1607) of Claudio Monteverdi. Both works were based on the ancient Greek myth of Orpheus.

11. Lully, Italian by birth, found favor at the court of the French King Louis XIV. As master of music to the royal household, he was responsible for the opulent spectacles which were presented for the amusement of the King and his nobles. Lully's music is graceful and elegant; its fundamental purpose was to serve as the accompaniment for lavish visual displays (in opera, ballet, and comédie-ballet).

12. The style of Lully was admired by the English King Charles II, during his visits to Versailles as an exile from England. After the Restoration of Charles to the throne in 1660, he encouraged dramatists and composers to create works in the style of such French masters as Molière and Lully.

13. A virtuoso is a star soloist on a musical instrument, admired for outstanding technical mastery. The first composer of virtuoso works was Biagio Marini, who performed his own complex and difficult compositions on the violin.

14. Molière (pseudonym for Jean-Baptiste Poquelin).

15. Henry Purcell was England's last great composer until the start of the twentieth century. He is a master of the Baroque style, and wrote in a wide variety of forms: harpsichord suites, works for the royal band, and incidental music for Restoration plays. Two of his best-known works are the opera *Dido and Aeneas* (1689) and the choral *Ode on St. Cecilia's Day* (1692).

16. St. Cecilia is the traditional patron saint of music.

Chapter 5

The Reformation

The Reformation

Alongside the growth of secular music in Elizabethan England and the development of opera in seventeenth-century Italy, a very different set of musical traditions was evolving in Germany, the home of the Protestant Reformation. In 1517, Martin Luther (1483–1546) pinned his ninety-five theses to the door of the church in Wittenberg. Luther, who had been a monk and choirmaster, demanded reforms in nearly every aspect of Church doctrine, practice, and liturgy. He was treated as a heretic by Rome, and expelled from the Church in 1520; thus was Protestantism born. In the succeeding decades, Luther's example was followed by others: the austere teachings of John Calvin (1509–1564) became the cornerstone of the Presbyterian Church, and the English monarch, Henry VIII, broke with Rome to found the Church of England.

Calvinist doctrine gave little scope to the growth of music, since only Biblical texts were permitted to be sung in Church, and these without accompanying harmony. However, the Church of England proved hospitable to both Latin and English texts, and Anglican sacred music flourished with William Byrd, Orlando Gibbons, and Henry Purcell (see Chapter 4, above). But the most impressive stream of purely religious inspiration in music was found in Germany, from the sixteenth to the eighteenth centuries; and this stream found its glorious culmination in Johann Sebastian Bach.

In order to understand the music of Bach, it is necessary to review the principal objectives of Lutheranism, and also to survey the main characteristics of the Baroque style in music. Luther was no enemy of the use of music in church services: he himself was an accomplished composer and instrumentalist (he played the flute and the lute). But he insisted that the texts of vocal music should be in the German vernacular, and that the settings be simple and attractive enough to encourage the full participation of worshipers. To this end, he completed the famous translation of the Bible into German; and he composed a number of church hymns, called *chorales*. He often borrowed folk tunes and other secular songs for chorales; one story has it that he once asked rhetorically, "Why should the devil have all the good tunes?" One of Luther's most celebrated chorales is his setting of Psalm 46, known by the title *Ein' feste Burg ist unser Gott (A Mighty Fortress Is Our God)*.

Luther's emphasis, then, was not a rejection of either secular or Roman Catholic styles in music; his goal was a more personal involvement of the congregation, an objective which could only be achieved if specially trained choirs singing polyphonic music in Latin were replaced by the broad spectrum of the worshipers themselves, who could celebrate their faith in words they understood and melodies they could sing. This explains why, despite the divisions of doctrine, Protestant Germany continued to remain abreast of Italian musical developments in the sixteenth and seventeenth centuries; the Roman Church in turn, eager to encourage a more accessible style in music, promulgated a simplified approach to the liturgy during the Counter-Reformation [see Chapter 3 on Palestrina].

Two illustrations of the ways in which Italian styles continued to influence German music are furnished by the careers of early Protestant composers. **Hans Leo Hassler** (1564–1612), who was born in Nuremberg within the lifetime of Hans Sachs, the famous Meistersinger, studied in Italy with Andrea Gabrieli, the organist of St. Mark's Cathedral [see Chapter 3]. Hassler later became organist of churches in Augsburg, Nuremberg, and Dresden. He composed madrigals, Masses, and motets; but his chorale tunes were his most notable contribution to music of the early Reformation. Like Hans Sachs, a follower of Luther whose guild of bourgeois singers, the Meistersingers, inspired many Protestant hymn tunes, Hassler believed in an accessible—and yet dignified—style of congregational singing. His success at composing in such a style is signaled by the fact that one of his Passion chorales is used several times by Bach in the *St. Matthew Passion*, written over a century after Hassler's death.

Heinrich Schütz (1585–1672), one of the greatest of Bach's predecessors, also studied in Italy with Giovanni Gabrieli [see Chapter 3]. From Gabrieli, Schütz learned the technique of writing for multiple choirs, as well as the art of interpolating organ solos during church services at points when no congregational singing was required. He returned to a distinguished career in Germany, serving the courts in Kassel and Dresden. Schütz produced a variety of sacred works; perhaps most notable are his settings of the Passion for unaccompanied voices. These compositions were performed in the vernacular, and possess a powerful dignity that distinctly foreshadows the great Passions of Bach. Schütz also combined some of the operatic techniques of Claudio Monteverdi with the Protestant tradition in his *Sacred Symphonies*, oratorio-like works in which Latin and German texts were sung by soloists and choirs to instrumental accompaniment.

German contact with Italy in the early seventeenth century insured the spread of the Baroque style in music across Northern Europe. The term "Baroque" comes from a Portuguese word used to describe an irregularly-shaped pearl. It means "rough" or "irregular", and was used in a derogatory sense in the later eighteenth century. The literal meaning of the term is misleading, since Baroque music is the first music in the West to exhibit consistently the ordered notions of tonal harmony that we take for granted. From the later viewpoint of Classicism, however, music of the Baroque seemed restlessly dynamic and insufficiently polished. Grandeur was the keynote of the Baroque, whether in the sculptures of Bernini, the painting of Velázquez or Rubens, or the poetry of John Milton or Pierre Corneille. The Baroque adored the splendor of overwhelming detail. In its pure form, the Baroque sought to express the inner essence through elaboration of the surface detail; eventually, it lost its meaning in the welter of detail.

The principal characteristics of Baroque music—whether in Monteverdi, Purcell, Bach, Handel, or Vivaldi—are the following:

1. Greater intensity of expression than in Renaissance music, particularly in compositions for solo voice.

2. A growing awareness of the structural possibilities of a harmonic language based on the major and minor scales.

3. The integration of polyphony into that harmonic language.

4. An ever-increasing use of regular, metric rhythms, many of them derived from popular dance rhythms.

5. The presence of *basso continuo* (literally, "continuous bass"), performed by a bass viol or bassoon in conjunction with a keyboard instrument (harpsichord or organ) to reinforce the harmonic structure of the music.

6. A new preoccupation with idiomatic—and often virtuosic—writing for solo instruments.

7. The emergence of new and well-defined forms like the concerto

grosso, trio sonata, choral prelude, oratorio, etc.

8. The increasing importance of operatic aria over recitative.

9. The appearance and cultivation of complex forms of keyboard music like the prelude, fugue, toccata, partita.

10. The use of "terraced dynamics"—alternating loud and soft passages consisting of identical thematic material.

The great Reformation organist and composer **Dietrich Buxtehude** (1637–1707) developed a number of keyboard forms (primarily for organ) which played important roles in the Lutheran service. Born in Denmark, Buxtehude came to Lübeck in Northern Germany in 1688. His improvisations on the organ swiftly assured for him a wide reputation; the young Johann Sebastian Bach walked two hundred miles from Arnstadt to Lübeck in 1705 to hear Buxtehude play. One of Buxtehude's favorite forms was the *toccata* (from the Italian, literally "touched" on a keyboard): a composition of great freedom in which the performer can display his virtuosity. The toccata had its origins in the music of the Gabrielis [see Chapter 4], and was brought to first maturity by **Girolamo Frescobaldi** (1583–1643), the organist of St. Peter's in Rome. Frescobaldi's keyboard style was brought to Germany (and thence to Paris) by his student **Johann Jacob Froberger** (1616–1667), a composer and keyboard player who spent four years in Italy in the 1630s. In time, the toccata and its close relative, the *prelude* (literally, "played before") became associated with the *fugue*, itself a descendant of the Renaissance ricercare [see Chapter 3].

There are many different types of fugue. A basic definition explains it as a form in which two or more instrumental voices successively introduce a main theme (the subject) and an answering theme (the counter-subject). The voices then develop the themes, in both tonic and dominant keys; tension is introduced through modulation and other harmonic devices; and the fugue is finally resolved in a grand intermingling of voices in the tonic. The rigid discipline of the fugue presented a striking contrast to the free, improvisatory form of the toccata. The contrast produced by pairing both forms in a single composition, unified by one key (and sometimes by melodic themes) well represents the spirit of the Baroque.

Buxtehude also composed a variety of choral music for the Lutheran Church: chorale variations, in which the melody of a well-known chorale would be elaborated by singers and instrumentalists; and cantatas, a more complex form in which an overture, arias, and choruses were combined.

The career and achievements of Buxtehude lead directly to the art of **Johann Sebastian Bach** (1685–1750), one of the great masters of the Baroque style, and (for many) the first household name in the history of music. Bach was born in North Central Germany, in the district called Thuringia; he was the son of a musician in the town of Eisenach. His father taught him to play the violin, and his elder brother trained him on the organ after the child was orphaned at the age of ten. The organ was the focus of his earliest composing efforts, and he visited Hamburg and Lübeck to hear famous virtuoso players, among them Buxtehude. By the age of eighteen, he had earned his first appointment of many as a director of music in the Lutheran Church.

Almost all of Bach's music was inspired by his deep religious faith. He represents the culmination of a stream of Protestant church music that had developed since the start of the Reformation in the early sixteenth century. Chorales, toccatas, fugues, cantatas, and Passions were all forms that existed before Bach was born; yet he managed to explore their possibilities so exhaustively that, in effect, he transformed them. He did not so much revolutionize the music of his time as bring to it a new depth and intensity of feeling. Neglected during his own lifetime—it was as if his craftsmanship and humble acquiescence to employers' demands had branded him as a conservative—Bach's work has outlived that of all his contemporaries.

Bach's early career involved a succession of church appointments: Arnstadt (1703–1707), Mühlhausen (1707–1708), Weimar (where he was court organist and music director in the Duke's chapel: 1708–1717). In 1717, he went to Cöthen, as music director of the prince's court; the six years he spent there marked the only period in his career when he concentrated exclusively on secular music. In 1723, Bach secured the post of cantor at St. Thomas' Church in Leipzig, where he remained for the rest of his life. He was nearing forty when he applied, and to demonstrate his fitness for the post, he offered a performance of one of his great choral works, the *St. John Passion*. Even so, the authorities were unimpressed; they originally preferred another candidate, **Georg Philipp Telemann**, who was at the time the most famous musician in Germany. Bach's appointment was only approved after Telemann declined the offer in favor of a higher-paying post.

Bach acquired a detailed knowledge of French and Italian musical styles early in his career. His posts at Arnstadt and Mühlhausen required primarily organ works; but he acquainted himself with other forms through the usual method of musical education at the time: copying out music by hand. He came especially to admire the work of Antonio Vivaldi [see Chapter 7], and adapted several of his violin concerti for solo performance on organ or harpsichord. Like Hassler, Schütz, and Buxtehude before him, Bach fashioned his style by eclectically combining the Lutheran tradition of church music with French and Italian elements: concentrated, brilliant melody and grand harmonic structures.

A marked characteristic of Bach's music, throughout his long career, is the detailed exploration of all the possibilities of a given form. Thus, he started early to compose toccatas and fugues, under the influence of Buxtehude. The famous *Toccata and Fugue in D Minor*, which dates from around 1709, is a good example of his youthful exuberance in the form. The *Toccata* immediately establishes tension, with its clarion-like opening gesture and syncopated rhythm. There follows a free improvisation on the D-minor chord, employing exciting runs, sequential imitations, dissonant chords that are built up on deep pedal-points (or single sustained notes), and sudden variations of rhythm. Cascades of sound alternate with brief, tense silences. A majestic cadence brings the *Toccata* to a close. The whole piece is less than five minutes in duration, but serves as an exciting introduction to the more complex *Fugue* which follows. The subject (which is closely related to the *Toccata*'s opening gesture) is heard in a sequence of different voices; the subject is then exploited in several developmental episodes; volume and tension increase to a thrilling climax, in which the brilliant figuration of the *Toccata* itself returns. Listening to this work, one may find it difficult to imagine how Bach could continue to exploit the form in even more complex, ingenious ways. Yet he continued to write toccatas and fugues for forty years, bringing to the form ever new dimensions.

Bach also delighted in incorporating complex elements of musical symbolism in his work. Take as an example, his great *Prelude and Fugue in E-Flat Major*, later nicknamed the "*St. Anne*" *Prelude and Fugue* because its opening theme is by coincidence identical with the

93

English hymn-tune for St. Anne, *O God, Our Help in Ages Past*. The piece employs the key signature of three flats: Bach saw in it a pictorial sign of the Holy Trinity, for whose glory he composed the work. The numerological symbolism is also manifested by the musical structure of the fugue, a gigantic tour de force of counterpoint in which three subjects are successively introduced and then combined. In his settings for the *Magnificat*, the traditional church canticle of Mary ("My soul doth magnify the Lord"), Bach sought appropriate musical effects for key phrases: for example, at the words "He hath exalted the lowly and put down the proud," the music's ascending and descending scales emphasize the contrast in the text. This compositional technique is often called "word-painting".

Bach's large and varied output can best be understood as his response to the demands of his various jobs. Thus, in his position as the organist at Weimar (1708–1717), he composed many of his great organ works. For example, the *Toccata and Fugue in D Minor* described above was composed during this period. At this time he also composed a number of *cantatas* (sung works to religious texts, from the Italian "cantare", to sing); these were largely works for solo voice and orchestral accompaniment, not the choral cantatas which he was to write at Leipzig [see below]. Although Bach wrote no operas, these works draw on the same forms and principles—alternations of recitatives with arias.

Much of his secular instrumental music—for orchestra, or solo harpsichord, or chamber ensembles—stems from his service at Cöthen (1718–1722), where he served as music director. Although less numerous than his sacred compositions, Bach's secular works are equally remarkable for their fertile ingenuity and impeccable craftsmanship. The most famous, perhaps, are the six *Brandenburg Concerti*, composed in 1721 for the Margrave Christian Ludwig of Brandenburg. These pieces are in the Italian style of the *concerto grosso* (literally, "large concerto"). The term *concerto* had originally applied to any music composed for more than one group of performers (instruments and/or voices)—like the compositions of the Gabrielis in Venice early in the seventeenth century [see Chapter 3]. During the latter part of the Baroque period, the term—especially when modified with the adjective *grosso*—came to have a more specialized meaning. In such a work, a small group of solo instruments (sometimes as few as one) called the *concertino* (literally, "little group") is contrasted with the larger string orchestra, called the *ripieno* (literally, "full"). Bach wrote concerti grossi for one or more harpsichords, one or more violins, and other combinations. George Frideric Handel and Antonio Vivaldi also composed large numbers of such works.

Bach, however, rarely composed in a form without making his own personal modifications to it. It is therefore not surprising that each of the six *Brandenburg Concerti* possesses a distinct personality, and that none of them is wholly typical of the genre. In the First Concerto, the usual clear distinction between *concertino* and *ripieno* is somewhat blurred—the "solo" instruments consist of the relatively large group of two horns, three oboes, and bassoon. This full scoring gives the work an unusually rich texture. The Third Concerto, composed for three groups of strings only (plus the omnipresent harpsichord continuo), features only two movements (rather than the usual three). In the Fourth Concerto, perhaps the most charming of the six, the *concertino* consists of solo violin and two recorders (though these parts are often played on modern flutes).

From the Cöthen period also come many of Bach's most celebrated works for harpsichord: the so-called *"English"* and *"French" Suites*, a number of Toccatas, but above all the first volume of 24 Preludes and Fugues—one for each major and minor key—known as *The Well-Tempered Clavier*. (The second volume, similarly a set of 24 Preludes and Fugues, was completed in 1740 at Leipzig.) Bach was one of the first composers to recognize the potential of the modern method of tuning a keyboard instrument. Older methods had caused some keys to be "in tune" at the expense of others which were "very out of tune". Bach's method rendered all keys "slightly out of tune" but left none unusable. More important, however, the 48 compositions which comprise the two volumes of this masterpiece form a virtual encyclopedia of the styles of keyboard composition of the late Baroque (as well as a great many styles which Bach improved upon so greatly that they are truly his own inventions). The fugues comprise every known variety and technique available in the genre, and reveal Bach as the consummate master of this extraordinarily difficult form of composition. *The Well-Tempered Clavier* has been nicknamed the "Old Testament of music" (Beethoven's Piano Sonatas being the "New Testament"), for the reason that it sums up with such clarity the entire tradition of Baroque keyboard music.

Bach held the post of cantor of the city of Leipzig from 1723 until the year of his death in 1750. While he was primarily responsible for playing the organ and directing the choir of the most important church in the city, St. Thomas', he was also responsible for overseeing all of the music in the city's three other major churches. If this were not enough, he was required to compose the great majority of the music performed, as well as to supervise the musical education of the boy choristers at St. Thomas' choir school. It is therefore not surprising that Bach returned to the composition of sacred music: in his first few years at Leipzig, he assembled two complete cycles of *choral cantatas* and part of a third for the Liturgical Year. These works comprise some 200 examples. Unlike the earlier solo cantatas [see above], these compositions include movements for the full choir, in addition to recitatives and arias for solo voices.

Bach was also required to compose musical settings of the story of the Passion of Christ for the Lutheran Good Friday services. It is in these works, called the *Passions*, that Bach most closely approaches the musical and dramatic values of Baroque opera. There are three *Passions* surely by Bach—one each for the Gospels according to St. John, St. Mark, and St. Matthew. The *St. Mark Passion* is adapted from music written for another purpose; but the *St. John Passion* (1723) and the *St. Matthew Passion* (1729) are two of the greatest works of choral music ever composed.

Both works are based on the story of Christ's suffering and death. They are of operatic length, and conform to the fundamental requirements of opera: a dramatic narrative combining recitative, aria and choral movements into an integral whole. Although the *Passions* were not staged, Bach accentuated the dramatic possibilities of the story by assigning the parts of individuals to soloists, and the role of the crowd to the chorus.

The *St. Matthew Passion*, in particular, is regarded by many as Bach's greatest work. The text is based on Chapter 26 and 27 of St. Matthew's Gospel in the German translation of Martin Luther. Some sections are quoted directly from the Bible; others, written by the Leipzig poet C.F. Henrici (1700–1764, wrote under the pseudonym Picander), are interpolated to provide a smoother dramatic flow. The *St. Matthew Passion* is divided into two major segments, much as an opera might be divided into acts. The first tells the story of the Last Supper, the agony in the Garden of Gethsemane, and the betrayal of Christ by Judas. The second deals with the trial, crucifixion, death, and burial. The musical forces required to perform the work include solo voices (a tenor represents the Evangelist, St. Matthew), two choruses, two organs, two orchestras, and harpsichord. In addition to the central narrative, at various points the choruses and soloists portray the reactions of the crowd and of individual witnesses. The work includes fifteen chorales (Lutheran hymns) to be sung by all of the performers as well as the congregation itself, in keeping with the important Lutheran principle of congregational involvement in the service. Perhaps the most famous of the chorales is *O Haupt voll Blut und Wunden (O Sacred Head Sore Wounded)*, which recurs in the *Passion* no fewer than seven times. This recurrence unifies the entire work.

The *St. Matthew Passion*, although it is the culmination of Baroque sacred music, might be taken as a touchstone for the fortunes of Bach in the latter half of the eighteenth century and the early years of the nineteenth. This masterpiece had to wait one hundred years for its second performance, when it was revived by the young Romantic composer, Felix Mendelssohn, in Berlin. Ironically, the great genius who consolidated nearly every Baroque form with such clarity and power was to be re-discovered and admired by the Romantics, one of whose chief objectives was a definitive break with the past.

Remarkable as it may seem, Bach appears to have composed the majority of the Leipzig sacred vocal music during the first several years of his tenure there, leaving himself free to compose additional secular instrumental music. During the last twenty years of his life, he was particularly interested in large-scale works which explore the musical possibilities inherent in a rather small amount of thematic material. Each of these works—we shall mention three—displays his unequalled inventiveness and consummate mastery of the contrapuntal style.

The *Goldberg Variations* were written in 1742 at the request of Count Kayserling, a patron of Bach's who suffered from insomnia and wanted a composition which his harpsichordist Goldberg could play for him on sleepless nights. The theme (called "aria" though it is not for voice) was originally composed about 1725 in the form of a slow dance called a *sarabande*. Bach composed thirty variations or transformations of this air, all of which preserve the same harmonic progression. The fertile imagination with which Bach explored the musical possibilities of the relatively simple theme is matched only by the majesty of the architectural structure of the work as a whole.

In 1747, Bach visited the court of King Frederick the Great of Prussia, where his son Carl Philipp Emmanuel had been appointed as royal harpsichordist. The King was a devoted amateur flutist, and invited the elder Bach to improvise upon a simple theme that Frederick played for him on the flute. Bach's harpsichord performance on the spot did not disappoint. When he returned to Leipzig, he wrote an entire series of pieces (three- and six-part fugues for keyboard, and a trio sonata for flute, violin and harpsichord), all of which incorporated Frederick's original air. He sent the works to the King under the title *A Musical Offering*. Once again, it is an example of a large-scale work derived from simple material.

One of Bach's last works—left incomplete at his death—is considered the last word on fugal writing. Bach intended *The Art of the Fugue*, as he called it, to be a systematic demonstration of all the various techniques and possibilities which could be applied to fugal composition. He constructed a simple subject in D minor, and proceeded to construct eighteen different types of fugue, always employing the same subject. Sometimes he used the subject in its original form, at other times he played it backwards, or upside-down, or even backwards and upside-down (the technical names for these techniques are retrograde, inversion, and retrograde-inversion, respectively). Additional transformations were achieved through rhythmic means: playing the theme twice as fast or twice as slow as the original. To write even a single fugue on a theme is one of the most difficult of all compositional tasks, and often requires the composer to take liberties with the "rules". Bach's eighteen examples on but one theme—and without a single liberty—reveal Bach's enormous mathematical insights. The work stands beside any mathematical proof as one of the great creations of Western thought; not coincidentally, each of the fugues is a moving and beautiful musical work in its own right.

Questions for Review

1. How did the objectives of the Protestant Reformation affect the development of German music during the sixteenth and seventeenth centuries?

2. What was Martin Luther's attitude toward music?

3. Briefly identify:
   a) Heinrich Schütz
   b) Dietrich Buxtehude
   c) *A Musical Offering*

4. What is the literal meaning of the term "Baroque"? Which dates are usually selected to define the Baroque period in music?

5. List as many characteristics of Baroque music as you can.

6. What is the relationship between Johann Sebastian Bach's music and the positions which he held during his lifetime?

7. What were Bach's objectives in music? What was his primary inspiration?

8. Name at least three forms in which Bach composed.

9. What were the *Brandenburg Concerti*? When were they composed?

10. What were some of Bach's duties as cantor of St. Thomas' Church in Leipzig?

11. Identify the subject of Bach's most monumental work. Which Romantic composer played a crucial role in reviving it in the nineteenth century?

12. Describe the structure of Bach's *Goldberg Variations*.

13. Briefly define the following:
   a) *basso continuo*
   b) Toccata
   c) *The Art of the Fugue*
   d) chorale

Answers

1. The Protestant Reformation, initiated by Martin Luther, did not object to the use of music in church services; but, since one of its chief goals was the more personal involvement of the congregation, it required a new type of

music. The most prominent early form was the chorale (or "church song"), in which the congregation sang a hymn in the vernacular, set to a simple (yet dignified) melody.

2. Luther himself was a distinguished musician; before he became the leader of the German Reformation, he was a monastic choirmaster, and also a skilled lutenist and flutist. He composed one of the most popular church chorales (*A Mighty Fortress Is Our God*), and freely borrowed from secular tunes in his works. He is said to have quipped, "Why should the devil have all the good tunes?"

3. a) Heinrich Schütz was one of the greatest of Bach's predecessors in the tradition of Protestant church music. He studied with Giovanni Gabrieli in Venice, and played a major role in combining Italian elements with the German musical tradition. His major works include motets, Passions, and the oratorio-like compositions called the *Sacred Symphonies*.

b) Dietrich Buxtehude was a renowned Danish-born organist who reached the height of his fame as composer and virtuoso player during the youth of Bach. Bach walked two hundred miles to hear Buxtehude's organ improvisations in Lübeck, and was significantly influenced by the older composer, especially in the forms of Toccata and Fugue.

c) *A Musical Offering* is the name of the collection of pieces which Bach presented to the Prussian King Frederick the Great in 1747. Consisting of keyboard fugues and a trio sonata for flute, violin, and harpsichord, the works originated in the King's invitation to Bach to improvise on a simple theme which Frederick played on the flute.

4. "Baroque" is probably derived from a Portuguese word meaning "rough" or "irregular". It was used as a derogatory term in the later eighteenth century. The dates which are usually selected to define the Baroque period in music are 1600–1750.

5. Characteristics of Baroque music:

a) Greater intensity of expression than in Renaissance music, particularly in compositions for solo voice.

b) A growing awareness of the structural possibilities of a harmonic language based on the major and minor scales.

c) The integration of polyphony into that harmonic language.

d) An ever-increasing use of regular, metric rhythms, many of them derived from popular dance rhythms.

e) The presence of *basso continuo* (literally, "continuous bass"), performed by a bass viol or bassoon in conjunction with a keyboard instrument (harpsichord or organ) to reinforce the harmonic structure of the music.

f) A new preoccupation with idiomatic—and often virtuosic—writing for solo instruments.

g) The emergence of new and well-defined forms like the concerto grosso, trio sonata, choral prelude, oratorio, etc.

h) The increasing importance of operatic aria over recitative.

i) The appearance and cultivation of complex forms of keyboard music like the prelude, fugue, toccata, partita.

j) The use of "terraced dynamics"—alternating loud and soft passages consisting of identical thematic material.

6. In each case, Bach composed music to meet the immediate needs of his employers. At Weimar (1708–1717) he served as court organist and composed a great deal of music for that instrument. His secular musical works mostly date to his employment as Music Director at the court of Cöthen (1717–1723). The majority of his sacred vocal compositions date to his first several years as Cantor of the city of Leipzig (1723–1750).

7. Bach's primary inspiration in music was his deep religious faith. He wrote most of his music explicitly for the glorification of God. His career is characterized by methodical, complex investigations of the potential of every form in which he worked.

8. Forms in which Bach composed: Chorale, Suite, Toccata and Fugue, Choral Prelude, Mass, Passion, Concerto Grosso, Theme and Variations, etc.

9. The *Brandenburg Concerti* were six compositions in Italian, *concerto grosso* style, composed by Bach in 1721 for the Margrave of Brandenburg. They are perhaps the most celebrated secular works of Bach.

10. Bach's duties in Leipzig included supervising services each week (and on many special occasions) at the four principal churches in town, composing new works for liturgical use, playing the organ, directing the choir at St. Thomas' Church, and supervising the musical education of the choirboys at the church choir school.

11. Bach's most monumental work is the *St. Matthew Passion*, a religious drama in music, written for the Lutheran Good Friday service in 1729. Felix Mendelssohn first revived the work in the Romantic period, after it had suffered a century of neglect.

12. The *Goldberg Variations* consist of thirty different treatments of the same melody, in all of which the same harmonic progression is employed.

13. a) *basso continuo*: the "continuous bass" which characterizes much Baroque music. It can be played on a variety of instruments (called "continuo" because of their function in the piece, and not because the term refers to a specific instrument).

b) toccata: a free, fantasia-like form for keyboard instruments (most commonly the organ). Developed by Frescobaldi in Italy in the early seventeenth century, and further refined by Buxtehude and Bach in Germany, the toccata (from Italian for "touched") commonly displays the organist's virtuoso powers of improvisation. It was frequently paired with the stricter form of the fugue.

c) *The Art of the Fugue*: the composition which Bach left unfinished at his death. It illustrates eighteen different varieties of fugue constructed on a single theme.

d) chorale: literally, a "church song" or hymn: the simplest form of unison singing (often employing popular tunes from secular music) in the Lutheran Church.

Chapter 6

The Advent of Fashion

The Advent of Fashion

The music of the German reformed Church, beginning with Martin Luther's own hymns in the 1520s, reached a culmination in the works of Johann Sebastian Bach. Bach's death in 1750 is often singled out as a turning point in the development of musical styles: for around the middle of the eighteenth century, the highly ornate Baroque yielded to a simpler, more consciously elegant style called Classicism. The important foundations for Classicism, however, were not laid by composers such as Bach, who was regarded as insular and conservative during his lifetime, and was long neglected after his death. It was the advent of fashion in the great European courts of the Baroque period that played a more important role in creating for music a wider public. New forms of secular music (for example, the sonata) were developed in the early eighteenth century; musical instruments (and playing techniques) continued to be refined; the public for music became wider and more various. Composers still enjoyed the support of powerful patrons; but public taste, as well, became a factor in their inspiration and appreciation.

We may summarize these trends by singling out a Baroque tradition in secular music: compositions which were written solely to entertain. This tradition was embodied in such composers as Jean-Philippe Rameau and François Couperin in France, Georg Philipp Telemann in Germany, and the Italian-born Domenico Scarlatti, who spent his mature years in the service of Queen Maria Barbara at the Spanish court in Madrid. These Baroque composers significantly enlarged the scope and appeal of non-liturgical music in their time. Their efforts reached a culmination in the works of George Frideric Handel—a composer whose approach to the purpose and occasions of music pointedly contrasts with that of Bach.

Jean-Philippe Rameau (1683–1764) was a significant musical theorist, as well as a composer whose works found favor at the court of Louis XV in France. Rameau taught himself both harmony and counterpoint. He visited Italy in his youth, and his early career consisted of a series of appointments as an organist. In 1722, he published in Paris his *Traité de l'harmonie (Treatise on Harmony)*, an important textbook on methods of chord progression.

At the age of fifty, Rameau wrote his first opera. Its failure did not deter him from continuing in this form; and he became so adept at opera and opera-ballet that he was eventually named composer to the King. Rameau's operas, like those of his predecessor Jean-Baptiste Lully [see Chapter 4], were highly stylized, and therefore appealed greatly to a court whose absolute sense of social hierarchy was exceeded only by its taste for elegant spectacles. The typical Rameau opera was divided into a series of discrete numbers, almost always organized into the same pattern. A grand overture introduced the performance. Then a prologue, usually with characters derived from ancient Greek and Roman mythology, established the main lines of the plot for the audience. A series of acts followed, interspersed by elegant ballets which were usually only tangentially relevant to the main action. Many of the mythological characters of the prologue were understood to represent contemporary figures: for example, Jupiter (the Roman King of the gods) was understood to stand for Louis XV himself, while Neptune (Jupiter's brother and lord of the sea) symbolized the English King George II. The agreement of the two "gods" over their respective domains symbolized the conclusion of a peace treaty between France and England; the concord of mythological deities was dramatized as an elegant parallel to harmony in real life. Such a scenario by Rameau celebrated the signing of the Treaty of Aix-la-Chapelle in 1749.

François Couperin (1668–1733), somewhat older than Rameau, complemented the large-scale works of his contemporary through his work in shorter forms. From a musical family (his uncle Louis Couperin was also a distinguished composer), François Couperin became organist to King Louis XIV at the age of twenty-five. Later, under Louis XV, Couperin entertained the sovereign every week with chamber-style concerts, usually featuring the popular form of the suite. The suite (French for "following") presented a series of short movements for instruments; often written in the same key, these movements were distinguished by their rhythms, derived from popular court dances. The typical framework for suites consisted of the Allemande (a dance of German origin, most often in four-four time), the Courante (a lighter, more rapid dance in triple time), the Sarabande (a slower, statelier movement), and finally a

Gigue (a lively conclusion, in compound duple time).

The basic framework of suites was capable of numerous interpolations; often, for example, other dance forms would be inserted, e.g. the minuet, the bourrée, the musette, or the gavotte. As many as eighteen movements could be included in a single suite, although Couperin's little orchestra (consisting of violin, viola, oboe, bassoon, and harpsichord) did not usually perform all of these at a single concert, but rather made a selection. The basic structure of the suite, however, was clear; it corresponded to the form of Italian chamber music established by Couperin's contemporary, **Arcangelo Corelli** (1653–1713). Corelli greatly influenced Couperin; and the success of the Baroque suite laid the groundwork for the more refined form of the sonata: a short composition for a solo instrument, usually in three or four contrasting movements.

Couperin was also important as a theoretician. In 1716, he published *L'Art de toucher le clavecin (The Art of Playing the Harpsichord)*, one of the first textbooks to discuss the concept of touch and the techniques of fingering for a keyboard instrument. J. S. Bach knew this book, and was much influenced by it. Couperin was profoundly concerned with the delineation of proper playing techniques for the two leading instruments of his day, the harpsichord and the organ. On the harpsichord, with its mechanical action of plucking the strings, sustained notes were impossible: a long note had to be emphasized by such figures as the trill. The organ, in contrast, demanded a quite different approach from both composer and player, since keyboard and pedalboard were connected to a windchest, which would sustain a tone through the pipes for as long as a player depressed any given key.

Younger than Couperin, and an almost exact contemporary of Rameau, was the German composer **Georg Philipp Telemann** (1681–1767). Telemann taught himself music by the study of scores; among his models was Jean-Baptiste Lully. A friend of Handel's, he excelled as a performer on both the harpsichord and the organ; indeed, he was originally preferred to Johann Sebastian Bach, when the authorities at St. Thomas' Church in Leipzig set out to engage a new cantor in 1721. (Telemann accepted instead a higher-paying post as music director of the Johanneum in Hamburg.) Telemann was extraordinarily prolific in a broad variety of forms: he wrote forty operas, over one hundred concerti for various combinations of instruments, forty-four settings of the Passion, hundreds of overtures, numerous cantatas, suites, and miscellaneous orchestral music. Although popular in his own time, Telemann is now regarded as a somewhat superficial composer; his music possesses both charm and skill, but cannot be compared in its depth of feeling to Handel's or Bach's. Nevertheless, he is memorable for the facility which he managed to bring to the requirements of music-making in the early eighteenth century. Composers were not required to touch the sublime; in an era of fashion, their audiences demanded wit, elegance, and—above all—entertainment.

It is no accident that many of Telemann's works (and those of most composers of this period) required a substantial degree of improvisation from the players; the speed at which this music was produced, for such a variety of occasions, simply did not afford a composer the time to linger over every detail. In particular, the *basso continuo* [see Chapter 5] that underlies the melody in many of Telemann's works (such as his *Sonata for Oboe and Harpsichord*) must be reconstructed by modern performers, since the composer supplied only a bare harmonic outline for the original instrumentalists. (The practice was quite similar to modern popular music, where usually only the melody is written out, along with "chord symbols" to indicate the proper harmonics.

In Italy, the most prominent composer of the late Baroque period was **Domenico Scarlatti** (1685–1757). He was the son of the distinguished musician and opera composer, **Alessandro Scarlatti** (1660–1725), and studied with his father. In 1709, during George Frideric Handel's extended stay in Italy, Handel's patron, Cardinal Ottoboni, arranged a virtuoso competition between Handel and Domenico Scarlatti on keyboard instruments; on the harpsichord, the contest was judged to be a tie, although Handel was deemed superior on the organ.

Scarlatti led an international career: he worked in Rome, Naples, London, Lisbon, and Madrid. He composed Masses, concerti, and cantatas; but he is remembered today, not as a composer of vocal music, but for his significant innovations for keyboard. He composed a series of over 500 *essercizi* ("exercises") for harpsichord—they were actually sonatas in one movement. In these works, he introduced many features of playing technique; for example, certain passages required the player to cross his right hand with his left, or vice versa; in others, rapid repetitions and modulations skillfully built up tension to a climax, and posed a considerable challenge to the performer.

Toward the end of his career, Scarlatti arranged many of his sonatas in pairs; each pair seems to have been conceived as an integrated unit, or as a longer piece in two movements. Both movements were normally written in the same key (although one might be composed in the major, the other in the minor). This, combined with the structure of each individual movement—in which a theme in the tonic gave way to a development in the dominant key, and then returned to the tonic—anticipated the form of the Classical sonata of three movements. In particular, the experiments of Scarlatti in keyboard music, together with those of his younger contemporary, **Carl Philipp Emmanuel Bach** (1714–1788) (the third son of J. S. Bach), foreshadowed the sonata-allegro form of Haydn and Mozart. This form (often called first movement form) was employed in symphonies, concerti, and other types of music besides the sonata; its basic structure of exposition, development, and recapitulation (with a final cadence in the tonic key) remained a fundamental feature of musical form for over a century.

George Frideric Handel (1685–1759) was born in the same year as Domenico Scarlatti and Johann Sebastian Bach. The son of a barber-surgeon, Handel was not encouraged by his father to make music a career; it was only reluctantly that the father permitted him to take lessons on the organ from the music director of Halle, where Handel was raised. In his youth, it seemed that Handel was destined for the same type of career as Bach, i.e. as a cantor (organist and music director) at an important church. But at the age of eighteen, the young man left Halle for Hamburg, where he hoped to learn more of opera—the form that excited him most from the beginning. It is significant that Handel was attracted to the most ambitious and spectacular of musical forms so early in life; whereas Bach never attempted an opera, Handel was to display a progressively greater mastery of it as his career unfolded.

In 1705, Handel's first opera (*Almira*) was produced in Hamburg. The following year he left for Italy, where he remained until 1710, improving his knowledge of opera in Rome, Naples, Florence, and Venice, and associating with the leading Italian composers and patrons. His opera *Agrippina*, based on an episode of ancient Roman history, was a great success in Venice in 1709. Although he composed some sacred music in this period (several Latin motets and some cantatas), his style had been formed by the time he returned to Germany at the age of twenty-five. Drama and grandeur in music attracted Handel; he frankly wrote to entertain his public.

Handel's return to Germany proved short-lived. He had been appointed music director to the Elector of Hanover, an important city near Hamburg. But within months, he was granted a leave of absence to journey to England, where he produce a new opera to great success (*Rinaldo*, 1711). This English visit was soon followed by another, even lengthier one. In 1714, when the Elector of Hanover became the English King George I, Handel was confronted by an awkward dilemma: his former employer was now the sovereign of his adopted country. After a short period of frosty relations, the composer returned to favor; one legend records that the turning point was Handel's composition of a suite of instrumental pieces for a royal boating party on the Thames—a collection now known as the *Water Music*.

Handel remained in England for the rest of his life. Italian opera was the rage in London in the opening decades of the eighteenth century. The fact that audiences could understand few of the words did not diminish their delight in spectacle, or their admiration for virtuoso singing; especially notable were the *castrati*, eunuchs who were trained for male roles in the upper register. Employed by the Royal Academy of Music in London, Handel produced a string of successes, including *Ottone* (1723), *Giulio Cesare* (1724), *Orlando* (1733), and *Serse* (1738). (The "Largo" or slow first aria in *Serse*, remains one of Handel's most popular melodies.)

Most of these operas, like those of Lully and Rameau in France, derived their plots from ancient or medieval history or legend. Characters were highly romanticized; plots were fragmented and static—mere frameworks for an appropriate set of virtuosic arias for the singers. The genre was called *opera seria* (or opera on "serious" subjects), but it required an unusually willing suspension of disbelief. Despite the constraints under which he worked, however, Handel often managed to transcend the limitations of the genre. His arias admirably conveyed a given emotion or mood, with a poetic resonance that exceeded that of all his contemporaries. Several of his operas have been successfully revived in modern productions.

In addition to opera, Handel was much in demand for ceremonial music on a variety of public occasions. This aspect of his work placed him in the tradition of **Henry Purcell** (1659–1695), whose large-scale choral works (often called anthems or odes) had been much admired thirty years before. Handel, like Purcell, combined the talent of composing for solo voice with a superb gift at choral writing. His anthem *Zadok the Priest* first performed at the coronation of King George II in 1727, is a perfect illustration of the genre; a master of stirring pageantry, Handel became an unofficial composer-laureate with this work, and it has been performed for over two centuries at every subsequent coronation of a British monarch. The *Water Music*, one of his most popular instrumental works, has already been mentioned; in 1749, he complemented that work with *Music for the Royal Fireworks*, composed for the grand, outdoor celebration of the Treaty of Aix-la-Chapelle [cf. Rameau's music for the same treaty, above]. In addition, the eleven *Chandos Anthems* (composed for Handel's patron, the Duke of Chandos, 1716–1719) should be mentioned.

In 1728, the poet John Gay produced a new type of popular work entitled *The Beggar's Opera*. Ironically, the composer was Johann Christoph Pepusch (1667–1752)—like Handel, a German-born composer who had settled in London. *The Beggar's Opera* is a satire which acerbically parodies both the witty comedy of manners and the stylized *opera seria*. The plot concerns the low life of eighteenth-century London: pickpockets, "fences" and highwaymen. Unlike the operas of Handel, it was sung in English; the music included a number folk tunes. Pepusch even even went so far as to filch (the plot concerned petty thieves, after all) the most popular aria from Handel's opera *Rinaldo*. *The Beggar's Opera* was nothing less than a smash hit. And its popularity quickly eliminated the fashion for Italian opera.

The following year, the Royal Academy of Music ceased to sponsor productions of Handel's Italian operas. For eight years he attempted to produce them privately, together with a partner; but by 1737 his company was virtually bankrupt. He suffered a paralyzing stroke in this year, and only slowly recovered. But two years later, he turned with renewed vigor to another large-scale form of music, which he hoped would replace *opera seria* in the affections of the public. This was the *oratorio* (derived from Italian, and literally meaning "a place of prayer").

The oratorio is a musical setting of a religious libretto, employing orchestra, soloists, and chorus—but not requiring scenery or costumes, since it is performed in the concert hall. The form of the oratorio offered Handel several advantages. Its dramatic character naturally appealed to him; it was far cheaper than opera to produce; and the libretti were in English, and could thus attract a larger, middle-class audience. Even before the failure of his opera company, Handel had experimented with oratorio-like works, in *Esther* (1732) and *Alexander's Feast* (1736)—the latter a setting of a celebrated ode by John Dryden. Oratorios had been written by Heinrich Schütz, Alessandro Scarlatti, and a number of other composers of the early Baroque; but Handel was to make the form indisputably his own.

Saul and *Israel in Egypt* (1739) inaugurated Handel's full-scale efforts in the new form. Both were based on passages from the Old Testament, and were a resounding success. As an added attraction, Handel offered improvisations on the organ during the intermissions. In the next twenty years, he wrote 26 oratorios in English, including *Samson* (1743), *Judas Maccabaeus* (1746), *Solomon* (1749), and *Jephtha* (1751). Of all these works, none has surpassed *Messiah* in popularity (first performed in Dublin, 1742). *Messiah* is actually atypical for Handel in one respect: unlike the other oratorios, it does not relate a narrative, but rather consists of a series of reflections on the meaning of Christian redemption. It resembles the other oratorios in that its libretto is based directly on passages of the Bible, a book that was far more familiar to the middle-class Englishman of Handel's time than the works of the classical poets and historians. Handel did indeed compose oratorios on classical subjects (e.g. *Hercules*, 1744), but these are a distinct minority.

In oratorio, Handel found even greater scope for his dramatic gifts and supreme choral writing. He combined features of Italian opera and oratorio with the German and English traditions; he used pictorial effects splendidly; his harmonic language was rich and expressive. Although he did not radically alter his musical style, he essentially adjusted his manner of expressing emotion: operatic arias commonly express an individual's emotions, while the content of oratorios usually involves communal feelings. Above all, Handel continued to exploit grandiose effects and striking contrasts; listen, for example, to the quietly beautiful descending passage "The wonders of his love" in the *Hallelujah* chorus of *Messiah*, suddenly followed by the great crescendo of drums and trumpets.

In addition to operas and oratorios, Handel wrote a large number of organ concerti, concerti for strings and woodwind, suites for harpsichord, and delightful sonatas for solo flute and oboe.

If we compare Handel's musical style to that of Bach, the other great master of the late Baroque, we are immediately struck by a set of contrasts. For Bach, musical inspiration came from religious faith; for Handel, it proceeded from popular taste. Handel's style, not surprisingly, is plainer and more outwardly dramatic; the tensions and resolutions of his music are accomplished through broad strokes. Although he was pre-eminently gifted at complex, contrapuntal forms (such as the fugue), he seldom explored them with the overwhelmingly detailed precision of Bach. Handel's choral writing tends rather to clearly etched melodies, supported by solid blocks of chordal harmony—a style which is also apparent in his concerti. The two composers, of course, often sound alike, especially in their suites and concerti grossi—in which Bach was brought closer to Handel by the French and Italian forms that were common coin in eighteenth-century Europe. But, listening to Handel, one senses a powerful dominance of spirited rhythm and the major mode; the style of Bach, even in the *Brandenburg Concerti*, often contains more deeply subjective, meditative elements.

When Handel died in 1759, he was accorded the signal honor of burial in Westminster Abbey. His musical influence in his adopted country had no rival for over a century; and one outstanding reason for Felix Mendelssohn's success when he revived the oratorio in nineteenth-century England was that he wrote in the tradition of Handel [see Chapter 10, on Mendelssohn's *Elijah*). Meanwhile, the advent of fashion in music on the Continent led to further important changes in musical form. The most notable of these were the concerti of Antonio Vivaldi, the new style in the operas of Christoph Willibald von Gluck, and the development of the symphony—pioneered by Johann Stamitz, and joyfully nurtured by the first master of Classicism, Joseph Haydn.

Questions for Review

1. What do we mean by the Baroque tradition in secular music? Name three or four of the outstanding composers of this tradition.

2. Which important musical forms were developed in the eighteenth century?

3. Identify the essential differences, in action and sound, between the harpsichord and the organ.

4. Briefly describe the typical pattern of court opera which was set by the French composers Jean-Baptiste Lully and Jean-Philippe Rameau.

5. What was the typical framework for the French suite, as developed by François Couperin?

6. How did the French composers Rameau and Couperin significantly enlarge the body of musical theory, especially with regard to keyboard instruments?

7. What problem exists for modern performers of much Baroque music (as illustrated by Telemann's *Sonata for Oboe and Harpsichord*)?

8. What was the importance of the keyboard sonatas of Domenico Scarlatti?

9. What musical form most attracted the young George Frideric Handel?

10. Identify and describe the circumstances surrounding the first performance of a) *Zadok the Priest* and b) *Music for the Royal Fireworks*

11. Comment on the sorts of subjects favored by Italian *opera seria* in Handel's time.

12. Name one of Handel's notable operas.

13. Comment on the style of John Gay's *The Beggar's Opera*. How did works like *the Beggar's Opera* contrast with *opera seria*?

14. Define the musical form of the oratorio.

15. Why did Handel virtually abandon Italian opera for the oratorio in the late 1730s?

16. Briefly contrast the inspiration and style of Bach and Handel.

17. Name at least two oratorios by Handel.

Answers

1. We distinguish a Baroque tradition in secular music to summarize musical developments in style and form that were most influential in the development of Classicism (as opposed to the sacred tradition of Lutheran composers like Bach, who were long neglected). The chief composers in the secular Baroque include Jean-Philippe Rameau and François Couperin in France, Georg Philipp Telemann in Germany, Domenico Scarlatti in Italy and Spain, and George Frideric Handel, who spent his entire mature career in England.

2. Important musical forms that were developed in the eighteenth century include: the sonata, the suite, the concerto grosso, and the symphony.

3. The organ produces tones by means of a wind action through pipes; when the player depresses a key, the tracker connected to that key opens the end of a pipe, and air is forced into it from the wind-chest. The sound is steady and continuous, for as long as the key is depressed. The keys of a harpsichord, on the other hand, are connected to a plucking mechanism; when a key is depressed, the string is plucked, and the sound gradually dies away. It is therefore impossible to sustain notes on the harpsichord; and long notes must be emphasized through a trill, or some other ornamental figure. In general, the organ is capable of far grander, more majestic effects than the harpsichord, and it possesses a broader range of tone-quality.

4. The operas of Lully and Rameau generally featured an overture, which was followed by a prologue, clearly outlining the action for the audience. Often the prologue presented a group of divinities from classical mythology (the plots of the opera were frequently derived from ancient myth or legend); the gods would pose as onlookers to the ensuing action. The opera itself was divided into a number of discrete numbers, featuring in turn the soloists, the choral ensemble, and the ballet. Settings and characters were highly stylized, and the plot was typically no more than a series of loosely connected episodes, strung together as a showcase for the talents of virtuoso singers.

5. The French suite, as developed by François Couperin in the early eighteenth century, was a composition for small, chamber orchestra. It was usually divided into four movements, based on the dance forms of the Allemande, Courante, Sarabande, and Gigue (in alternating slow and fast rhythms).

6. Rameau and Couperin both published technical treatises for keyboard composition and performance: Rameau's *Traité de l'Harmonie* (1722), which treated proper methods of chord progression, and Couperin's *L'Art de toucher le clavecin* (1716), which discussed concepts of touch and fingering. The latter book had an important influence on J. S. Bach.

7. Much Baroque music (e.g. Telemann's sonata) does not specify the exact manner in which the bass line is to accompany the melody; only general indications of harmony are provided, since composers and players were normally expected to be adept at improvisation. Therefore, modern performers are forced to reconstruct the *basso continuo*.

8. Domenico Scarlatti's keyboard sonatas (which number over 500) were composed as exercises to improve various aspects of player technique. They were usually written in one movement; but toward the end of his career, Scarlatti started to conceive the sonatas in pairs. These pairs, in structure and in the contrasting use of the tonic and dominant keys, anticipate the development of the three-movement sonata, and are also an embryonic illustration of sonata-allegro (first movement) form: exposition, development, and recapitulation.

9. Opera was the musical form which attracted the young Handel.

10. a) *Zadok the Priest*: coronation anthem composed by Handel for the accession of George II to the English throne in 1727. It has been played at every subsequent coronation of a British monarch.

b) *Music for the Royal Fireworks*: Handel's orchestral suite, written for the outdoor celebrations that marked the singing of the Treaty of Aix-la-Chapelle in 1749.

11. *Opera seria* ("serious opera") usually favored subjects from Greek and Latin mythology, or from classical history. Although few members of the English audiences in Handel's day could understand many of the words, *opera seria* enjoyed a tremendous vogue as aristocratic entertainment in the opening decades of the eighteenth century.

12. Handel's notable operas include: *Rinaldo* (1711), *Ottone* (1723), *Giulio Cesare* (1724), *Orlando* (1733), and *Serse* (1738).

13. *The Beggar's Opera* was a deliberately irreverent spoof of *opera seria* and of the leading genre on the English stage, the comedy of manners. Its plot recounted unsavory incidents in the London underworld of thieves, prostitutes, and other "low types"; its music consisted of catchy tunes, many of them borrowed from ballads and other folk-music of the day. The text was, of course, in English. Audiences identified quickly with this genre, and it severely cut into the popularity of *opera seria*.

14. The oratorio is a musical setting of a libretto (nearly always religious in character), employing orchestra, soloists, and chorus. Unlike the opera, it does not require scenery or costumes; and it is usually performed in the concert hall, rather than in the theater or the church.

15. Handel abandoned Italian opera for the oratorio because the success of *The Beggar's Opera* and other similar works convinced him that the popularity of Italian opera was waning. Oratorio, in contrast to opera, were performed in English; their plots were derived from Biblical texts, which were more familiar to middle-class audiences than the literature and mythology of Greece and Rome. Oratorios thus had the potential for attracting a large middle-class audience. In addition, they were considerably cheaper to produce than operas.

16. Bach was primarily inspired by his German Protestant heritage; most of his works were written for the explicit glorification of God at church services. Handel, on the other hand, possessed a showman's temperament and a sure sense of the dramatic in music; hence, he was the master of public spectacle. Religious faith was the keynote of Bach's work; it was popular taste that dic-

tated Handel's efforts. In style, Handel is plainer and less intense than Bach—especially in his choral writing, which relies on clearly etched melodies and solid blocks of chordal harmony, rather than on intricate counterpoint.

17. Handel's well-known oratorios include: *Saul* (1739), *Israel in Egypt* (1739), *Messiah* (1742), *Samson* (1743), *Judas Maccabaeus* (1746), *Solomon* (1749), and *Jephtha* (1751).

Chapter 7

The Seasons and the Symphony

The Seasons and the Symphony

By the time Bach and Handel reached artistic maturity in the early eighteenth century, a number of different national styles had developed all over Europe. Regardless of their own nationality or that of the patrons for whom they worked, composers often adopted the mannerisms of these styles: witness Handel's Italian operas, and Bach's "French" and "English" suites [see Chapters 5 and 6]. During the last half of the century—a period stretching from, say, Antonio Vivaldi to Franz Joseph Haydn—a new internationalism developed in European music. This development is most clearly manifest in the evolution of that most international of large-scale orchestral forms: the symphony.

All of the composers whom we discuss in this chapter—Vivaldi, Gluck, Stamitz, and Haydn—were great innovators. Whether from practical necessity or out of theoretical belief, they all helped to shape a revolution in music. Vivaldi brought the *concerto grosso* to the peak of perfection; Gluck rescued opera from a static celebration of vocal virtuosity and introduced elements of theatrical drama; Stamitz created new orchestral techniques; Haydn established the string quartet as the primary form of chamber music and—above all—the symphony as the primary form of orchestral music.

The lifetimes of these composers span over a century: Vivaldi was born in 1678 and Haydn died in 1809. During this period of 130 years, much about musical life in the great courts of Europe remained unchanged. Composers were often still forced to travel the continent in search of commissions and powerful patrons. Music was still regarded by such patrons as "occasional": its function was largely to amuse. There was no such thing as a "standard repertory" consisting of popular works which were played repeatedly. A composer was continually expected to furnish something new for the enjoyment of aristocratic audiences.

But there were some changes. In the early part of the eighteenth century, the great age of the violin was ushered in by Stradivarius and the school of Cremona, a town not far from Vivaldi's Venice.

Though the violin already had a long history, it had—because of its humble origins as a folk instrument—been somewhat looked down upon. In the hands of the Cremonese masters, however, the instrument was brought to a degree of splendor never since equalled; through its greater flexibility, expressiveness and, above all, its greater dynamic range, the violin (and its relatives the viola and violoncello) rapidly displaced the family of viols which had been the primary bowed string instrument since the Renaissance.

In the 1740s, the adventuresome Johann Stamitz developed a new, bigger, and richer sound in his orchestra at Mannheim. And toward the end of our period, the effects of the Industrial Revolution, the political unrest which led to rebellions in America and France, and the search for a new freedom in literature and art combined to produce the international movement of Romanticism: a movement that would profoundly influence the course of music, literature, painting, philosophy—indeed, every aspect of man's thinking and expression.

Antonio Vivaldi (1678–1741) is one of the last great masters of the Baroque period. His music is constantly active, dynamic; his themes are vigorous, and he often utilizes a far broader dynamic range than some of his Baroque contemporaries. He is most famous today for the violin concerti nicknamed *Le quattro stagioni (The Four Seasons)*; they constitute the first four compositions of Opus 8, which is a collection of twelve concerti for strings entitled "The Contest Between Harmony and Invention" (1725). *The Four Seasons* celebrates the Italian countryside at every time of year. It is an early example of descriptive music, in which the beauties of nature are held up to mankind as a model for pleasure and enjoyment. As one listens to the first concerto, "Spring", the music presents a superb description in sound of the landscape: birds, breezes, flowers, rustling leaves, a sudden storm. Here is the poem that was prefixed to the composition (the author is unknown):

> Spring is here, greeted by happy birdsong,
> while streams run murmur softly murmuring
> to the breath of gentle breezes.
> Then the sky is black; thunder and lightning
> hold sway; and after the storm is quiet,
> the little birds return to their harmonious song.
>
> In this flowering meadow, leaves sweetly rustling,
> the goat-herd sleeps beside his faithful dog.

> Beneath the bright sky, nymphs and shepherds
> turn to the festive sound of the pastoral dance.

The sound of Vivaldi's music is distinctive. Sharp juxtapositions of loud and soft (measures are frequently "echoed" for contrast) are typical of much of his work; melodies of infinite sweetness stand side by side with forceful, masculine expression.

At first, Vivaldi seemed destined for a career in the Church. Taught music by his father, who was a violinist in the orchestra of St. Mark's Cathedral, the young Antonio studied for the priesthood, and was in fact ordained in 1703. The same year marked the beginning of his remarkable association with the Ospedale della Pietà, a foundation for orphaned girls run by the Church. Here he taught violin, had his works performed, and presided as *maestro* for more than three decades. Unable to fulfill his ecclesiastical duties because of chronic ill health, he turned more and more to music. Gradually, his unconventional life (he had a relationship with a woman singer) brought him into conflict with Church authorities.

Among Vivaldi's first major compositions were operas. He is reputed to have written 94 operas, usually based on episodes of ancient Roman and Persian history) are largely forgotten today, Vivaldi's interest in large-scale composition is significant. His instrumental music reflects his sense of orchestral potential—his *sonatas* were written for a range of instruments, some of which had been largely ignored by major composers. One story asserts that Vivaldi composed sonatas for so many instruments—cello, oboe, flute, mandolin, recorder, and the horns—because he wrote to order for the diverse performing talents of the children in his orphanage.

Vivaldi's sacred compositions are also important. These include cantatas, a Mass, an independent setting of the *Gloria*, and the oratorio *Juditha Triumphans*. The early work entitled *L'Estro armonico* ("Harmonic Inspiration"), a collection of twelve concerti for various combinations of strings, is also notable. Vivaldi was greatly admired by Johann Sebastian Bach, who transcribed a number of his concerti for harpsichord and organ. Vivaldi's music fell into a long period of neglect shortly after he died in Vienna in 1741. In our own time, with the revival of interest in the original performance techniques of Baroque music, and with the discovery and publication of hitherto unknown works, the music of Vivaldi has finally taken its rightful place alongside that of Bach and Handel.

Just as the enormous variety of Vivaldi's instrumental works opened up new possibilities in orchestral composition, **Christoph Willibald von Gluck** (1714–1787) pioneered a new style in opera. In the seventeenth and early eighteenth century, opera had served largely as a showcase for the talents of individual singing artists. Dramatic values were almost totally ignored; libretti were often mere skeletons; the orchestra itself was entirely subordinate to one instrument—the singing voice. Gluck set out to change all this. His theory and practice resulted in two notable operas: *Orfeo ed Eurydice* (1762) and *Alceste* (1767). While these works are still highly formal in style and classical in subject, Gluck's fusion of musical and dramatic values distinctly anticipates the boldness of some operas of the Romantic period a century later—in particular, the works of Richard Wagner.

Gluck was born at Erasbach in Germany. When he was eighteen, he traveled to the University of Prague to study music and philosophy. Finding a patron in Prince Lobkowitz, he moved to Vienna, and thence to Milan and London (where he met Handel). His early career was nothing out of the ordinary: a peripatetic apprenticeship, in search of teachers, commissions, and patrons. Meanwhile he composed a series of early operas. But in 1754, the Empress Maria Theresa appointed him the Kapellmeister of the court theater in Vienna; it was here that he started to develop the full scope of his audacious new theory of opera. He aimed to transform the form from a purely musical to a musico-dramatic one.

Opera before Gluck—from the pens of such composers as Alessandro Scarlatti (1660–1725), Pietro Francesco Cavalli (1602–1676) (the pupil of Claudio Monteverdi, generally recognized as the father of opera [see Chapter 4]), and George Frideric Handel (1685–1759)[see Chapter 5]—had largely ignored the dramatic potential of the libretto (the text). In structure, their operas focused to such an extent on elaborate and lengthily repetitious solo arias that dramatic continuity was practically non-existent. Gluck's novel ideas included eliminating *da capo* repetitions, so that the action could proceed in a relatively unbroken flow; strengthening the accompaniment to recitative; and restoring the chorus to a prominent role. He also insisted on a certain element of psychological realism in the music drama. These ideas found expression in two great works, both based on classical mythology.

Orfeo ed Eurydice (1762) was inspired by the Greek myth of the singer Orpheus. According to the myth, Orpheus sang so beautifully that man and beast alike were charmed by his voice. He married the lovely girl Eurydice, but their happiness ended abruptly when she died from the bite of a poisonous serpent. Orpheus descended to the underworld to try to bring her back. The gods of the underworld, in recognition of his great art, promised to restore Eurydice to life on the condition that Orpheus not turn back to look at her as he led her up to daylight. But the impatient Orpheus could not keep his promise: he looked back at his bride, and so the shade of Eurydice returned to the underworld forever.

In Gluck's version, Orfeo is first seen at Eurydice's tomb, lamenting her death. The great Second Act contrasts the terrifying demons of Hades and the pastoral spirits in Elysium (that part of the underworld which the ancients believed to be the abode of blessed spirits). Orpheus charms the nether powers with his music. The Third Act is notable for the characterization of Eurydice: Gluck and his librettist, Raniero Calzabigi, injected a psychologically interesting tension between hero and heroine, Eurydice mistaking Orfeo's apparent coldness for rejection. The most famous aria in the opera is *Che farò senza Eurydice? (What shall I do without Eurydice?)*, sung by Orfeo after the flight of Eurydice's spirit. The aria's noble simplicity is only superficially at odds with the hero's despair: its combination of dignity and anguish is a dramatic masterstroke.

Five years after *Orfeo* came the first performance of Gluck's *Alceste* (1767). This opera was also based on classical myth. King Admetus is warned that he will die unless he can find someone to die in his place; his wife Alcestis volunteers to make this ultimate sacrifice. Gluck prefaced the score with an essay in which he declared his aims for opera: "To confine music to its proper function of serving the poetry in order to further the expression and the situations of the plot... I believed that my greatest effort should be directed to seeking a beautiful simplicity... and there is no accepted rule that I have not thought should be gladly sacrificed in favor of effectiveness." Gluck's theory was also reflected in the subtitle of *Orfeo*, which he described as an *azione teatrale per musica* ("a dramatic action in music"): note that the dramatic element is named first. Some critics have pointed out that Gluck's emphasis on drama and plot in opera foreshadow, to some extent, the more elaborate and complete synthesis of music-drama by Richard Wagner in the nineteenth century.

Gluck's operas were so successful in Vienna that he was amply rewarded by the Empress Maria Theresa. He spent the 1770s in Paris, where he composed a number of new operas in the grand style (including *Iphigénie en Tauride*) and supervised the production of revised versions of *Orfeo* and *Alceste*. In 1779 he returned to Vienna, where he spent the last years of his life. (According to one story, he precipitated his own death by ignoring the orders of his doctor and enjoying an after-dinner drink.) In addition to serious operas (the genre known as *opera seria*), he composed several lighter, comic pieces (*opera buffa*) for the court of Maria Theresa, as well as sonatas, the choral work *De Profundis*, and the important ballet *Don Juan* (1761), in which he incorporated his theories of music supporting, rather than eclipsing, the dramatic action. However, it is for the pioneering works *Orfeo* and *Alceste* that Gluck is best known today; both operas are parts of the standard operatic repertory.

Gluck's theory and practice welded classical harmony and style to a new realism, a new energy in drama. He is thus a major transitional figure in the history of opera. Not coincidentally, such a transition was occurring in the mid-eighteenth century in purely orchestral music as well. The *sinfonia* (or short concert overture) was on its way to becoming the symphony. To see how this happened, we must consider the careers of two other transitional figures: Johann Christian Bach and Johann Stamitz.

Johann Christian Bach (1732–1785) was the eighteenth child and youngest son of Johann Sebastian Bach. He is sometimes called the "English Bach" since he worked in London for the last twenty years of his life. A leading practitioner of the *galant* (or courtly) style in music, his sinfonias, sonatas, and piano concerti are notable for their grace, elegance, and melodic charm. He was born in Leipzig, where his father was cantor in St. Thomas' Church for the latter part of his career (1723–1750) [see Chapter 5]. After studies in Berlin and Bologna, Bach moved to Milan. His early attempts to compose opera were not successful, and he soon accepted an invitation from the King's Theater in London, where he composed such operas as *Orione* and *Zanaida*, well received in their time but now obscure. It was in London that he met the young Mozart, who visited England in 1764. Bach performed a sonata with the boy, who was then aged eight. It is now generally recognized that Bach's music exerted a fruitful influence, not only on Mozart, but also on Haydn and (early in the nineteenth century) on the young Beethoven.

For Johann Christian Bach, the symphony as we know it did not yet exist. The term *sinfonia* (literally, "played together", i.e., an instrumental work) was used to denote a concert overture that led to a more important attraction, such as an opera, cantata, or suite. The *sinfonia* was therefore an introductory piece, hardly the major focus of a composer's effort, and certainly not the focus of attention for an eighteenth-century audience.

Yet during J.C. Bach's lifetime, the *sinfonia* developed into the symphony. Bach found the process underway when he paid a visit in 1772 to the court of the Elector Palatine at Mannheim in Germany. The "Mannheim school" of composers and musical performers had initiated a great change in the sound of the orchestra, starting in the 1740s, when the Elector Palatine had invited the Bohemian violinist **Johann Stamitz** (1717–1757) to Mannheim. Stamitz directed the orchestra from 1745 to 1757. During a short career, he developed startlingly new ideas for the sound of the players, the number of instruments, and the composition of the symphony. In this enterprise, other composers joined him, including Ignaz Holzbauer (1711–1783), F. X. Richter (1709–1787), and Stamitz' own sons, Karl (1745–1801) and Anton (1754–1809). Karl and Anton Stamitz settled in Paris in 1770; gradually, the influence of the Mannheim school was felt throughout Europe: in France, Italy, Bohemia—and, above all—in that perennially musical city, Vienna.

Stamitz' principal innovations concerned the size and balance of the orchestra, and the form of the symphony itself. The typical mid-eighteenth-century orchestra, the type which played the music of Gluck and Johann Christian Bach, consisted of strings, double woodwinds, horns, and an instrument to play the "continuo" (or "continuous" harmonic accompaniment): often, this was the harpsichord. The sound of such an orchestra could be graceful and elegant. But by today's standards, it was confined to a relatively narrow dynamic range. Stamitz gradually expanded the orchestra to include 60 players, including a violin section of 20. His Symphony in D Major called for numerous strings, a large woodwind section, four horns, two kettle-drums, and a trumpet. Something like the modern orchestra was taking shape.

Stamitz wrote over 70 symphonies, ceaselessly experimenting

with what came to be known as the "Mannheim sound". A rich new spectrum of effects emerged: e.g. the "Mannheim rocket" (a series of rapidly ascending scales), the "Mannheim sigh" (an elaborate and prolonged "leaning" from one note to the next), and great dynamic range between loud and soft. Stamitz borrowed horns from the Elector Palatine's military band to enrich and deepen the brass section. He doubled and re-doubled string and woodwind parts. The Mannheim orchestra displayed a new, far more varied set of colors.

Although Franz Joseph Haydn is often called the father of the symphony, some of the credit for inventing the symphony form rightfully belongs to Stamitz. For it was Stamitz' innovations that made it possible for the *sinfonia* to become the symphony: melodies could now be repeated and varied in an almost endless series of combinations; different instruments, or groups of instruments, could be used for thematic subjects; and as the orchestra expanded, so did the forms that were composed for it.

Of all the innovative composers of this period—indeed of any period—one of the greatest is **Franz Joseph Haydn** (1732–1809). With Haydn, the symphony and the string quartet (the most enduring and challenging forms for orchestral music and chamber music) were definitively established. Musical styles, in consequence, became international, since composers—regardless of their nationality or seat of patronage—continued to develop these two most flexible forms of music. Haydn himself, like Antonio Vivaldi, was extraordinarily prolific: he wrote over 100 symphonies and 83 string quartets, not to speak of operas (20), masses (13), oratorios, cantatas, 52 keyboard sonatas, concerti, and assorted works for solo voice. Practically all his works are marked by gaiety and exuberance; there has never been a composer who sounded so consistently happy in his music. Classical form and the *galant* style (elegant, refined, symmetrical) are fused in music that combines exuberance with deep feeling, sparkling wit with grandeur and emotion. Haydn's range was enormous. Yet his music, during a long career, was continually inspired by a wish to provide—as he expressed it—"a source of relief and joy for those oppressed by care."

Haydn was born in the village of Rohrau, in lower Austria. Although he did not come from a musical family (his father was a wheelwright), he was a true child prodigy. At three, he rubbed sticks together in time with the singers and dancers at local festivals. At five, he began to study music with the village schoolmaster. And at eight, he went to St. Stephen's Church in Vienna to spend the rest of his childhood as a choirboy. As a young man in the 1750s, he endured poverty, eking out a living by giving lessons and serving as an accompanist. It was not until 1761 that he found a niche as assistant Kapellmeister for the aristocratic Esterházy family—passionate music lovers, and one of the richest noble houses in Europe.

Consider the requirements of a wealthy music lover before radio or recordings or even public concerts: music at meal times, to dance by, for chapel, for entertainment, for performance by adult practitioners of one or another instrument, and for study by children. Not all of this music would be heard with strict attention—some of it served as background for conversation and the clatter of dishes. Prince Paul Esterházy and his successor, Prince Nikolaus, assigned the overall supervision of music-making to the young Haydn. He performed a variety of duties for their court: conducting the orchestra, producing operas, composing music in a wide variety of forms, and performing in chamber works. Elaborate entertainments, family celebrations, intimate gatherings after dinner: all were graced by Haydn's works. The confidence of the Esterházys in their Kapellmeister was well placed, since Haydn used their thirty-year association to move forward constantly in his art. As he wrote: "My Prince was always satisfied with my works. I not only had the encouragement of constant approval but, as conductor of an orchestra, I could make experiments, observed what produced an effect and what weakened it, and was thus in a position to improve, alter, make additions or omissions, and be as bold as I pleased. I was cut off from the world, there was no one to confuse or torment me, and I was forced to become *original*."

Haydn became a friend and admirer of Mozart in the 1780s, and the works of the two composers in this period display mutual influence. In 1790, the Esterházy family interrupted its patronage; Prince Nikolaus had died, and his successor dismissed the orchestra. But luckily for Haydn, his fame had spread, and it insured several invitations. He traveled to Vienna from the Esterházy palace on the border of Hungary and Austria; he then spent a year and a half in England (1791–92), where he was warmly received with royal honors and an honorary degree from Oxford University. He returned to Vienna, where the young Beethoven became his pupil (although friction soon developed between the grand old man and the young revolutionary [see Chapter 9]). In 1794–95, he paid a second visit to England, even more successful than the first. In the first years of the nineteenth century, the Esterházys revived their patronage, and allowed Haydn to concentrate on composing. To this period belong the oratorio *The Creation* and several magnificent masses. Haydn died in Vienna in 1809, full of honors, as the troops of the Emperor Napoleon entered the city. The last piece he played was the Austrian national anthem (*The Emperor's Hymn*), which he himself had composed, believing that his native land deserved a national melody with the stirring dignity of Britain's *God Save the King*.

Of all his achievements, none is more important than the way in which Haydn forged the musical language of the Classical style. It is probably true that no single element of that language is strictly original with Haydn—indeed, we have already seen the contributions of such composers as J.C. Bach and Johann Stamitz. Yet Haydn's particular genius was for musical architecture. Almost single-handedly, he established the principles of form which were adopted by Mozart, then Beethoven, and finally by many of Beethoven's followers.

Haydn grasped as no one before him the significance of certain formal relationships between individual musical phrases and the harmonic structure of an entire movement. In many Baroque dance movements and in almost all the movements of Haydn's immediate predecessors, a very simple structural procedure had been followed. A movement began with an easily recognized theme in the home key, and—at the close of the first half—*modulated* (changed key) to another key, usually the "Dominant", five scale-steps away. The first half of the movement was then repeated. In the second half of the movement, which commenced in the "other" key, another modulation takes place which returns to the original "home" key. This second half of the movement is also repeated.

Haydn modified this common procedure, and thereby produced one of the most fertile fields for musical composition which has ever been invented. Haydn's procedure is called *sonata-allegro* form, because it is most commonly found in the first (allegro) movements of sonatas, symphonies, and concerti. Haydn's modification essentially consisted of superimposing a three-fold structure upon the dual harmonic division of the movement. This is how the sonata-allegro form works:

Exposition: The movement begins with a section called the *Exposition*. Here, the basic thematic material of the movement is stated in the home key.

Bridge: A short modulation, called the *Bridge*, moves to another key (again, usually the "Dominant"), and introduces a second theme which contrasts with the first. The first half of the movement concludes in the "other" key, and is then repeated.

Development: Next, a section known as the *Development* begins the second half of the movement. Here, the thematic material of the first half is fragmented, transformed, and amplified. Typically, a large number of different keys are touched on, giving this section a great deal of tension and vigor. At the conclusion of the Development, a last modulation takes place which returns the music to the original "home" key.

Recapitulation: At this point, Haydn re-introduced the original material which had made up the first half of the movement, but without its own internal modulation. Thus, the entire *Recapitulation* remains in the home key.

Haydn's invention is very flexible because the harmonic tension achieved through the process of changing keys allows sufficient time for the exploration of thematic material. As Haydn himself began to understand the complex relationships inherent in this structure, his sonata-allegro movements grew longer and more intricate. Beethoven [see Chapter 9] would eventually be able to construct single movements by this procedure which were longer than entire Haydn symphonies, but he did so by visiting keys which were "more distant" than those used by Haydn.

This procedure was the basis of almost all of Haydn's composition. It is to be found in his symphonies, string quartets and other chamber music, even some of his Mass movements.

If there is any characteristic that unites all of Haydn's diverse works, it is liveliness. The second movement of one of his best-known symphonies, No. 94, the *Surprise*, illustrates his sense of wit perfectly. A simple melody, built on the C-Major chord, is announced by the violins: it is soft, relatively slow, and staccato. At the end of each phrase, the orchestra thunders an echo of the last note, *fortissimo*. (Haydn is reported to have remarked to a friend that at these points all the ladies in the audience would scream.) In the *Military* Symphony (No. 100), horn-calls in the second movement vividly evoke the ceremony of trooping the color which Haydn had seen the royal guards perform in London on one of his English visits. The *Echo* Symphony (No. 38) exploits some of the effects which Stamitz had developed at Mannheim. Many of Haydn's other symphonies acquired expressive nicknames reflecting the direct and charming picturesque abilities of the composer. (This practice continued in the symphonies of Mozart, Beethoven, Schubert, and later composers of the nineteenth and twentieth centuries.) To cite only the best known: the trilogy known as *Le Matin, Le Midi,* and *Le Soir (Morning, Noon,* and *Evening)* (Nos. 6–8), *Philosopher*(No. 22), *Farewell* (No. 45), *Schoolmaster* (No. 55), *Hunt* (No. 73), *Hen* (No. 83), *Queen* (No. 85), *Clock* (No. 101), and *London* (No. 103).

The wittiness of the *Farewell* Symphony is especially characteristic. The Esterházy family fostered the composer's genius. But their love of music created extraordinary demands on the time and energy of Haydn and his orchestra. For months at a time, the Esterházys retreated to their grand palace; they expected a different musical entertainment almost every evening. When the musicians grew restless, Haydn protested indirectly to his patrons. In the last movement of the *Farewell* Symphony, the score calls for the players to leave their posts one by one while the orchestra is playing, until only two musicians remain at the end. Legend records that the Prince took the hint and granted the orchestra a vacation.

Haydn's symphonies gradually increased in dynamic range and depth of musical expression; the last twelve symphonies, in particular, can be compared with those of Mozart in their combination of elegance and passion. While bringing to the symphony a new range and power, Haydn also transformed the string quartet into the premier form of chamber music.

Chamber music is smaller, more intimate, more compact than symphonic music. There are few instruments, and only one instrumentalist for each part. Because there are fewer musical lines, the structure of the piece is clearer; whereas one may be surrounded by orchestral sound, one is more apt to be conscious in a chamber work of the individual instruments and their musical parts. The number of musicians is small: the four members of a string quartet (two violins, a viola, and a cello); piano and three stringed instruments; flute or clarinet and three strings; a string quartet plus cello or piano. Other combinations, smaller or slightly larger, are also possible. The most common form is the string quartet.

Like the symphony, the classical string quartet normally consists of four movements. But the quartet emphasizes the individuality of each instrumental voice. Haydn's early quartets emphasized the solo first violin; but he gradually developed the form into an almost equal partnership of the four players, and endowed it with such sprightliness and lyricism that critics have dubbed his quartets "elegant, four-way conversations". Haydn is the first great exponent of a form that has continued to challenge composers down to the present day: the quartet's flexibility and popular appeal have made it the symphony of chamber music. That Haydn was capable of solemnity and passion in the form, as well as of wit and sparkle, is illustrated by the moving variations on the *Emperor's Hymn* in the *Emperor* Quartet (Opus 76, No. 3).

Haydn also invented a form of chamber music closely allied to the string quartet: the piano trio. In this combination of instruments, the violin strengthens the upper register of the piano, while the cello reinforces the bass and makes it more lyric. In Haydn's age, the piano was in its infancy. Like the orchestra before Stamitz' innovations at Mannheim, the instrument lacked resonance and power. With the invention of the piano trio, Haydn initiated a series of musical experiments that would lead to far-reaching development of the piano, until it attained the status of one of the premier solo instruments, early in the nineteenth century [see Chapters 8–10].

No account of Haydn's importance would be complete without mention of his sacred and choral music. His visits to England inspired the *Nelson Mass* (No. 9), which the British admiral himself heard performed as he stopped at the Esterházy palace on his return to England from doing battle against Napoleon. The trumpets and kettle-drums of the Sanctus in this Mass speak of military victory while the words are of thanksgiving. One of Haydn's greatest works is *The Creation* (1797–98), an oratorio based on the Book of Genesis and John Milton's epic poem *Paradise Lost*. Here Haydn's fusion of joy and majesty touches the sublime. Another notable composition of sacred music is *The Seven Last Words of Our Saviour from the Cross* (1785); originally commissioned by the Cathedral of Cádiz in Spain, these orchestral interludes were later variously arranged by Haydn as string quartets and as cantatas for chorus and soloists.

Johann Stamitz had preceded Haydn with great originality in the form of the symphony; and other composers had at least anticipated the string quartet. But it was Haydn who developed these two forms of instrumental music to exploit the full range of feeling and form. The isolated, hard-working genius, who never lost either his sense of humor or his bold willingness to experiment, had made music a truly international language.

Questions for Review

1. What requirements for musical composers in Vivaldi's time help to explain his uncommonly large output?

2. Why is Vivaldi, in one sense, the last major figure in one period of music? How is he original, foreshadowing changes in the conception of musical objectives?

3. Describe some of the ways in which Vivaldi's music can be said to be "picturesque".

4. Identify the Ospedale della Pietà.

5. Name the Italian musical forms which Vivaldi brought to perfection.

6. What did Gluck consider to be the objectives of opera?

7. Who was the "English Bach"? What was his influence?

8. Explain why composers and musicians of the eighteenth century traveled so regularly and widely.

9. What is a *sinfonia*? Name some of the composers of the *sinfonia* in this period.

10. How big was the Mannheim orchestra in the 1740s? What made it unusual among orchestras of the period?

11. Characterize specifically the "Mannheim sound".

12. What was the importance of Johann Stamitz in the development of musical forms in this period?

13. Define the string quartet. Who invented this form?

14. Comment on the characterization of Haydn's string quartets as "witty and elegant four-way conversations".

15. What explanation did Haydn himself give for his own originality

in the development of the symphony?

16. What famous composition by Haydn served as the basis for a set of variations in his *Emperor* Quartet?

17. What is a piano trio? Who invented this form? What instruments (besides the piano) are involved?

18. How do the other two instruments in a piano trio specifically support the dynamic range of the piano?

19. Explain the joke in the finale of Haydn's *Farewell* Symphony. What working conditions prompted this semi-humorous protest?

20. Why is Haydn's Symphony No. 100 called the *Military* Symphony?

21. How were musical styles becoming "international" in this period?

Answers

1. In Vivaldi's time, composers were expected to furnish new music for a variety of social occasions (weddings, christenings, visits by dignitaries, or simply after-dinner concerts). There was no such thing as "repertory", in which a group of standard works were regularly revived. Thus composers were under continuing pressure to furnish new works.

2. Vivaldi is the last major figure in the Baroque period because he brings to perfection the standard forms of his time: *sinfonia*, concerto, sonata, and early Italian opera. These forms would all continue (for example, the *sinfonia* developed into the symphony); but without major changes in their development they threatened to become stale. Vivaldi initiated some of these changes by his original conception of "picturesque" music, and by his inventiveness in writing for a wide variety of solo instruments.

3. Vivaldi's music is "picturesque" in that it often celebrates the joys of nature and the landscape. An especially popular example is his group of four string concerti devoted to the "Four Seasons".

4. The Ospedale della Pietà was the Venetian orphanage for girls which Vivaldi served as music director for the greater part of his career; some of the surprising combinations of instruments for which he wrote are perhaps explained by the availability of student instrumentalists.

5. The early forms of the sonata, concerto, *sinfonia* (orchestral overture), and opera.

6. Gluck believed that opera should unite music and drama, i.e. that the music should serve the elements of the dramatic action, rather than dominate the action as a showcase for the talents of virtuoso singers.

7. The "English Bach" was Johann Christian Bach (1735–1782), who com-

posed in London in the 1760s and 1770s. The melodic charm and supple harmonies of his *sinfonias*, sonatas, quartets, and concerti were especially admired by Haydn, Mozart, and the young Beethoven.

8. Composers and musicians of the eighteenth century had several compelling reasons to travel: for study and apprenticeship, for patronage (the support of a noble or royal figure), and for commissions (i.e. special invitations to compose or perform works for a specific occasion).

9. A *sinfonia* was originally a short orchestral overture to a major piece (such as a cantata, suite, or opera). It then became a detached form in the works of Vivaldi, J.C. Bach, and others in the late Baroque and early Classical periods.

10. The Mannheim orchestra was expanded by Johann Stamitz and his followers to sixty players. Its ample, varied sound and broad range of dynamic effects distinguished it from other orchestras of the period.

11. The "Mannheim sound" included sudden shifts from *forte* to *piano* (loud to soft), and vice-versa; rapid ascending scales (the so-called "Mannheim rocket"); and an effect known as the "Mannheim sigh" (leaning from one note to the next).

12. Johann Stamitz' expansion of the Mannheim orchestra, and his experiments in his own symphonies with its larger, more varied sound, paved the way for the *sinfonia's* development into the symphony.

13. A string quartet is a form of chamber music scored for two violins, viola, and cello. In form, it generally features four movements, like the symphony. Indeed, the string quartet has become the "symphony of chamber music" in several respects: the flexibility and challenge of the form, its continuing attraction for great composers over several centuries, and the appeal of quartets to the public. Haydn is usually credited with inventing the form. This may not be literally true; but it was certainly Haydn's 83 quartets that mark the form's first significant development.

14. In Haydn's early quartets, the first violin dominated as the solo instrument; but increasingly, the composer endowed each part with equal importance. The interplay of themes, echoes, and re-statements of Haydn's generally elegant and sprightly music gave rise to the characterization of his quartets as "four-way conversations".

15. Haydn emphasized that at the court of the Esterházys he was cut off from other influences; this, combined with the resources and encouragement of his patrons, gave him the freedom to experiment with his orchestra.

16. The *Emperor's Hymn* (later the Austrian national anthem) served as the basis for variations in the *Emperor* Quartet. Based on a folk melody, the hymn was inspired by Haydn's belief that Austria should have a national tune with a dignified melody, such as Britain's *God Save the King*.

17. The piano trio is a light form of chamber music, involving the piano, the violin, and the cello. Haydn is generally credited with inventing the form.

18. Since the piano was in its infancy during Haydn's lifetime, he strengthened its resonance in the piano trio, with the violin contributing to

the sound of the higher registers (the treble), and the cello reinforcing the bass.

19. In the last movement of Haydn's *Farewell* Symphony (No. 45), the musicians are directed to leave their posts one by one as the movement is played, until only two players remain at the end. Haydn's work was prompted by the long hours of hard work which the Esterházy family demanded of him and his musicians. We are told that the Prince, his patron, took the hint and allowed the orchestra some time off.

20. Haydn's *Military* Symphony is so called from the horn calls of the second movement. The composer is reported to have written the symphony shortly after he had watched an impressive ceremony of "trooping the color" put on by the royal guards in London.

21. Musical styles became "international" during the late eighteenth century because of the development of forms in orchestral and chamber music that transcended the national forms of the late Baroque and early Classical eras. Chief among these were the forms of the symphony and the string quartet, both pioneered by Haydn.

Chapter 8

Vienna

Vienna

Vienna, the capital of modern Austria, was the most important European city in the history of Western music during the eighteenth and nineteenth centuries. The city of Joseph Haydn, Wolfgang Amadeus Mozart, Ludwig van Beethoven, and Franz Schubert, it was the capital of the powerful Austro-Hungarian Empire and a cosmopolitan magnet of culture. The court of the Emperor was the social center of Europe, and the wealthy nobility—many of whom were themselves musical—vied with one another in attracting talented artists to create their entertainments. Generous aristocratic patronage drew musicians from all over Europe.

Vienna had wealth, glamor, and cultural appetite. It also had a long musical tradition. The famed Vienna Boy Choir, for example, traces its history back to 1498. The first operas to be performed in the city date to 1641, very shortly after the invention of the form by Claudio Monteverdi. By the late eighteenth century, there were two established opera houses in Vienna. Christoph Willibald von Gluck's landmark opera, *Orfeo ed Eurydice*, had its premiere in Vienna in 1762 [see Chapter 7].

The city was at once grand and intimate. In this chapter we discuss two great composers whose careers illustrate a contrast in the artist's relationship to society. Wolfgang Amadeus Mozart, born in Salzburg, came to Vienna in 1781 with the hope that he could find influential patrons and a wider public. To some extent, he succeeded. Mozart, the darling of kings and princes during the European tours of his childhood, moved easily among the aristocracy. He was an essentially "public" composer whose works achieved substantial exposure and recognition during his short lifetime, though not even Mozart could be assured of a permanent post in Vienna—the fickle public regarded some of his masterpieces, such as the opera *Don Giovanni*, as too advanced and complex. And he rarely made enough money through freelancing to support his family. One of Western music's true giants, the genius who brought the Classical style to perfection, Mozart was buried in a pauper's grave.

Franz Schubert's career contrasts with that of Mozart. He too was poor. But he was sustained in his composing, not by the irregular commissions of aristocrats, but by a small circle of devoted friends who gathered in cafés or in private houses in the evenings to perform his works. These occasions, known as "Schubertiades", were far different from the elegant gatherings in aristocratic salons where Mozart performed. But despite the differences in circumstance, and the tragically short lives of both composers, each changed the course of music in the pivotal decades between 1780 and 1830.

Wolfgang Amadeus Mozart (1756–1791) was a genuine child prodigy. He was an accomplished pianist at the age of three and mastered the violin when he was five; at eight he wrote his first symphony, and at eleven his first opera. His genius was instantly recognized by his family and by those for whom he played; he is the classic example of the musical *Wunderkind*, and one of the very few child wonders whose gift was sustained into adulthood.

Mozart's music represents the summit of the Classical style, displaying symmetry, wit, elegance, and perfect grace. But it is far more than this. Others, including Johann Christian Bach, had already perfected the *galant* or elegant style. While their music is, on the whole, elegant and pleasing, it is also often superficial. The distinctive character of Mozart's music derives from its sweetness of melody and from a haunting interplay of playful and melancholy themes—of surface gaiety and deeper, darker moods. These, in turn, are ambiguous: at times they seem impersonal, and at times (as in the *Requiem*) to represent personal statements by the composer. It was hard to blend Classical elegance with statements of the broad range of human emotion, but Mozart succeeded in achieving exactly that. His instinctive sense of form makes his music eminently "predictable" in one sense; yet the intricate interweaving of melodies and the variations of his musical moods lend endless fascination to his works.

Besides the intrinsic perfection of such a high proportion of his music, Mozart occupies a formidable place in musical history because his genius expanded and changed many of the traditional forms. Along with Joseph Haydn (who befriended him), Mozart is largely responsible for establishing the symphony as the principal form of large-scale orchestral composition. His first symphonies were influenced by J.C. Bach and Haydn; but by the time we get to the last symphonies (No. 38, the *Prague*, No. 39, No. 40, and No. 41, the *Jupiter*), we are close to the passionate expressiveness of Beethoven. In opera, Mozart's masterpieces—*The Marriage of Figaro, Don Giovanni, Così Fan Tutte*, and *The Magic Flute*—represent a giant step beyond the achievements of even such innovators as Gluck. In Mozart's operas, the orchestra no longer simply accompanies the stage action and the singing of the principals; it comments on the actions and emotions of the characters.

Mozart is also the inventor of the the piano concerto as we know it. Just as he focused on the dramatic interplay of orchestra and singers in his works for the stage, his cycle of 27 piano concerti featured the dramatic interplay of orchestra and the solo instrument. Previous concerti, such as those of J.C. Bach, had used the orchestra far less forcefully—as an accompaniment, almost as a minor appendage to the piano. With Mozart, it became a full and equal partner of the piano.

Mozart was born in Salzburg, a provincial town some 100 miles from Vienna. He was the son of Leopold Mozart, the Kapellmeister to the Prince-Archbishop of the city. In contrast to the young Beethoven, whose cynical father seems to have exploited his son's musical talent, Mozart enjoyed a spirited and happy childhood. Leopold nurtured the boy's gifts; awed by Wolfgang's talent and that of his sister Maria Anna (also a brilliant keyboard player), Leopold arranged for lessons, and also for leave for himself so that he could conduct his children on a series of European concert tours. In 1762, when Mozart was six, they visited Munich and Vienna. The following year, they set out on a three-year journey through Germany, France, and England. At all the great courts, the young Mozart awed the aristocracy with his performing virtuosity, his ability to improvise in any key and in any form, and the charm of his personality. In London, where the Mozarts remained for several months, Johann Christian Bach performed and composed with the *Wunderkind*. It was Bach who introduced Mozart to the Italian style in opera, which Mozart was in turn to transform.

The family returned to Salzburg in 1766, when Mozart was ten years old. He had already composed three symphonies and—more important—he had been exposed to many of the great courts and musical styles of Europe. With Mozart as with Haydn, European music transcends regional and national forms and combines them into something new. For example, the opera *The Marriage of Figaro* was based on a contemporary comedy by the French playwright Beaumarchais; the opera was composed in Vienna to an Italian text; and it had its first performance in Prague.

Aside from some contemporary letters which tell us that Mozart was solemn and intensely concentrated when he played the piano, there is no indication that he had anything but a normal childhood in other respects than music. Indeed, when he was six he is said to have climbed into the lap of the Empress in Vienna and to have proposed marriage. He appears to have had an optimistic, extrovert personality; in adolescence and young manhood, his favorite hobby was playing billiards (at which he was also a genius).

During his adolescent years, Mozart composed a prodigious number of pieces in almost every form. By 1776, when he was twenty years old, he had written nearly thirty more symphonies, several piano concerti, five concerti for violin, several operas, over a dozen string quartets, some piano sonatas, songs, and short pieces for solo piano, and an impressive collection of sacred music. The Austrian cataloguer Ludwig von Köchel (1800–1877), whose chronological arrangement of Mozart's works is widely used to designate them by "K" (or Köchel) number, listed seven symphonies for the year 1773 alone. In a period without repertory, when patrons expected new works from court composers for a wide variety of occasions, such an output was not unparalleled; composers like Vivaldi and Haydn were also forced to write at high speed. What is extraordinary about Mozart is that he produced these works when he was so young, and that such a high proportion of them are works of superb quality.

In 1778, Mozart and his mother visited Paris. The composer hoped to establish himself abroad, beyond the narrow confines of Salzburg, where a new Prince-Archbishop was relatively indifferent to Mozart's efforts. But Mozart's mother fell ill and died in France. And although Mozart the child prodigy had been an object of wonder for Louis XV and the court of Versailles, Mozart the adult composer did not much impress the French public. The French trip was a failure and he returned to Salzburg to serve as organist for the Archbishop. In 1781, he protested his treatment as one of the liveried servants and was ignominiously dismissed from the Archbishop's service, thrown out with (as he described it) a kick on the backside. He left Salzburg for Vienna the same year, determined to succeed in the capital of eighteenth-century music as a freelance composer.

Mozart married in Vienna in 1782. He met and became friends with Joseph Haydn, over thirty years his senior, who deeply admired him. And he struggled to support a growing family. The so-called "Vienna period" (1781–1791) marks the last ten years of Mozart's life. It was a period of uneven fortunes which sometimes drove the composer to the brink of despair, and it saw the composition of his greatest music.

Although Mozart was the master of almost every musical form, he loved opera best. In his time, there were two kinds of opera, called by their Italian names *opera buffa* (light, comic matters—the English analogue is "buffoon") and *opera seria* (so-called "serious opera" dealing with the affairs of mythological gods and heroes). The plots and stage action were stylized and unrealistic; the orchestra functioned merely as a thin and conventional accompaniment for the beautful voices of the singers. Even Christoph Willibald von Gluck [see Chapter 7], who championed an audacious new emphasis on the continuity of dramatic action, had not progressed beyond typical *opera seria*, as the plot of his *Orfeo ed Eurydice* illustrates.

Mozart's early operas were in the traditional style, but his mature works display a revolutionary series of stylistic changes. He was fascinated by the ways in which the operatic medium—unique among the arts—could be employed to dramatize the fortunes and feelings of several stage characters simultaneously. Such a dramatic interplay could be heightened and intensified if the orchestra were made the equal partner of the singers. (He had also given the orchestra a far more important role in the concerto form.) It could comment on, deepen, or even contradict the sentiments of the characters on stage. Libretto and score could be mobilized to present a psychologically penetrating whole.

For an appreciation of Mozart's originality in opera, there is no better work to study than *Don Giovanni* (1787), often called the perfect opera because of its dramatic plot, its distribution of vocal parts, its profound orchestral score, and its naturalistic (or believable) use of the stage. Mozart had visited Prague in 1786 on the occasion of that city's production of his *Marriage of Figaro*. (Prague, which is today the capital of Czechoslovakia, was in Mozart's day a part of the Austro-Hungarian Empire; the language, taste and style of its upper class were those of the capital city, Vienna.) The whole of Prague, Mozart gleefully wrote, was "Figaro-crazy". The success of *Figaro* (which had met a lukewarm reception in Vienna), and the popularity of his Symphony No. 38 in D (K504), the so-called *Prague* Symphony, won him a commission for a new opera based on the legend of Don Juan, the unregenerate seducer of ladies. In collaboration with Lorenzo da Ponte (1749–1838), the poet to the court opera in Vienna who had written the libretto for *Figaro*, Mozart responded with *Don Giovanni*.

The story—originally dramatized by the Spanish playwright Tirso de Molina (1570–1648) in *El Burlador de Sevilla (The Trickster of Seville)*—concerns the rakish escapades of Don Juan, whose pleasure it was first to conquer and then to discard beautiful women; the hero is accompanied by his servant Leporello. Tirso's play and Molière's French adaptation in 1665 show us Don Juan's exploits; at the end, Don Juan is punished through the intervention of the supernatural.

Mozart and his librettist da Ponte transformed this plot into a profound drama, which combines wit and gaiety with tragic seriousness, and cynical sophistication with charming naïveté. Leporello sings the famous "catalogue aria" in Mozart's opera, humorously detailing the Don's conquests: one thousand and three in Spain alone! But the light beginning comes to a dramatic and dark end. In Act I, Don Giovanni (Giovanni is the Italian form of Juan) kills the Commendatore, who is trying to save his daughter from abduction; in Act III, Don Giovanni, ever boastful, invites the dead man's stone monument to dinner. Mysteriously, the statue comes to life. The Commendatore warns the libertine to repent; the terrified Leporello hides under the table as Don Giovanni adamantly refuses to change his ways. In a dramatic and striking end, the statue grasps Don Giovanni by the hand and drags him down to everlasting torment in hell.

Musically, Mozart's arias combine his superb talent for creating melodies with a dramatic sense which heightens the action. Humor and lightness balance the darkness of death and damnation. In addition, Mozart's use of the orchestra introduced chromatic harmonies and bold passages for brass instruments which prefigure some of the techniques of Beethoven, Wagner, and many other composers in the nineteenth century.

Don Giovanni was a great success in Prague, but the audiences in Vienna were less enthusiastic, deeming the work too massive and the orchestral music too complex. As a gesture to the Prague audience which had so loved *The Marriage of Figaro*, Mozart included a musical quotation from the earlier opera in *Don Giovanni*, a light, chamber-style melody which has become a kind of signature tune. Perhaps both operas, in which a satirical portrait of contemporary aristocratic ways could be discerned, struck too close to home for the Viennese nobility, who were accustomed to the *opera seria* plots on mythological themes.

Mozart gained little money from *Don Giovanni*, and in the last four years of his life he was increasingly beset by financial problems and failing health. We can only speculate on the relationship between personal adversity and the masterpieces which Mozart composed during these years. The last three symphonies—Numbers 39, 40, and 41—anticipate Beethoven in their passionate melody, the increased range of their dynamics, and new touches of chromaticism and harmonic dissonance. The operas *Così Fan Tutte* (1790) and *The Magic Flute* (1791) carry forward Mozart's fusion of the charming with the spiritually profound. They are even more psychologically incisive than *Don Giovanni*. The Finale of Act I of *Così Fan Tutte* is a particularly good example of Mozart's powers in exploiting the potential in opera for simultaneous revelation of characters' emotions, motives, and reactions; six characters (the young heroes Ferrando and Guglielmo, their fiancées Fiordiligi and Dorabella, Don Alfonso, and Despina) address the audience directly, and sing of their disparate emotions at the same time.

The strange ironies surrounding the composition of the great *Requiem Mass* (1791), which Mozart left unfinished at the time of his death, seem to typify the sharp contrasts of Vienna in this period. An anonymous nobleman approached the composer through an intermediary, offering a commission for this work. The nobleman who was willing to pay for the *Requiem* intended to pass it off as his own composition, since he fancied himself a gifted musician. But Mozart, who in 1791 was increasingly obsessed with thoughts of his own death, came to imagine the *Requiem* as a symbol for his own funeral, and hastened against time to complete it. In the event, Mozart died so poor that no Requiem was played, and at the funeral only a few friends were present. His wife was ill, and could not attend the simple service. He was buried in an unmarked pauper's grave.

Mozart's music reflects the crises of his life in no specific fashion, but rather in an inspired blending of light and tragic motifs and moods (especially the Symphony No. 40 in G minor). He is capable of the most ethereal gaiety and of the most sublime melancholy. The quality that distinguishes Mozart's music from Haydn's—at least in Mozart's late works—is its heartfelt passion. Whereas Haydn always preserves the innate joy of making music, in Mozart this joy is complemented, and made more profound, through passages of infinite sadness. On the other hand, Mozart's temperament, although it is sometimes held to prefigure the spontaneity of the Romantics, never stays with one mood for long. He is not given, as is Beethoven, to thoroughly sustained passages of emotional turbulence. If clouds can be discerned in his musical landscape, the warm sunlight is almost always quick to break through to disperse them. Basically conservative, he did not transform the music of his time through radical innovation as much as through the inherent superiority of every note. In his symphonies, the traditional minuet form can still be heard in the third movement; it remained for Beethoven to substitute the freer scherzo. In his mature operas, he achieved so musically perfect an expression of the subtlest psychological insights into his characters that it was not until the operas of Giuseppe Verdi and Richard Wagner in the nineteenth century [see Chapter 12] that the form would develop beyond the boundaries established by Mozart.

Franz Schubert (1797–1828), although not so comprehensive a genius as Mozart, is now reckoned as among the greatest composers of the early nineteenth century. Schubert's distinction derives from his extraordinary sense of melody, and from his ability (like that of Haydn, Mozart, and Beethoven) to transcend the limitations of classical forms when he found them unduly restrictive. Schubert's life, like Mozart's, was tragically short and he had to struggle to win acceptance, let alone suitable recognition, for his music. Whereas Mozart was a public composer, in the sense that a number of his large-scale works (symphonies, operas, masses, and piano concerti) were performed during his lifetime, Schubert was an essentially private composer. Supported and encouraged by a limited circle of devoted friends, he relished the evenings of music-making (or "Schubertiades" as they were called) with his friends in private houses and cafés. It was on such occasions that his chamber music, his songs, and his short piano pieces were performed. His larger works—for example, the eight symphonies and several operas—were either failures during his lifetime, or were simply neglected; he never heard any of his symphonies properly performed. If Mozart's sound is pre-eminently Classical, symmetrical, and ordered, Schubert's music contains the stirrings of Romanticism. The two composers were born only forty years apart, but between them lies the giant shadow of Beethoven, a figure whom Schubert revered like an idol in the Vienna of his youth, but whom he could never summon the courage to approach.

Franz Schubert was the son of an impoverished schoolteacher. His musical training was uneven and relatively informal. Mozart had been dead for six years when he was born. The city of Vienna had changed: the enlightened leadership of the Emperor Joseph II (who had suggested the concept of *Così Fan Tutte* to Mozart and da Ponte in 1790) had given way to a more repressive atmosphere. The French Revolution of 1789–1794 had swept away the old aristocratic order in France, and nervous tremors were being felt all over Europe among the traditional patrons of music. Schubert was twelve when the armies of Napoleon menaced the gates of Vienna and Viennese aristocrats fled the city for their country estates.

In some ways, Schubert was as precocious as Mozart. By the time he was seventeen, he had composed a large number of impressive works. But although he aspired to writing large-scale works for the stage, his greatest contribution was simultaneously to inaugurate, and to provide the greatest exemplars of, the unique form of the German art-song, or *Lied*. Fascinated by the poetry of the Romantic writers Goethe and Schiller, he experimented with this form while still in adolescence. He continued to write songs (more than 600 of them) during his entire career.

The essence of the *Lied* (the plural is *Lieder*) is difficult to define. One critic has defined it as the "elusive art of expressing the dramatic quality of a poetic text in non-operatic form." It differs from the folk song in the far greater complexity of both the text and music. A folk song rarely has a text other than a four-verse rhymed stanza, and a simple melodic line which non-musicians can readily sing. An art song, on the other hand, combines a serious text with a melodic line which follows the rhythmic and thought patterns of the words. The quick, short phrases and simple repetitions of the folk song are gone; the art-song, following its text, is "through-composed".

Schubert's *Lieder* tell a story, express a mood, or create an atmosphere with the vocal line (for solo male or female voice) and the piano score as equal partners. The piano becomes more than a mere accompaniment; it acts as an expressive voice in its own right, commenting on and reinforcing the dramatic emotion of the singer. The same principles that Mozart had brought to the composition of opera were exploited, on a less grand scale, by Schubert in the art-song. Ironically, all of Schubert's operas were failures. But in the miniaturist vignette of the *Lied*, he has no rival.

Some art-songs are self-contained and last only two or three minutes; others he built up into extensive cycles in which both the text and the music explore the same, or closely related, themes. The moods of Schubert's songs range from intense, declamatory emotion to gentle nostalgia, from uninhibited joy to dream-like melancholy. Their harmonies are often boldly untraditional and frequently illustrate a favorite device of the composer: hovering between the major and the minor triads, so that the tonality remains suspended, or unresolved, for a relatively long time. The subjects of the songs are vignettes of common emotions and experiences. In one song, *Frühlingstraum*, the poet dreams of spring but awakens to find that it is still winter. In another the poet, alone at dawn, longs for spring when he will hold his beloved in his arms. In the famous song *An die Musik (To Music)*, the poet thanks the art of music itself, which consoles him and transports him to a better world whenever the troubles of life threaten to overwhelm him. Other notable Schubert *Lieder* include: *Gretchen am Spinnrade (Gretchen at the Spinning Wheel)* (1814); *Erlkönig* (1815); *Der Wanderer (The Wanderer)* (1826); *Seligkeit (Happiness)* (1816); and the cycles *Die schöne Müllerin (The Fair Maid of the Mill)* (1823) and *Winterreise (Winter Journey)* (1827). Over fifty songs are based on the poems of Goethe. But Schubert was capable of metamorphosing the poetic texts of relatively minor poets as well: some of his most memorable songs (including the cycle of twenty *Lieder* of *Die schöne Müllerin*) were based on poems by the second-rate poet Wilhelm Müller (1794–1827), who readily acknowledged that his poetry needed Schubert's music to make it complete.

Schubert also brought his gift for melody to the composition of piano works: notably the late sonatas and the "musical moments" that he called Impromptus. He wrote chamber music and symphonies. His first string quartets were modeled after those of Mozart and Haydn. The *Trout* Quintet, so called because it developed from his song *Die Forelle (The Trout)* is now one of the most often performed works in the entire repertory of chamber music. Written in

1819, it is scored for piano and strings. Some critics have judged the String Quintet in C major (1828), composed for the usual quartet instruments (first and second violins, viola, and cello) and an extra cello part, to be Schubert's masterpiece in this genre. But equally impressive is the quartet movement in C minor which Schubert left unfinished, possibly because he felt that he could not match the standard of composition.

The best known of Schubert's symphonies is the *Unfinished* No. 8 in B Minor. No one is certain why the composer put it aside after he completed two movements in 1822. The symphony itself had to wait for its first performance until 1865, well after Schubert's death. But it is a tribute to the remarkable character of its melodic invention that it is regarded as a complete work of art. Like Beethoven, Schubert experimented with orchestral tone color in notable ways in his symphonies. In both the *Unfinished* Symphony and in the C Major Symphony of 1825 (No. 9, called the *Great*), passages for cello, horn, trombone, and clarinet broke new ground.

The Symphony No. 9 exemplifies Schubert's failure to achieve recognition in his own time for his large-scale works. Discovered by Schumann, the symphony received its first performance in 1839. The conductor was Felix Mendelssohn. We have only lately come to recognized that the *Great* C Major Symphony influenced not only the early Romantics, but also the later Romantic Anton Bruckner [see Chapter 10]. Thus, even though Schubert failed to attract a large public in the Vienna of his day, the rediscovery of his music had important, long-term consequences throughout the nineteenth century.

Schubert died in 1828, at the age of only thirty-one. Some of his works remain unpublished to this day. The chaotic disorder of his manuscripts and the obscure chronology of their composition have posed major problems for music scholars. Just as we refer to the works of Mozart by their "K" (Köchel) number, it is customary to designate the works of Schubert by their "D" number, from the catalogue of O.E. Deutsch (1883–1967).

During Schubert's lifetime, the single concert solely devoted to his music (held in Vienna in 1826) inspired an enthusiastic reaction from foreign music critics; but the critics of the city of Vienna, who could have greatly aided his prospects, were conspicuous by their absence. Vienna, the home of music and musicians, often treated its greatest sons with an alarming, capricious disregard. Schubert's influence after his death was very great, however, and his place in the repertory is unshakable in our own day. Such Romantic composers as Schumann, Chopin, and Mendelssohn were deeply indebted to his innovations in short piano pieces. And all subsequent composers of the art-song, from Schumann and Brahms through the twentieth century, have had to reckon with the remarkable achievement of Franz Schubert.

Questions for Review

1. Briefly characterize the Vienna of the time of Mozart and Schubert. Why was Vienna such a musical center?

2. How do the careers of Mozart and Schubert exhibit a contrast in the relationship of the musical composer with society?

3. Give a short description of the music of Wolfgang Amadeus Mozart. What words would you use to characterize his style?

4. What is the meaning of *Wunderkind*? How was Mozart's childhood the classic example of a musical *Wunderkind*?

5. How did Mozart's genius transform the musical forms which he inherited? Give two specific examples.

6. Briefly describe the circumstances which led to Mozart's departure from Salzburg for Vienna.

7. Which musical form did Mozart invent, as we know it?

8. What musical concept links Mozart's piano concerti with his work for the stage?

9. Name two of Mozart's mature operas. What was *opera seria* in Mozart's time? How did Mozart's work in this form depart from tradition?

10. How does the Finale of the First Act of *Così Fan Tutte* illuminate the unique artistic potential of opera?

11. Was Mozart financially successful as a freelance musician in Vienna?

12. What poignantly ironic circumstances surrounded the composition of Mozart's *Requiem*?

13. Define the *Lied*, or art-song. Name two of Franz Schubert's best known *Lieder*.

14. Identify the poet Wilhelm Müller. What was his importance in the career of Franz Schubert?

15. What are some of the distinguishing characteristics of Schubert's music?

16. What was Schubert's importance for such later composers as Schumann, Chopin, and Mendelssohn?

17. Name Schubert's best known symphony. When was this symphony first publicly performed?

18. Briefly summarize the plot of Mozart's *Don Giovanni*. When and where was the opera first performed?

Answers

1. No other city can match the importance of Vienna in the history of music. As the capital of the Austro-Hungarian Empire in the days of Haydn, Mozart, Beethoven, and Schubert, it was a cultural center, a magnet for composers, artists, and poets. The enlightened Emperor Joseph II headed a group of rich aristocrats who were vitally interested in patronizing the arts.

2. The careers of Mozart and Schubert display a contrast in the relationship of the composer to society. Mozart was a "public" composer who moved easily among aristocrats, kings, and princes. Schubert's Vienna, several decades later, was more repressive. The city had been shocked by the invasion of Napoleon's troops. Many of the wealthy patrons of the arts retreated to their country estates. Schubert was essentially a "private composer" at the center of a limited circle of devoted friends. He never heard many of his large-scale works publicly performed.

3. The style of Mozart is characterized by elegance, grace, Classical symmetry, an endlessly inspired flow of melody, wit, and an interplay of joy with darker, more melancholy themes.

4. *Wunderkind* is the German word for "child prodigy" (literally, "wonder-child"). Mozart played the piano at the age of three, was taken by his father Leopold on tours all over Europe by the time he was ten, and started to compose serious works in his teens.

5. Mozart (along with Haydn) established the symphony as the premier orchestral form. His mature operas transformed that form as well, by virtue of Mozart's naturalistic use of the stage, his psychological insight into characterization, and his use of the orchestra to comment on the action rather than merely to accompany the singers.

6. Mozart was dissatisfied and restless in the service of the Prince-Archbishop of Salzburg, who treated him like a liveried servant. Against his father's advice, he protested and was dismissed from the Archbishop's service for his pains. He set off for Vienna to make a career as a freelance com-

poser.

7. Mozart invented the form of the piano concerto as we know it. His cycle of 27 piano concerti forms one of his most impressive musical achievements.

8. What interested Mozart most in his mature operas was the dramatic interplay of personalities on stage and the ways in which the orchestra could be used to comment on the characters' emotions. Similarly, there exists in his piano concerti a dramatic interplay between the solo instrument and the orchestra, which are given approximately equal importance.

9. Mozart's mature operas include *The Marriage of Figaro, Don Giovanni, Così Fan Tutte,* and *The Magic Flute. Opera seria* ("serious opera") in Mozart's time dealt with mythological heroes and gods. But Mozart's *Marriage of Figaro* and *Così Fan Tutte* dealt with contemporary characters and situations, and used the stage in a naturalistic (i.e. thoroughly credible) way.

10. In the finale of the first act of *Così Fan Tutte*, six characters sing simultaneously to the audience of their various emotions: the two heroes (Ferrando and Guglielmo), their fiancées (Dorabella and Fiordiligi), the cynical Don Alfonso, and the maid Despina. Only opera among art forms can present simultaneously the lives and emotions of such a group.

11. Mozart was intermittently successful but never acquired a permanent post. He was often plagued by financial worries and died destitute. He was given a pauper's funeral and buried in an unmarked grave.

12. A stranger approached Mozart with a commission for a Requiem Mass in 1791. The stranger was the emissary of an anonymous nobleman, who is said to have intended to pass off the Requiem as his own work, since he imagined himself to be a talented composer. But Mozart, ill and increasingly in debt, came to think of the Requiem as symbolic of his own death. He died before he completed it, on December 5, 1791, two months short of his thirty-sixth birthday.

13. The art-song (German, *Lied*) is a brief, dramatic musical treatment of a poetic text, written for piano and solo voice. In the *Lied* the music is as important as the words in establishing a mood and commenting on the text itself. Some of Schubert's best-known *Lieder* are: *Seligkeit (Happiness), An die Musik (To Music), Frühlingstraum (Dream of Spring), Der Wanderer (The Wanderer), Gretchen am Spinnrade (Gretchen at the Spinning Wheel),* and the cycles *Die schöne Mullerin (The Fair Maid of the Mill),* and *Winterreise (Winter Journey).*

14. Wilhelm Müller was a relatively minor German poet whose works were especially important for Schubert's *Lieder* (e.g. the cycle of 20 songs for male voice entitled *Die schöne Müllerin (The Fair Maid of the Mill).*

15. Distinguishing characteristics of Schubert's music include: sustained, eminently lyrical melodies hovering between the major and the minor triad, thus suspending the tonality of a passage; and the poetically expressive, direct statement of emotion.

16. Schubert's melodic gift, untraditional harmonies, and perfection of short piano works (such as the Impromptus) were all important for Chopin, Mendelssohn, and Schumann. They regarded him as a precursor of the Romantic movement which they championed.

148

17. Schubert's best known orchestral work is the Symphony No. 8 in B Minor, called the *Unfinished* Symphony. Schubert completed two movements of the symphony in 1822, six years before he died, and then put them aside, perhaps because (as in the case of the quartet movement in C minor) he felt he could not continue to match the standard he had set. In any case, the *Unfinished* Symphony is now recognized as a work of art on its own terms. It was not publically performed until 1865.

18. The plot of Mozart's *Don Giovanni* (first performed in Prague in 1787) concerns the libertine Don Juan, who seduced and abandoned ladies all over Europe. Ultimately he is urged to repent but refuses, and is dragged down to hell for his sins.

Chapter 9

The Revolutionary

The Revolutionary

By the year 1800, a series of great changes were sweeping over Europe. The Industrial Revolution was leading to a massive upheaval in the settled assumptions of societies and economies. The replacement of hand labor by machine labor caused the growth of factories and the rise of a well-to-do middle class; this, in turn, influenced the development of new forms and styles in the arts, and even affected society's larger concept of the purpose of art. In Beethoven's lifetime, for example, music was democratized. Its very purpose changed from the entertainment of a select few to a universal language that could appeal to many. Music passed from the elegant, aristocratic salon to the public concert hall.

Along with social and economic changes, there were political ones. The revolt of the American colonies from Britain in 1776 was sparked by predominantly economic motives. But the French Revolution (1789–1794), which had been nearly a century in the making, was founded on great social ideals, and it swept away forever the aristocracy's way of life. The French Revolution, which proclaimed the goals of "liberty, equality, and fraternity" for all citizens, played a crucial role in shaping the vanguard of a new movement in the arts all over Europe: Romanticism.

Romanticism was an international movement that affected styles in music, poetry, and painting. The term does not primarily refer to "romantic" subjects, although romantic love (and universal, human love) were important themes for many Romantic writers and composers. Romanticism refers to a broad cluster of attitudes towards nature, the human mind, and man's experience. The concept of freedom was paramount for the Romantics: political freedom, personal freedom, and the artistic freedom to break away from conventions, fixed styles, and traditional "rules" in the arts. Romanticism prized spontaneity, individualism, and authenticity of personal emotion. Indeed, the expression of such emotion was more important to the Romantics than its control, or suppression, in traditional forms. The Romantics broke new ground by insisting that many subjects and themes which had hitherto been thought inappropriate for art were the very stuff of poetry and music: dreams, semi-conscious states, feelings of personal exultation or melancholy, emotions inspired by the natural landscape, and the revolutionary struggle for justice.

Romanticism developed at different times in different countries, and did not develop evenly and consistently among the various arts. In England, for example, the Romantic movement in poetry was not fully under way until 1798, when William Wordsworth and Samuel Taylor Coleridge published their short volume, *Lyrical Ballads*. Wordsworth was born the same year as Beethoven (1770). In the preface to *Lyrical Ballads*, he argued that poetry should spring from "emotion recollected in tranquillity;" a poet should choose "incidents and situations from common life" and compose in a "selection of language really spoken by men." By the 1820s, Wordsworth, Coleridge, Shelley, and Keats had demonstrated the workings of such a prescription in poetry of extraordinary vitality; and the personality and verse of George Gordon, Lord Byron (1788–1824), gave Europe a quintessentially Romantic figure, the "Byronic hero"—a character-type of remarkable talent and deep melancholy, capable of great good and great evil.

In France, Romantic poetry lagged behind the development of the Romantic novel. But France also furnished a hero-type that fired the Romantic imagination: Napoleon Bonaparte (1769–1821). Napoleon's series of military victories left a continent in awe. To some he seemed the epitome of evil; others, including Beethoven for a brief period, idealized him as the savior who would curb the worst excesses of the Revolution in France and institute a new order of justice and love.

In Germany, the land of Beethoven's birth, two great poets prefigured the Romantic movement in literature during the composer's childhood: Johann Wolfgang von Goethe (1749–1832) and Friedrich von Schiller (1759–1805). Goethe's highly personal novel of doomed love and youth, *The Sorrows of the Young Werther* (1774), played an important role in the development of German Romanticism. Almost as significant were Schiller's plays, including *Die Räuber*(The Robbers) (1781), *Don Carlos* (1787), and *Wallenstein* (1799). It was Schiller's "Ode to Joy" (originally entitled "An Ode to Freedom") that Beethoven adapted as the text for the choral movement of his Symphony No. 9.

Ludwig van Beethoven (1770–1827) is the musical revolutionary who stood astride the transition from Classical to Romantic. He is too great a figure to be wholly comprehended by either of these labels; indeed, an essential ingredient of his style is that he holds the Classical values and the stirrings of Romanticism in dynamic tension. Even as he largely accepted the principles of the Classical style, his music transcends them. Beethoven revolutionized every musical form in which he worked.

Beethoven's career reveals a fundamental change in societal attitudes towards music, and new fashions regarding its performance. With the rise of the middle class, music was no longer solely an ornament for aristocratic entertainments (although that function did continue throughout the nineteenth century). Public concert halls and opera houses began to provide composers with an alternative to the salon. Haydn had worn a servant's uniform at the palace of the Esterházy family [see Chapter 7]; it was only in the last few years of his life that his reputation had become sufficiently established to allow him to give public concerts in London and Vienna. Mozart, though he derived some income from the public performances of his operas, was still forced to seek patronage to avoid starvation. Beethoven's relationship with the aristocracy was more complex, and a good indicator of both his personality and the changing role of the artist in Viennese society.

Throughout his life he was to enjoy the company of princes, counts, and archdukes. Yet he saw himself as a member of a different kind of aristocracy: the aristocracy of genius. An anecdote illustrates this view of the role of the creative artist. As he was taking a walk with his friend, the poet Goethe, a nobleman happened to pass by on the road. Goethe paused and respectfully tipped his hat, while Beethoven walked on, apparently oblivious to the nobleman's presence. "*They* should be tipping their hats to *us*", he remarked when Goethe caught up with him.

Paradoxically, Beethoven also identified strongly with his own humble origins and therefore with the "common man" (there was probably never a man so *un*common as Beethoven!).

Beethoven, who came from a line of court singers, was born in Bonn (today the capital of West Germany). His father was an irresponsible lout who hoped to exploit the son's talent. The young Beethoven endured a harsh and unhappy childhood, and left school when he was eleven; at fourteen he took a job to help support his family. When Beethoven was seventeen, he traveled to Vienna, where legend records that he improvised on the piano for Mozart. Mozart is reputed to have said: "Watch out for that young man. He will make a noise in the world some day." Returning to Bonn, Beethoven held a series of jobs in the Elector's court orchestra. His mother died in 1787, and it fell to him to support his father and two younger brothers. In 1792, Haydn passed through Bonn and invited the young musician to study with him in Vienna. Beethoven, encouraged by his friends the von Breunings and Count Waldstein, accepted. He must have been eager to escape the provincial town of his youth and the trying circumstances of his family life. He was to remain in Vienna until his death.

Beethoven's first years in Vienna coincided with the culmination of the French Revolution. While in France itself the original ideals of liberty, equality, and fraternity had degenerated into the bloody repression of the Reign of Terror, the spirit of revolution continued to spread all over Europe. It is clear that Beethoven espoused the lofty principles of this spirit, and equally clear that he was naïvely ignorant of the darker uses to which other men sometimes put them.

In his personal relationships, Beethoven was often overbearing, impetuous, and downright rude. His high principles often led him to expect superhuman loyalty from his friends, though it is fair to say that he expected no better than he was willing to give. He never married, and his relationships with women were a great source of personal agony: invariably, the objects of his affections were aristocratic, idealized beyond reason, and unattainable.

Beethoven combined humanistic principles with an intense preoccupation with the self, and broad generosity with petty avarice. His idealistic artistic goals were constantly threatened (though never overcome) by intense personal suffering. In every imaginable way, Beethoven's personality manifested the paradoxical mixture and conflict of darkness and light. The light triumphed.

Throughout Beethoven's music, there is ample evidence of the tensions of his personality and of his struggle to resolve those tensions. A dynamic, propulsive energy constantly stretches the bounds of the Classical language inherited from Haydn and Mozart. This energy is most strongly marked in works composed after about 1802, but it is present even in the first Piano Sonata in F Minor (Opus

2, No.1), which Beethoven dedicated to Haydn and published in 1796. The nature of the artistic relationship between Beethoven and his illustrious predecessors Haydn and Mozart is epitomized in his personal relationship with Haydn himself.

In 1792, at Haydn's invitation, Beethoven journeyed from his hometown Bonn to the great capital of the musical world: Vienna; he was to study composition with the master. Haydn had just returned from his first trip to London [see Chapter 7] and was at the peak of his career, respected all over Europe as the greatest composer of the age. Mozart—whom Haydn befriended and clearly saw as his artistic heir—lay in an unmarked pauper's grave. What Beethoven expected from Haydn is not entirely clear—though it seems likely that the devout and kindly "Papa" Haydn expected a more docile and respectful pupil than Beethoven proved to be. Beethoven arranged secret lessons for himself with another teacher (of nowhere near the stature of Haydn), did not do his assignments and instead passed early compositions off as recent work, and, finally, refused to identify himself as a pupil of Haydn. Precisely what Beethoven learned directly from Haydn has never been ascertained; the lessons terminated in 1794 when Haydn returned to London.

Whatever Beethoven may have learned directly from the elder composer, it is clear that he inherited the musical language which had been forged by Haydn and refined and amplified by Mozart. By the 1780s and 1790s, both Haydn and Mozart had become more deeply concerned with a broader range of feeling in their music; Mozart's later symphonies and concerti, and Haydn's last twelve symphonies, explore a broader dynamic and harmonic world than their earlier works. It was this music that Beethoven heard most keenly. Although he was to break far more radically than they with the formal strictures of Classicism, there is nonetheless a clearly discernible line of continuity with the past. In this sense, Beethoven is the last of the Classical composers, just as he is the first of the Romantics.

After his promising early years in Vienna, in his late twenties, Beethoven discovered that his hearing was gradually growing fainter. By 1802, he was forced to abandon any hope of improvement; by the time he was thirty-five, he was stone-deaf. The dimensions of his profound spiritual crisis can be inferred from an extract of a letter to his brothers, written in 1802 and meant to be read after his death:

> My misfortune is doubly painful, since it is the cause of my
> being misunderstood. For me there can be no relaxation in
> human interaction, no conversation, no exchange of thoughts
> with my fellow men. I am compelled to live in solitary exile.
> Whenever I meet strangers, I am overcome by a feverish dread
> of betraying my condition. That is the way I have felt for the last
> six months, which I have spent in the country. The orders of my
> doctor, to spare my hearing as much as possible, well suited my
> state of mind, although my longing for company has often
> tempted me into it. But how humbled I feel when someone near
> me hears the distant sounds of a flute, and I hear *nothing*; when
> someone hears a shepherd singing, and again I hear *nothing*!
> Such events have brought me to the edge of despair, and I came
> very near to putting an end to my own life. Art alone restrained
> me. It seemed impossible for me to quit this world forever be-
> fore I had done all I felt I was destined to accomplish.

Besides the fear of deafness, Beethoven's failure to find happiness
in marriage and a family caused him particularly acute anguish at
this time. Lonely and depressed, he grew increasingly more eccentric in his middle years. He communicated with others through a
"conversation book" in which his visitors would write down their
comments or questions, and he would reply. But his deafness, and
the self-consciousness which it caused in him, led him to become
more and more withdrawn and irascible. The struggle of Beethoven
to find hope amid despair is part of the great drama of his music.

Napoleon was for Beethoven a revolutionary hero—at least for a
time. The composer dedicated his Symphony No. 3 in E-flat major
to the French leader. The composition itself was a revolutionary one;
it is called the *Eroica* because Beethoven specifically intended for it
to celebrate the heroic ideals of revolutionary leaders. When Beethoven received news that Napoleon had had himself crowned as Emperor of France, he angrily erased the dedication, since he was disillusioned: his hero had become just one more politician. Happily,
however, he did not change a note of the symphony itself. Colossal
in scale—the first movement alone was longer than all four movements of many contemporary symphonies—the *Eroica* broke new
ground in this orchestral form. First performed in 1804, the *Eroica*
was received with mixed reviews; some critics thought that it piled
up too many colossal ideas on top of one another. Despite the controversy, however, it remained a highly influential landmark

throughout the nineteenth century, and is today one of the most frequently performed symphonies in the repertory.

Beethoven followed the *Eroica* Symphony with another, equally revolutionary work: his only opera, *Fidelio*. Its subtitle was "Conjugal Love," which the composer himself yearned for, but never found. The opera's central idea was a radical statement about the power of love to loosen political chains and change the world. The plot features an unconventional heroine, Leonore, whose husband Florestan has been unjustly imprisoned by the tyrant, Don Pizarro. Leonore disguises herself as a man with the name Fidelio (meaning "faithful"); she manages, through the assistance of Rocco the jailer, to find her husband behind the prison walls. When Don Pizarro threatens to murder Florestan, Leonore steps forward to shield him. The Minister of Justice arrives at the last moment, pardons Florestan, and imprisons the evil Pizarro. The opera ends with the celebration of Leonore's courage and unwavering loyalty. Despite the thrilling plot and Beethoven's inspired music, *Fidelio* was a failure when it was first performed in Vienna in 1805. Ironically, the audience which might have filled the theater with applause had fled the city in panic at the news that Napoleon's troops were near.

His Symphony No. 6 in F Major (1808), commonly called the *Pastoral* Symphony, was inspired by Beethoven's walks through the woods and along the streams in the outskirts of Vienna. The symphony celebrates nature, and the four movements bear these subtitles: "Awakening of happy feelings on arriving in the country", "By the brook", "Joyous gathering of country folk—storm", and "Shepherd's song; happy and thankful feelings after the storm". Note that Beethoven's symphony represents a quite different approach to the landscape from Vivaldi's *Four Seasons* or from some of the music of Haydn. The earlier composers treated nature as "picturesque" and such compositions as *The Four Seasons* attempted to reflect the beauty of nature in music. For Beethoven, what mattered were the human feelings which the landscape inspired; the feelings, not the imagery, formed the subject of music. In this, Beethoven was a true Romantic; the poet Wordsworth, for example, had emphasized that nature was not his subject, so much as the emotions which nature prompted in the poet's own imagination.

Most critics customarily divide Beethoven's works into three great periods:

The "Early Period" extends from his early piano trios and first sonatas (published in 1795 and 1796) to 1802. This period includes the six string quartets (Opus 18), Symphonies Nos. 1 and 2, and the first three piano concerti. The music of this period exhibits ebullience, joy, and a playful lyricism.

The "Middle Period" extends from 1802 through 1816. It includes Symphonies Nos. 3–8, the *Egmont* Overture, the opera *Fidelio*, the Fourth and Fifth Piano Concerti, the Violin Concerto in D, and a large number of quartets and piano sonatas (including, among the latter, the *Appassionata*, Opus 57). This is the mature Beethoven, in which the composer liberated music. No single set of adjectives suffices to characterize the music of this period. It ranges from volcanic energy in the Fifth Symphony to lyrical sweetness in the Eighth, from the passionate portrayal of married love in *Fidelio* to the titanic splendor of the *Eroica* Symphony.

The "Late Period" extends from 1816 to his death in 1827. The music of this phase combines the composer's restless energy with a meditative wisdom that reaches the sublime. Representative works of the late style are: the last five piano sonatas, the *Diabelli* Variations for Piano, the *Missa Solemnis* in D, the late string quartets and the Symphony No. 9 in D minor, the *Choral*. When Beethoven died in 1827, he had plans for a tenth symphony and numerous other works.

Beethoven's musical innovations span all three periods of his career. We can only list the principal ones here:

a) Beethoven expanded the *length* of many musical forms. Symphony No. 3, for example, is nearly twice as long as the typical symphony of Mozart or Haydn. The same holds true for the piano concerto, especially Beethoven's Fourth Concerto in G (1806) and his Fifth Concerto in E-flat (1809), the *Emperor*. In his piano concerti, Mozart had begun to elevate the status of the third movement. Formerly treated as a light Rondo, Mozart made it as important as the first movement in duration and in thematic content. Beethoven continued this tendency, and the dynamic finale of works such as the *Emperor* Concerto definitively established the importance of the last movement. In chamber music Beethoven boldly experimented with the number of movements in the form of the string quartet; one of his later quartets, for example, boasts seven distinct movements, as opposed to the usual four.

b) Beethoven expanded the *size* of the orchestra for symphonic works, even beyond the dimensions established at Mannheim in the mid-eighteenth century by Johann Stamitz and his successors [see Chapter 7]. Beethoven introduced trombones and the contra-bassoon; he made far more extensive use of the clarinet and kettledrums; and he augmented the woodwinds' high register with the piccolo.

c) With a larger orchestra, Beethoven (like the Mannheim musicians) could afford to exploit *dynamic ranges* more broadly. Even in passages scored for all the instruments, he sometimes called for them to play softly, as in some passages of the Ninth Symphony.

d) Beethoven made numerous innovations of *form* and *structure*. He incorporated new material into the recapitulation and coda sections of the sonata-allegro form. He replaced the relatively strict minuet-trio form with the freer form of the scherzo for the third movement of symphonies and quartets. He occasionally varied the placement of the slow movement in these forms (which was expected always to stand second), and he lengthened the duration of the movements themselves. He was the first composer to establish a cyclic treatment of themes in the symphony, in which one or more themes recurred from movement to movement, instead of being confined to the movement in which they were introduced. The most famous example of the cyclic technique is the celebrated four-note introductory theme of Symphony No. 5, which recurs in various transformations in all the movements of the work. Finally, Beethoven extended Mozart's practice of balancing the orchestral and the keyboard part in piano concerti. He permitted the piano to introduce principal themes, departing from the traditional practice of stating the theme first in the orchestra. In this he was followed by many Romantic composers, including Schumann and Grieg.

e) Beethoven's innovations in *harmony* and *rhythm* are numerous and complex. He explored unusual key relationships. He allowed crashing chords to be followed by silences, or rests, instead of immediate continuation or resolution. For an introduction to Beethoven's originality in this area, there is no better exercise than listening to a movement from a symphony of Haydn or Mozart, and following it with the fourth movement of Beethoven's Symphony No. 9.

f) Finally, Beethoven's *style for the piano* must be mentioned, since it played a considerable part in the development of the modern instrument as we know it. In Beethoven's day, the piano was relatively new. The invention of the instrument is generally credited to Bartolomeo Cristofori, whose instrument, completed in Florence around 1710, was the first to feature a mechanism of hammers striking the strings (rather than a plucking mechanism, as in the harpsichord). But it was not until Beethoven's era that the piano came into its own. He is the first composer, for example, to have taken full advantage of the sustaining pedal. His piano sonatas, which span the three periods of his composing career, featured violent contrasts of mood, and were so difficult technically that at first only Beethoven could perform them. (He is supposed to have said about one sonata that if it were performed properly, the piano would break apart.) Beethoven's sonatas were of crucial importance in the development of later Romantic piano music, e.g. that of Schubert, Chopin, Mendelssohn, and Liszt. Some of the best known sonatas are: No. 8, Opus 13 (*Pathétique*), No. 14, Opus 27 (*Moonlight*), No. 21, Opus 53 (*Waldstein*), No. 23, Opus 57 (*Appassionata*), and No. 29, Opus 106 (*Hammerklavier*).

If we compare the Ninth Symphony with the First or Second, the late piano sonatas with the early ones, and the final string quartets with the youthful series that Beethoven dedicated to Haydn, we can see the composer's remarkable musical growth over the span of thirty years. Like most great geniuses in the arts, from Shakespeare to Picasso, Beethoven never settled comfortably into any one "style": he was always boldly experimenting with new ideas and techniques. An anecdote from his final years, in conjunction with one of the late string quartets (Opus 135), helps us to understand the inner struggle of the composer to fulfill the "destiny" to which he refers in the letter to his brothers. Beethoven's housekeeper informed him that some bills—for which he apparently lacked the money—had to be paid. Shocked, he asked her, "Muss es sein?" (Must it be?) "Yes," she said, "Es muss sein." (It *must* be). Beethoven inscribed her answer on the score of the final movement of his string quartet, and transferred the three-syllable question and answer into the music. The trivial incident was transformed into sublime music; it seems to have symbolized, in Beethoven's own mind, a profound questioning, and a final acceptance, of his suffering fate.

Probably no composer boasts a greater number of frequently performed compositions. Symphonies 3, 5, 6, 7, and 9 are especially popular; Piano Concerti Nos. 4 and 5 are familiar fare on every orchestral schedule; the Violin Concerto in D has been a basic work in the repertory of every virtuoso since it was first performed by Franz Clement in 1806. *Fidelio*, despite its inauspicious premiere, is now familiar to opera-goers the world over. The string quartets, the piano sonatas, and the *Missa Solemnis* are similarly popular. If the works of Beethoven were subtracted from today's musical repertory, many concert halls would be as empty as when his own *Fidelio* was presented in 1805.

Questions for Review

1. What great changes swept over Europe during the youth of Ludwig van Beethoven?

2. Define Romanticism in the arts. Name some of the principal artistic values of the Romantic poets, painters, and composers.

3. Identify the following: a) William Wordsworth; b) Napoleon Bonaparte; c) Friedrich von Schiller. What is the significance of each of these figures in the study of Beethoven?

4. Why can Beethoven not be characterized by either of the terms "Classic" or "Romantic"?

5. What did Mozart say about the young Beethoven?

6. Comment on the ways in which Beethoven changed the course of music, with specific reference to the following:
    a) the purpose of music
    b) the circumstances of musical performance
    c) the position of the composer in society

7. Why was the Symphony No. 3 of Beethoven such a musical landmark? To whom was this symphony first dedicated? Why did Beethoven remove this dedication? By what name is the symphony now generally known?

8. What tragedy struck Beethoven in his late twenties and early thirties? How did he comment on it in his letter to his brothers?

9. Why did Beethoven leave Bonn to live in Vienna?

10. With what great composer did Beethoven study in Vienna?

11. Briefly summarize the anecdote concerning Beethoven, the poet

Goethe, and the nobleman on the road. How does this anecdote illuminate for us Beethoven's attitudes toward the traditional patrons of music?

12. Characterize the style of Beethoven's piano sonatas. Name two of the most famous sonatas.

13. What was the subtitle of Beethoven's opera, *Fidelio*? Why is the title ironic within the context of the composer's own life?

14. Was *Fidelio* a success when it was first presented? Briefly summarize the plot and identify the principal theme of the opera.

15. Contrast Beethoven's treatment of the landscape in Symphony No. 6 (the *Pastoral*) with Vivaldi's picture of the countryside in *The Four Seasons*.

16. How does the late string quartet (Opus 135, *Muss es sein*) contrast in style with Beethoven's early string quartets? What anecdote lies behind the title of this quartet? How does it illuminate Beethoven's spiritual development?

17. Identify at least two innovations in form and structure in the Beethoven symphonies.

18. It is traditional to divide Beethoven's career into three periods. Define these periods chronologically, characterize the style of each as specifically as you can, and name one principal work from each period.

Answers

1. During the youth of Beethoven (who was born in 1770), a number of important changes—social, economic, and artistic—were transforming Europe. These occurred at different rates in different countries. In general, the effects of the Industrial Revolution radically re-shaped patterns of wealth and work; the French Revolution swept away the old order of privileged aristocracy and clergy; and Romanticism, a new international movement in all the arts, replaced the old doctrines of Classicism.

2. Romanticism in the arts implies, not just a focus on themes of romantic love, but a cluster of attitudes toward man's experience, the functionings of human imagination, and nature. The principal Romantic values included: personal and artistic freedom, spontaneity, individualism, authenticity, expressive and personal emotion, subjectivity, and an exploration of untraditional styles and forms.

3. a) William Wordsworth (1770–1850) was the great English poet who, with Samuel Taylor Coleridge, announced the advent of a new poetry in the Pre-

face to *Lyrical Ballads* (1798). This poetry was not at first called "Romantic"; Wordsworth and Coleridge did not think of themselves as belonging to a school, or movement. But their call for a poetry on "common subjects" in "common language", whose substance was to spring from "emotion recollected in tranquillity", became one of the chief touchstones of later poets, and an important parallel for musicians who, like Beethoven, wrote for a mass audience in musical language that was addressed to the common man.

b) Napoleon Bonaparte (1770–1821) brought a certain stability and unity to France after the turmoil of the French Revolution and its bloody excesses. His military genius and the ideals he professed inspired a continent; many felt that it would be through Napoleon that the noble goals of the Revolution—liberty, equality, and fraternity—would become established in a new, universal world order. Among Napoleon's admirers was Beethoven, who dedicated the Symphony No. 3 (*Eroica*) to him. But when Beethoven heard that Napoleon had had himself crowned as Emperor, the composer was outraged. Disillusioned that he had honored yet another ambitious politician, Beethoven erased the dedication.

c) Friedrich von Schiller (1759–1805) was, with Beethoven's friend Goethe, one of the two most important poets of the early Romantic movement in Germany. Author of lyric poetry and verse plays, Schiller's notable works include the dramas *Die Räuber (The Robbers)* (1781), *Don Carlos* (1787), and *Wallenstein* (1799). Associated with the *Sturm und Drang* ("storm and stress ") movement in German literature , Schiller's work was characterized by highly moving, personal conflict. Beethoven based the text for the choral part of his last symphony (No. 9) on a poem of Schiller. It is called *Ode to Joy (An die Freude)* in Beethoven's version; the original poem was entitled "An die Freiheit" ("To Freedom").

4. Beethoven cannot be wholly comprehended by the labels "Classical" or "Romantic"; an essential element of his greatness is that his style holds the classical values of symmetry and balanced form and the Romantic values of individualism in such powerful tension.

5. When Mozart heard Beethoven improvise on the piano when the young composer was seventeen, Mozart is supposed to have remarked: "Watch out. This young man will make a noise in the world some day."

6. a) Beethoven was the first composer to conceive of music as a political and social vehicle. His Symphony No. 3 (*Eroica*) was dedicated to the ideals of revolutionary heroes; his opera, *Fidelio*, was a hymn to the blessings of marriage and the power of married love to overcome obstacles; his Symphony No. 9 was explicitly a praise of universal love and the brotherhood of man.

b) With Beethoven's music, we come for the first time to circumstances of performance resembling those of our own day. No longer was music written for the private, aristocratic courts of the nobility. Music was composed for the masses and publicly performed in concert halls. Beethoven meant his music to speak to men and women of every class in society.

c) Beethoven's career also marks a break with the traditional place of the composer in society. He refused to be "Haydn's scholar". He declined to show deference to noble patrons. With Beethoven, the modern era of the freelance composer in society begins.

7. Symphony No. 3 was a landmark because of its grand scale. The first movement alone was longer than many contemporary symphonies. Beethoven defied tradition by writing the second movement in the form of a funeral march. The entire symphony was so overpowering and complex that it failed to win the approbation of many critics when it was first performed; some complained that it piled up too many musical themes and was insufficiently "rounded out". It is the first symphony in musical history to be explicitly intended for the praise of political revolutionaries, rather than in honor of the established nobility. Beethoven originally dedicated the symphony to the French general Napoleon. But when he heard that Napoleon had crowned himself Emperor, he angrily removed the dedication. The symphony is now called the *Eroica*.

8. Beethoven began to lose his hearing in his late twenties; by the year 1805 he was stone deaf. In a moving letter to his two brothers, which is called the "Heiligenstadt Testament" (after the town in which the composer was living), he tried to explain his growing withdrawal from social contact and his sense of humiliation. In this letter, written in 1802, he stated that only his art prevented him from seriously considering suicide.

9. Beethoven left Bonn to escape the confines of a small provincial town. Encouraged by his friend Count Waldstein (to whom the Waldstein Sonata is dedicated), he decided to seek his fortune in the musical capital of Europe in his day.

10. Beethoven studied with Joseph Haydn in Vienna, and dedicated a series of early quartets to him. But the old master and the young revolutionary clashed in temperament. Beethoven shocked Haydn by his refusal to abide by established social custom, and by his musical boldness.

11. Beethoven and Goethe are said to have been walking together when a nobleman passed them on the road. The older Goethe stood still quietly, and respectfully tipped his hat. Beethoven walked on, seemingly taking no notice. Afterward he remarked to Goethe, "*They* should be tipping their hats to *us*." The incident captures Beethoven's fierce sense of artistic independence, and his refusal to accept the "old order" of society, in which composers and poets were dependent on noble patrons for a livelihood.

12. Beethoven's piano sonatas are notoriously difficult in the demands they make on the performer. In the sonatas, classical elegance of form and beauty of melody are subordinated to the violent contrasts of mood. Beethoven is reputed to have said that the piano would break into pieces if one of his sonatas should be performed the way he intended. Two of the best-known sonatas are the *Moonlight* (Opus 27, No. 2) and the *Appassionata* (Opus 57). They were written in 1802 and 1806, respectively.

13. The subtitle of *Fidelio* was "Conjugal Love". The subtitle is ironic because one of the chief sources of Beethoven's unhappiness in life was his disappointment in love. He never married.

14. *Fidelio* was a disastrous failure when it was first presented in 1805. The theater was nearly empty, and the opera was withdrawn after only three performances. The principal theme of *Fidelio* is the power of married love to overcome political hatred and injustice. The plot concerns Leonore's courage to free her husband Florestan, who has been unjustly imprisoned by the ruthless tyrant, Don Pizarro. Leonore disguises herself as a man named Fidelio, and with the unwitting assistance of Rocco the jailer manages to get inside the prison. When Don Pizarro threatens to murder his prisoner, Leonore steps forward to shield him with her body. The crisis is resolved by the arrival of the Minister of Justice, who pardons Florestan and imprisons the evil Pizarro.

15. Vivaldi, in such works as *The Four Seasons*, was inspired by the landscape as a picturesque tableau to be painted. For Beethoven, as for most of the Romantics, the countryside was not to be rendered "literally" in music: the value of nature, rather, was that it inspired reactions and emotions in the composer, which in turn imaginatively suggested composition. The *Pastoral* Symphony, then, is not so much a portrait of nature as an exploration of the feelings that nature inspires in the composer.

16. The late string quartet *Muss es sein* (Opus 135) is far less symmetrical and classically elegant than Beethoven's early quartets. Its dynamic range is wider, and the personal feelings that it expresses are more compelling. Beethoven is said to have inscribed the German words "Muss es sein?" ("Must it be"?) on the score of the last movement, whose music reflects the question in a three-note theme, and is answered by another theme representing the answer, "Es muss sein." ("It must be."). His housekeeper is supposed to have told him that some bills needed to be paid. When he questioned her with "Muss es sein?" she replied: "Es *muss* sein." This trivial incident seems to have been transformed in Beethoven's own mind to a profound questioning, and final acceptance, of the fate which had brought him so much loneliness and suffering in life.

17. Beethoven's innovations in form and structure of the symphony:

a) expanded the length of the symphony as a whole, and of individual movements;
b) expanded the size and range of the orchestra by introducing instruments such as trombones, contra-bassoon, and piccolo;
c) replaced the minuet-trio form for the third movement with the freer scherzo form;
d) established a cyclical treatment of themes (as in the Symphony No. 5);
e) explored untraditional harmonies.

18. **First period (1795–1802)**: Characterized by joy and lyricism. Forms are most purely "classical" in this period, and music reflects the late Haydn and the late Mozart to some degree. Six String quartets of Opus 18, Symphonies No. 1 and 2, Piano Concerti Nos. 1–3.

Second period (1802–1816): Characterized by volcanic energy, brutal physicality, intense contrasts of mood, innovations in form, structure, and harmony, intense belief in music as a revolutionary force. Symphonies Nos. 3–8 (including the *Eroica*, No. 3, and the *Pastoral*, No. 6), *Fidelio*, Piano Concerti Nos. 4–5, Violin Concerto in D, middle string quartets, numerous piano sonatas (including the *Moonlight* and the *Appassionata*).

Third period (1816–1827): Characterized by propulsive energy that blends with a more profound vision: meditative and spiritual. *Missa Solemnis* in D, *Diabelli* Variations for Piano, last five piano sonatas, late string quartets (including *Muss Es Sein*), and Symphony No. 9 (*Choral*).

Chapter 10

The Romantics

The Romantics

The music of Beethoven is a decisive turning point: the passionate energy that he poured into his piano sonatas and symphonic works, and his innovations in structure and harmony, led to an ever freer approach to music. Although, strictly speaking, he cannot be called a Romantic, his music ushers in Romanticism in the nineteenth century.

The great era of Romantic music extends from the 1820s to roughly 1900. Even in our own century, some composers have written primarily in the Romantic vein, although the term "post-Romanticism" has been coined to designate a style of music that overlaps with the beginnings of Modernism, or the contemporary style. Romanticism is thus the outstanding style of Western music for nearly a century.

Whereas the eighteenth century avoided strong emotions, the Romantics of the nineteenth enthusiastically embraced them. They cared more about expressing their feelings, and less about the shape, or form, of music. Many of these composers, like Chopin and Wagner, led turbulent, unconventional lives filled with strong contrasts and often actively associated with political or nationalist causes. The nineteenth century was an era of revolutions in Europe; it was also an age in which some nations (notably Italy) strove for unity and freedom. Composers, artists, and painters were adopted by their countries as national symbols. Beethoven's conviction that art was a universal language, and that music could powerfully express the brotherhood of man, came to be shared by a significant number of the Romantics.

The leading Romantic values in all the arts—in music, painting, and literature—were spontaneity, authentic and personal emotion, and individualism. Romanticism proceeded at different rates in different countries in Europe: it was an international style, as well as a set of attitudes that permeated all the arts. But by the 1840s it was in full swing. In art, Ferdinand Delacroix (in France) and John Constable and Joseph Turner (in England) were the leading figures of the new style. In literature, the premier Romantics included the poet Heinrich Heine in Germany; Byron, Keats, Shelley, and Wordsworth in England; and the novelist and playwright Victor Hugo in France. For all these artists, politics, old legends, the natural landscape, and powerful feelings of romantic love were leading themes. The supernatural and the exotic, themes which had held no interest for the Age of Reason in the eighteenth century, captured the Romantic imagination: witness the short stories and poems of Edgar Allan Poe and the novels of Charlotte and Emily Brontë (*Jane Eyre* and *Wuthering Heights*).

An intriguing feature of Romanticism is that the previously separate arts came closer together. Romantic composers often created their music with specific works of literature and painting in mind; poets and painters were reciprocally inspired by music. Art spread to a wider public in this period. It was the era in which museums, conservatories, and orchestra societies began to be established, many of them the beneficiaries of the new wealth created by the Industrial Revolution.

The Industrial Revolution affected music in other ways as well. Cities grew enormously; the countryside became dotted with what the English poet William Blake called "dark, satanic mills"; the gap between rich and poor widened to the extent that the essayist Thomas Carlyle wondered if England might not undergo her own revolution, similar to that of 1789 in France. In 1846, Felix Mendelssohn (who was Queen Victoria's favorite composer) saw his oratorio *Elijah* first performed in the bleak, industrial city of Birmingham in the English Midlands: music for a vast new audience, which was thus transported from the bleak realities of their everyday existence, if only for the length of the concert. Instead of social entertainment for the upper classes, music was now spiritual therapy for the common man. Such works as Mendelssohn's oratorio were performed in the vernacular English; and it is significant that the participants were amateurs, rather than professional musicians. In almost every way, Romantic music became broader in purpose and appeal.

The Romantics were also more conscious of their predecessors in music than the composers of previous ages. The burden of originality—the necessity to break away from established styles, and to compose in new forms—was one result of the subjective and individualistic values they espoused. It is during the Romantic age that scholarly journals and conservatory faculties began to study previ-ous music systematically. Mendelssohn, for example, actively pro-moted the re-discovery of Bach's works; and Schumann founded one of the first critical journals in music, the *Neue Zeitschrift für Musik*.

The first group of Romantic composers we will study spans the years 1809 (the birth of Mendelssohn) to 1897 (the death of Johannes Brahms). Chopin, Schumann, Mendelssohn, Brahms, and Bruckner are enormously diverse; but each contributed in a highly individual fashion to shaping the legacy of Beethoven: the use of music as a powerful vehicle for expressing personal emotion.

Frédéric Chopin (1810–1849) was born near Warsaw of a French father and a Polish mother. He studied at the Warsaw conservatory, and soon displayed extraordinary precocity at composition. His first work (*Rondo in C Minor*) was published when he was fifteen. Before he was twenty he had written and performed his two piano concerti (No. 2 in F Minor, Opus 21, actually pre-dates No. 1 in E Minor in order of composition). In 1830 he set off on a round of concerts in Europe, visiting Dresden, Prague, and Vienna. Settling in Paris in 1831, he became a noted piano virtuoso, though he did not exploit theatrical virtuosity for its own sake, as did his contemporary and friend Franz Liszt [see Chapter 11]. Chopin, although a great pianist, disapproved of flashiness in composition and performance for its own sake; significantly, two of his models were Bach and Mozart.

Gradually, Chopin turned from performance to teaching and full-time composition, nearly exclusively for the solo piano. Robert Schumann hailed his genius. In 1837, he met the French novelist George Sand; for the next ten years he lived with her in an often tem-pestuous relationship. After the revolution of 1848, Chopin left Paris for England, where he gave concerts in a number of cities. He died the following year in Paris, having suffered for some time from tuberculosis.

Chopin never returned to his homeland, since Poland had come under Russian domination. But in his music he inaugurates an im-portant motif that we can trace in the works of many Romantic com-posers throughout the century: the nostalgic yearning in the heart of an exile for his motherland. The dance forms and songs of Poland, remembered from his childhood, provided Chopin with a rich vari-ety of forms in which to pour out his patriotic feelings. These in-cluded the *polonaise*, a slow dance measure in triple time; the *mazurka*, also in triple time, with a certain accentuation on the second beat; and, of course, the *waltz*. In Chopin's *Polonaise in A Flat*—which resembles a stately procession more than a dance—he seems to speak with pride of the elegance and sophistication of an oppressed people.

To the forms of the polonaise, mazurka, and waltz, Chopin added other, freer forms for solo piano: the *étude* (or "study"), which emphasized one particular aspect of the pianist's technique in each piece; and the *nocturne*, a short piece in free form with a placid lyricism suggesting night time. To all of his piano works, Chopin brought richly expressive ornamentation (some of which he derived from Italian opera, which he admired) and a rare intensity of passion. The *Polonaise in A Flat* forcefully attacks the piano with a driving rhythm and a majestic melody. Chopin could be delicate and graceful, too, as in many of the waltzes and mazurkas; his harmonies could suggest almost child-like simplicity or an atmosphere of dreaming, as in the *Preludes* (still a staple for all piano students). Chopin's piano works are among the most important in that instrument's repertory.

Felix Mendelssohn (1809–1847) was born in Hamburg, the son of a prosperous banker. Taught piano by his mother, he was even more precocious than Chopin. He made his performing debut at the age of nine, and at twelve he was introduced to the poet Goethe (then over seventy), who warmly fostered the boy's genius. By his mid-teens, he had composed his first opera, and also a major overture (to Shakespeare's *A Midsummer Night's Dream*). To these years as well belongs his *Octet in E Flat for Strings*, Opus 20 (1825), a remarkably mature work that shows how thoroughly Mendelssohn had assimilated the counterpoint of Bach.

Mendelssohn attended the University of Berlin in the 1820s. He traveled from Germany to England, where he inaugurated a long series of successful visits by presenting the English premiere of Beethoven's Fifth Piano Concerto (the *Emperor*). The early 1830s were spent in that great Romantic pastime, travel. Eager to explore distant lands, to assimilate their sights and sounds in his music, Mendelssohn set off for Scotland, Austria, and Italy. The landscapes that he saw inspired such compositions as the *Hebrides Overture* (1830; a portrait in music of the Western Islands off Scotland), the *Scottish Symphony* (No. 3 in A Minor, 1830), and the *Italian Symphony*

(No. 4 in A, 1833). In the finale of the *Italian Symphony*, we can hear two dance forms with galloping rhythms, which Mendelssohn had doubtless heard in the vicinity of Naples: the *saltarello* and the *tarantella* (a legend reports that the latter was named after the tarantula spider, whose poisonous bite would drive the victim to perform a hectic dance which drove out the poison).

Mendelssohn was appointed conductor in both Düsseldorf and Leipzig. In 1843, he founded a music conservatory in Leipzig, and served as its director; his friend Robert Schumann was on the faculty. A man of extraordinarily diverse talent, Mendelssohn was gifted at painting, literature, and conducting, and mastered several musical instruments. More than any other single figure in the early nineteenth century, he was responsible for the revival of Bach, who had been neglected in favor of Handel. For example, while still a youth in Berlin in 1829, he conducted Bach's *St. Matthew Passion* in the first performance since the composer's death in 1750. Yet Mendelssohn could also see that the times required some of Handel's showmanship. He took Handel as a model when he revived the oratorio. Just as Handel had provided the oratorio as an alternative to Italian opera for a larger audience in the first half of the eighteenth century, Mendelssohn reached out to even larger audiences with such works as *Elijah*, which he conducted at its first performance in Birmingham in 1846. The work transcended its Biblical roots, and was intended to be performed in English by amateurs. Mendelssohn's music provided a brief respite from the bleak realities of everyday life; it could be enjoyed, and performed, by groups from all classes of society.

Like Chopin, Mendelssohn died tragically young. His own music, like that of Bach, was to suffer from neglect after his death, with many dismissing it as superficial and insufficiently "heartfelt". Certainly the music of Mendelssohn lacks, on the whole, the intense subjective passion of Chopin and Schumann. But its essential Romantic qualities, and the subtlety with which he combined "pictorial" elements with elegant expressiveness, have led in turn to a reevaluation of Mendelssohn. Many of his works are now standard in the repertories of the world's leading orchestras. His principal works include: five symphonies, two concerti for piano and orchestra, numerous songs, incidental music to theatrical pieces, six string quartets, the several oratorios, and assorted works for piano including the eight books of *Lieder ohne Wörter (Songs Without Words)* (1834–1843), various capriccios, and the *Rondo Capriccioso* (Opus 14).

Robert Schumann (1810–1856) is the third great Romantic composer of this generation. Schumann was born in Zwickau, Germany, in the same year as Frédéric Chopin—whose genius he did much to promote from the time they both were in their early twenties. Schumann studied law at the universities of Heidelberg and Leipzig, but his true talent lay in composing and music criticism. He did not begin piano lessons until his late teens under the tutelage of Friedrich Wieck, whose daughter Clara he would later marry despite the bitter opposition of her father. Soon after he devoted himself seriously to music, he inaugurated a new periodical for music criticism in Germany: the *Neue Zeitschrift für Musik (The New Journal for Music)*, which Schumann edited for a decade.

Even if Schumann had written no music himself, the *Neue Zeitschrift für Musik* would have been sufficient to establish him as a major figure in the history of music. Today we take for granted an entire critical establishment: books, articles, learned journals, and reviews. Practically none of this existed in Schumann's time. His periodical helped to promote the highest standards in composition and performance, and was often of crucial assistance to struggling young composers. For example, Schumann wrote generously, and correctly, of the talent of the 20-year-old Johannes Brahms in 1853. Through the journal, Schumann contributed significantly to the musical life of his time and provided a model for the future development of music criticism.

The piano was always Schumann's favorite instrument, as it had been for Chopin. Experimenting with a device to improve his fingering, Schumann crippled one of the fingers of his right hand when he was in his twenties. This cut short the career he had hoped for as a professional pianist, though the instrument remained the focus of his composing efforts during most of his life. He also wrote for orchestra, voice, and the string quartet. Piano sonatas, fantasies, impromptus, and short occasional pieces like the celebrated *Kinderszenen (Scenes from Childhood)*, all give evidence of his originality and Romantic temperament. His piano music is less forceful, less full of violent contrasts than that of Beethoven, and generally less passionate than Chopin's. Schumann's music is distinguished by exquisite melody, flowing and lyrical harmonies, and sometimes an almost dream-like gentleness. In Schumann's exquisite *Lieder* (art-songs), the piano accompaniment often assumes an importance almost equal to that of the singer. Some were written to celebrate his love for his wife Clara at the time of their marriage—the song-cycles *Dichterliebe (A Poet's Love)* and *Frauenliebe und Leben (Woman's Love and Life)* both stem from this time, 1840. Schumann's *Lieder* are the equal of Schubert's in their range of emotion, exquisite melodic line, and perfectly crafted form. It is often hard to distinguish them from the art-songs of Schubert, so perfectly did Schumann assimilate the model of his great predecessor, though Schumann's harmonies tend to be more complex, slightly darker and more dissonant, than those of Schubert.

Schumann approached the challenges of composition in a highly distinctive fashion. He would plunge into a form and focus intensely on composing in it for about a year; then he would turn his attention to another form. Thus, from 1840 we have some of the major songs and song-cycles. In 1841 Schumann concentrated on symphonies, in 1842 on chamber music, and in 1843 on choral works. Three of the string quartets from 1842 were dedicated to his friend Felix Mendelssohn.

By the end of the 1840s, Schumann had completed most of his greatest works: the *Piano Concerto in A Minor* (1845), most of his songs and short piano pieces, and the choral works, including *Paradise and the Peri* (1843), a highly romantic fantasia for chorus and orchestra based on an episode of Persian mythology. (Schumann, like many of the Romantics, was vitally interested in literature and mythology; the works of the German Romantic poets Heinrich Heine and Joseph von Eichendorf served as the texts for many of his *Lieder*.) During this same period, Schumann assisted Mendelssohn in founding the Leipzig Conservatory. In 1844, during a stay in Dresden, he immersed himself in the study of Bach, perhaps prompted by Mendelssohn's great interest in that long-neglected master.

During most of Schumann's life, he experienced the tension of contrary pulls between the traditional and the innovative. He summed up these two sides of his nature (the impetuous and the meditative) in the two pseudonyms Florestan and Eusebius, which he used to sign articles in the *Neue Zeitschrift*. (Eusebius was one of the fathers of the early Church; Florestan was possibly an allusion to the revolutionary who was unjustly imprisoned in Beethoven's opera,

Fidelio.) Thus, while he was in Dresden, Schumann simultaneously assimilated Bach and admired the young Richard Wagner, whose opera *Tannhäuser* provoked a controversial reception when it was first performed in 1845. Perhaps it was his friendship with Wagner that led Schumann to compose his only opera, *Genoveva*, in 1847–48. Here Schumann, like Wagner, attempted to write a distinctively German opera, which would throw off the traditional influences of Italian style. But Schumann's effort was a failure. It remained for Wagner, whose talent Schumann had recognized, to write definitively German compositions in this form—and, in the process, to transform radically the settled assumptions of musical harmony [see Chapter 11].

In 1850, Schumann completed his Symphony No. 3 (*Rhenish*), and also his *Concerto for Cello and Orchestra*. The Third Symphony is a portrait in music of the beautiful Rhine valley; it is a joyous tone-picture. The Cello Concerto is now considered one of the most significant compositions for that instrument in the entire repertory (others include the concerti of Joseph Haydn and Antonin Dvořák); the lyrical motifs seem perfectly suited to the instrument. Schumann and his wife moved to Düsseldorf in this period, since Schumann hoped to earn a better living by conducting. But overwork and depression led to a nervous breakdown in 1853, and he tried to commit suicide by throwing himself into the Rhine. He spent his final years in an institution and died in 1856.

As we listen to the *Rhenish* Symphony (Schumann's last, in order of composition), we should note that the composer's four works in this form, although sometimes criticized for their "heavy" and unimaginative orchestration, experimented with formal innovations that significantly influenced later composers. These included the cyclic repetition of themes from one movement to the next [see Beethoven's practice, described in Chapter 9]; combining the development and recapitulation sections of sonata-allegro form; and introducing new material in the coda (or tail-piece to the recapitulation). Schumann's symphonies also tended to blur the break-points between movements, so that each major segment of a lengthy work leads more directly into the next segment. This is especially marked in his Symphony No. 4 in D Minor. A variation of the technique may be observed in the abrupt transition between the second and third movements of the *Piano Concerto in A Minor*, one of Schumann's best-known works and a staple of the concert repertory today.

With the career of **Johannes Brahms** (1833–1897), we move to German late Romanticism. Musical styles, like styles in poetry and painting, seldom move in a linear, easily traced development. They are more like spirals, curving backward and then advancing. Thus, Brahms—while he was the protégé of Robert and Clara Schumann—was perceived by his contemporaries as somewhat old-fashioned. Schumann remarked that he could hear "veiled symphonies" in Brahms' early piano sonatas. Yet when Brahms came to write his first symphony, at the age of forty, the critics called it "Beethoven's Tenth"—an allusion to his musical conservatism. (The symphony was first performed in 1876, nearly fifty years after Beethoven's death.)

Brahms avoided the flashiness of Franz Liszt, and the audacity of Richard Wagner; he insisted through his works that there was still room for the development of forms like the symphony, which the "progressive" composers of his time insisted were outmoded. His music has a rich, complex, expressive quality. His melodic lines are drawn out to an unusual length; sometimes they are fragmented, only to be re-combined and sustained. Large-scale works, such as the four symphonies and *Ein deutsches Requiem (A German Requiem)* (1868), look back to the past in an almost nostalgic, autumnal fashion. The fantastic, programmatic, or delicately lyrical flights of composers such as Liszt, Mendelssohn, and Schumann were not to Brahms' taste. His harmonies in the symphonies are generally rich and dark; there is extensive use of the brass section of the orchestra; the compositions are grand in scale and structure. But Brahms also had a lighter, jollier side, which we see in his shorter works like the chamber music, the piano sonatas and variations, the *Hungarian Dances* and especially the songs, which are in the tradition of Schubert and Schumann.

Brahms was the child of a string player in the orchestra at Hamburg. His father taught him to play a notable variety of instruments: piano, violin, cello, and horn. As a young man he played the piano in dance-halls and sordid cafés on the riverfront to make money for his family. By the time he was twenty, his virtuosity on this instrument was evident. Luckily, he met the Hungarian violinist, Eduard Reményi, at this time; Reményi invited Brahms to serve as his accompanist, and introduced him in turn to Robert and Clara

Schumann, both of whom fostered Brahms' career in important ways. Schumann hailed him as a young genius in the influential journal which he had founded; Clara Schumann performed his piano works at her recitals and maintained a life-long friendship with Brahms.

From the year 1860, Brahms' relatively uneventful life centered around Vienna. He regarded himself as continuing the tradition of Beethoven, whom he revered. But he taught, composed, and conducted without major success until his *German Requiem* was first performed in the Cathedral at Bremen in 1868. Unlike previous Requiems, this piece was not intended as a musical setting of the entire Latin liturgy for the dead; it was based instead on passages of Martin Luther's German translation of the Bible, selected by Brahms himself. The *Requiem* was inspired by the death of Brahms' mother in 1865. Like Mendelssohn's oratorio, *Elijah*, it was a deeply moving choral work in the vernacular, with which large audiences could easily identify. It was played in almost every major city in Germany during Brahms' lifetime, and it assured the composer's fame. Its somber, and yet lyrical, music transcended a specifically religious faith; Brahms' music seemed to speak, rather, of the universal issues of life and death, and to be inspired by a fatalistic acceptance of personal tragedy.

There followed Brahms' four symphonies, Nos. 1 and 2 in 1876–77, and Nos. 3 and 4 in 1883 and 1885. Relatively conservative in structure, they incorporate some chromatic and dissonant harmonies, and display unusual relationships of keys in their movements. Leonard Bernstein, the American composer and conductor, once compared the tense opening measures of the First Symphony to the stretching of a giant rubber band. The two piano concerti of 1859 and 1881 (Brahms was the soloist at the first performance of each) are also staple features of the concert repertory today, as is the Violin Concerto in D Major, first performed in 1879, with Brahms' good friend, the great virtuoso Joseph Joachim, as the soloist.

Anton Bruckner (1824–1896), one of the last composers in the German Romantic tradition, was born in Austria and resided quietly in Vienna; he served as a professor of harmony at the Conservatory in that city for most of his career. He was nine years older than Brahms, yet, musically speaking, he seemed to look over Brahms toward the future: whereas Brahms looked back to Beethoven as a hero and principal model, Bruckner admired the revolutionary music of Richard Wagner. He was thus inevitably compared with Brahms by the music critics who fanned the "Wagner-Brahms dispute" (Wagner representing the "progressives" in music, and Brahms representing the "conservatives"). An intensely religious man, Bruckner's aim was to transfer to the symphony the immense, epic breadth and richness of orchestration of Wagnerian opera.

His musical training was that of an organist and his several Masses and nine symphonies have an organ-like fullness. In the Masses, the rich vocal polyphony of Giovanni Palestrina (1525–1594), the great master of Italian sacred music, is an obvious influence. In the symphonies, the complex full orchestration and the continuous web of sound clearly owes much to Wagner. Many of the symphonies are over an hour in length; Bruckner, following Beethoven and Wagner, composed music of a new scale and amplitude. For many decades his work was belittled as derivative of Wagner; more recent audiences have learned to accept on its own terms the melodic beauty and majestic orchestration of Bruckner's compositions.

With Bruckner, we are close to the end of an era—one which had erupted in the first piano sonatas and string quartets of Beethoven; had progressed through the lyrical, subjective emotions of Chopin, Schumann, and Mendelssohn; and had been nostalgically revived in the music of Brahms.

Bruckner's symphonies, while they cannot be placed on the same level of originality with those of Beethoven and Brahms, are a last, eloquent witness to the artistic energies of Romanticism. In the next chapter, we turn to the works of those Romantic composers—Berlioz, Liszt, Verdi, and Wagner—for whom national roots and a sense of political and cultural unity were the driving forces behind their music.

Questions for Review

1. What were the primary artistic values for the Romantic composers?

2. Name at least three of the forms in which Frédéric Chopin composed for piano.

3. How did composers such as Chopin and Mendelssohn conceive the purpose of music?

4. What circumstances in Mendelssohn's life inspired the *Italian* Symphony?

5. Identify the following:
   a) Polonaise
   b) Industrial Revolution
   c) *Rhenish* Symphony
   d) *Elijah*
   e) George Sand

6. Despite the considerable evidence that the Romantics wished to break decisively with the past, there are ample indications of "conservatism" in some of these composers. Comment on this statement, with reference to Mendelssohn, Brahms, and Bruckner.

7. Which older Romantic composer encouraged and promoted the young Brahms?

8. How did Brahms' contemporaries characterize his First Symphony?

9. Why is Schumann's *Piano Concerto in A Minor* a significant landmark in the development of this musical form?

10. What were the circumstances of Brahms' composition of his *German Requiem*? Where was this work first performed? What were the effects of this performance?

11. What circumstances surround the remarkable output of *Lieder* by Robert Schumann in 1840?

12. What is the significance of Schumann's journal, *Neue Zeitschrift für Musik*, in the history of nineteenth-century music?

13. Briefly characterize the style and purpose of the symphonies of Anton Bruckner.

14. Which nineteenth-century composer did Bruckner especially admire?

Answers

1. The primary artistic values for the Romantic composers were: spontaneous expression of personal emotion, sincerity and authenticity, the picturesque value of exotic landscapes, individualism, and the freedom to explore and develop untraditional forms.

2. Some of the forms in which Chopin composed for piano: Polonaise, Mazurka, Waltz, Ballade, Prelude, Etude, Nocturne.

3. Chopin and Mendelssohn felt that music should channel the profoundly personal, subjective emotions of the composer to the audience. Music could also be the expression of patriotic feeling (as in Chopin's tributes to the pride and spirit of the Polish people), or a therapeutic "release" from the grim realities of everyday existence (as in Mendelssohn's oratorios).

4. The *Italian* Symphony was inspired by the composer's lengthy journey to Italy. It specifically reflects, in the last movement, Italian dance forms (such as the saltarello and tarantella) which were popular in the region of Naples.

5. a) Polonaise: a Polish dance in triple time, relatively slow, which suggests a solemn procession. Used by Chopin as the basis for piano pieces of short-to-medium length.

b) Industrial Revolution: the widespread transition from manual labor to machine labor and manufacturing, which transformed the social structure and economy of European countries in the period 1750–1830.

c) *Rhenish* Symphony: Schumann's Symphony No. 3 in E-flat Major (1850), inspired by the scenery along Germany's chief river, the Rhine.

d) *Elijah*: Mendelssohn's oratorio, based on a selection of Biblical texts, which was first performed in Birmingham, England in 1846.

e) George Sand: pen-name for Lucile-Aurore Dupin (1804–1876), French Romantic novelist, the mistress of Frédéric Chopin (and also of the Romantic poet, Alfred de Musset).

6. The conservatism of the Romantic composers may be illustrated by Mendelssohn's interest in the works of Johann Sebastian Bach (which he played a major part in reviving), in Brahms' devotion to Beethoven, and in Bruckner's profound religious faith, which looked to the example of Palestrina, among others, for inspiration in his sacred music.

7. Robert Schumann.

8. Brahms' First Symphony (first performed in 1876) was often called "Beethoven's Tenth".

9. Schumann's piano concerto blurred the transition between the second and third movements; the composer also allowed the piano to begin the concerto, with an introductory statement of the first movement's principal theme.

10. The *German Requiem*(1868) was inspired by the death of the composer's mother three years before. The work was first performed in Bremen Cathedral and had the effect of catapulting Brahms to fame.

11. In 1840, Schumann was struggling to win the hand of Clara Wieck, the daughter of the man who had been his musical mentor. Friedrich Wieck bitterly opposed the marriage. Schumann wrote many of the *Lieder* of this year to express his love for Clara.

12. Before Schumann's journal, there had been no formal criticism of music in print. Schumann performed a crucial service in evaluating performance, in the historical study of music, and in promoting talented young composers (e.g. Chopin and Brahms).

13. Bruckner wrote his symphonies to express his profound religious faith in God. They are as massive and complex in architecture as a cathedral—often longer than an hour in duration.

14. Bruckner especially admired Richard Wagner.

Chapter 11

Nationalism and Revolution

Nationalism and Revolution

Many of the Romantic composers felt it natural to devote their music to self-expression: Schumann poured out his love for Clara Wieck (later to be his wife) in superb *Lieder*; Mendelssohn translated his feelings of exuberance and wonder at foreign landscapes into works like the *Italian* Symphony; and Anton Bruckner's symphonies reflected his deeply personal sense of the majesty of God's universe. We now come to a group of composers in the nineteenth century whose music is equally personal: Hector Berlioz, Franz Liszt, Giuseppe Verdi, and Richard Wagner. From four different countries in Europe (France, Hungary, Italy, and Germany), they may be considered together as Romantic representatives of nationalism, since for each of these composers music was a vehicle to identify with nationalist causes. The memories of Poland which found their way into Chopin's piano works of the early 1830s prefigure the nationalist theme in music; art, for good or ill, had become allied with politics.

Hector Berlioz (1803–1869) was born near Grenoble in Southern France, and came to Paris in his early twenties. His family sent him there to study medicine, but he was more interested in going to the opera to see the still-popular works of Gluck, who had died half a century before. Berlioz studied at the Paris Conservatory. In music he revered Beethoven; in literature, the playwright William Shakespeare. At a performance of Shakespeare's *Hamlet* in 1827, he saw the Irish actress Harriet Smithson, with whom he fell passionately in love.

Although Berlioz did not meet the object of his affections until five years later, she dominated his thoughts and served as the inspiration for one of the most extraordinary symphonic works of the nineteenth century: the *Symphonie Fantastique (Fantastic Symphony)*, first performed in 1830. This symphony, subtitled "Episodes in the Life of an Artist", was frankly autobiographical. Although Berlioz believed that the work could stand on its own as a piece of music, he also provided it with a literary text to be distributed to the audience. This text explained the musical structure in narrative terms and is called a *program*. The *Symphonie Fantastique* called for an enormous orchestra and was organized in five movements, each containing the same melody—the *idée fixe* ("unchanging idea") which represented the obsessive image of the artist's beloved. The effects of orchestral color in the symphony had no precedent. Berioz was suddenly a controversial figure; and one of his most vigorous champions was a fellow Romantic who attended the premiere of this symphony, Franz Liszt.

Berlioz followed this work with a number of others of similarly grandiose scale; many of these also depended on programs for their inspiration, and several had literary subjects. His second symphony, *Harold in Italy*, for solo viola and orchestra (1834), was inspired by Byron's *Childe Harold*. A third symphony took Shakespeare's *Romeo and Juliet* as its subject and title.

All of Berlioz' undertakings met with mixed reviews from the critics. His champions were as vociferous as his detractors. But he stubbornly continued to write a series of epic and highly original works, many of them—like the Requiem of 1837 and the *Te Deum* of 1855—specifically inspired by nationalist themes. The Requiem, for example, was entitled *Grande Messe des Morts (Great Mass for the Dead)*, and was composed to commemorate the heroism of French revolutionaries. In the score, Berlioz called for a chorus of 500, an orchestra of 140 players, four brass bands, ten pairs of cymbals, and 16 kettledrums! The *Te Deum* required three choirs, a huge orchestra, and an organ. To say that "dramatic" is the key-word for the works of Berlioz is an understatement; never before had works been designed on such a titanic scale.

Opera was still the most important musical form in Berlioz' lifetime, and in the late 1850s he struggled to complete the opera that has since been judged his masterpiece: *Les Troyens (The Trojans)*. Based on the *Aeneid* of the Roman epic poet Virgil, the opera telescoped the action of the episodes of the fall of Troy, and of the hero Aeneas' tragic love affair with the Carthaginian Queen Dido. *Les Troyens* was written in five acts, and demanded a large chorus and many principal singers. Producers found it impossible to stage in its entirety during Berlioz' lifetime, and the composer was forced to divide the opera into two, relatively self-contained parts. The complete work was not performed on one evening without cuts until as recently as 1969.

While Berlioz struggled to win recognition, **Franz Liszt** (1811–1886) was taking Paris by storm. Liszt was born in Hungary; although he lived abroad for most of his life, he identified himself through his music with the Hungarian struggle for freedom from the rule of Austria. In fact, Liszt could barely speak Hungarian, and his orchestral *Hungarian Rhapsodies* (1860) really owe little to genuine Hungarian folk-music. They reflect, rather, what Liszt in his boundlessly fertile imagination conceived to be national themes. But revolutionaries often care less about academic precision than about ideals; and since Liszt was Hungarian—and famous—his countrymen were happy to adopt him as a cultural patron saint.

Liszt's genius was explosive. He was lionized in Paris in the 1830s and 40s for his good looks and for his virtuosity: some critics judge him to have been the most brilliant pianist who has ever lived. His command of technique was flawless; his sense of timing and showmanship was impeccable; and his compositions for piano were so fiendishly difficult that for years only he could play them. He was the first man to use the word "recital" for the public performance of a solo pianist; and (legend records) the first man to turn the piano at right angles to the audience, so that admiring ladies would have a full view of his handsome profile. Countesses and princesses swooned at his feet; and his fame (sometimes amounting to notoriety) spread throughout Europe. Following Beethoven and Chopin, Liszt transformed the piano from an instrument of the polite, aristocratic salon to an instrument of epic power, almost orchestral in the breadth of its sonorities.

But Liszt's nature, like Schumann's, was paradoxical. His worldliness was combined with a deep, religious mysticism; and his flamboyant instinct for performance co-existed with two quite different talents: a remarkable gift for composing, and an equally strong dedication to the teaching and encouragement of younger musicians. In 1848, he became music director at Weimar in Germany and turned that court into a center for promoting the music of revolutionary composers (both in the political and the musical sense). He championed Hector Berlioz and the young Richard Wagner (who later became Liszt's son-in-law). In 1860 he moved on to Rome, where he took holy orders in the Church, having forsaken his reputation as a playboy. He composed a number of visionary, quasi-mystical works in this period, experimented with chromaticism and impressionism in musical harmony (which are usually associated with the better-known works of Richard Wagner and Claude Debussy), and invented a new orchestral form: the symphonic tone-poem, a programmatic picture in music of a specific theme or place [see Chapter 14, on Debussy's *La Mer*].

Thus, the significance of Liszt in nineteenth-century music transcends his identification with Hungarian nationalist themes. He was a veritable Byronic hero for younger musicians, uniting the sacred and the profane—as fascinating in real life as in his own music. The list of composers whom he influenced or expressly encouraged is stunning: besides Berlioz and Wagner, it includes the Russians Borodin, Rimsky-Korsakov, and Tchaikovsky; the Czech composers Smetana and Dvořák; Edvard Grieg of Norway; the Spanish composer Isaac Albéñiz; the Belgian César Franck; and the French Camille Saint-Saëns. Many of these composers went on to become celebrated as the founders of—or important figures in—the national style of music in their own countries [see Chapters 12 and 13].

Giuseppe Verdi (1813–1901) is the preeminent composer of Italian opera. His career also constitutes a large part of the history of music in Italy in the nineteenth century. Of his 26 operas, more than half are basic repertory of opera houses all over the world today; all the works from *Rigoletto* (1851) onwards to *Falstaff* (1893) are familiar to lovers of this form. The heir to the tradition of *bel canto* ("beautiful singing") in the operas of Gioacchino Rossini (1792–1868), Gaetano Donizetti (1797–1848), and Vincenzo Bellini (1801–1835), Verdi managed to forge a style in opera that surpassed the achievements of all his predecessors. Aware of, and yet apparently untroubled by, the radical innovations of his contemporary Richard Wagner in Germany, Verdi pursued an independent course. Two factors, above all, were responsible for his remarkable success: his extraordinary feeling for melody (there are numerous anecdotes about the common people of Verdi's day humming the composer's tunes, a practice which continues all over Italy) and his sure mastery of what would "play" on the operatic stage. Other factors contributing to his popularity were his sympathy with Italian national feeling, his originality in breaking away from the idealization of *bel canto*, and the steady growth of psychological insight in his music.

Verdi was born into a poor family near Busseto, in north-central Italy. He failed his entrance examinations for the Milan Conservatory, and was forced to study privately. After a few inconsequential early pieces, he set about composing an opera, and was encouraged by the moderate success of his first work, *Oberto*, produced at La Scala in Milan in 1839. But this period severely tested Verdi. Within two years, his wife and two children died. And his second opera, *Un Giorno di Regno (King for a Day)* was a disastrous failure. This, besides his last work (*Falstaff*), was Verdi's only attempt at comedy; it is easy to see how the bereaved and disappointed composer avoided the genre for so long.

Verdi almost gave up opera altogether in the next few years. But the manager of La Scala urged him to look at the libretto for an opera on the Biblical King Nebuchadnezzar. Verdi agreed, and offered *Nabucco* (the Italian form of the name) for production in 1842. The stirring story and melodic fluency of the opera were a great success. Italians, who were then under the yoke of the Austrian Empire (and would not achieve liberty and unity until 1860, under Garibaldi), could identify with the plight of the ancient Jews in captivity. One chorus from the opera—"Va, pensiero" ("Fly, my thoughts, on golden wings")—was enough to catapult the young composer to fame. Before long, enthusiastic fans were even to turn Verdi's name into an acronym for political protest. The letters V-E-R-D-I were chalked up on walls, both in homage to the composer, and as a political statement: they were the first letters of "Vittorio Emmanuele, Re d'Italia"—Victor Emmanuel, King of Italy—a nationalist slogan which expressed the yearning for a unified Italy, under an independent, native monarch.

From *Nabucco* onward, Verdi's output can be divided into three great periods. First come the operas on national or heroic themes. *Ernani* (1844) was adapted from Victor Hugo's play *Hernani*, which had caused a sensation at its premiere in Paris in 1830. *Giovanna d'Arco (Joan of Arc)* (1845) was also based on a play of one of the great Romantic dramatists, Friedrich Schiller. Two other operas were derived from Schiller's plots: *I Masnadieri (The Robbers)* and *Luisa Miller* (1849). Punctuating these melodramas was a significant experiment: Verdi's adaptation of Shakespeare's play *Macbeth* (1847). The opera foreshadows Verdi's consummate renderings of Shakespearean tragedy in *Otello* and Shakespearean comedy in *Falstaff* at the end of his career.

Closing the first period are three of the most popular operas by any composer: *Rigoletto* (1851), *Il Trovatore (The Troubadour)* (1853), and *La Traviata (The Lost One)* (1853). *Rigoletto* was based on another play by Hugo, entitled *Le Roi s'amuse (The King Enjoys Himself)*.

The plot tells the story of Rigoletto, the ugly, misshapen court jester whose daughter is corrupted by the Duke whom he serves. Determined to avenge his daughter's honor, Rigoletto is brought inexorably to discover that he has arranged the assassination of his own daughter, rather than that of the rake who has corrupted her. As drama, *Rigoletto* exploits every opportunity for theatricality and irony, while humanizing its characters. The music is beautifully melodic and dramatically effective; the score boasts an unusual number of memorable arias, even for Verdi: the opening aria of the libertine Duke of Mantua (*Questa o quella*), the charming *Caro nome* of Gilda the heroine, the storm music and quartet of the final act, and the ever popular aria, *La donna è mobile (Woman is fickle)*. Verdi heightens his drama by the repeated uses of the curse motif of Monterone, the vengeance duet sung by Rigoletto and his daughter, and the terrifying effect of the Duke's reprise, off-stage, of *La donna è mobile*. The range of his writing for the baritone part of Rigoletto prefigures some of his best later work. Dramatically, the tender love between father and daughter is a theme that interested Verdi greatly: it finds notable expression in *Simone Boccanegra* (1857), and (with variations) in *La Traviata* and *Aida*.

Verdi's middle period extends from *I Vespri Siciliani (The Sicilian Vespers)* (1855) through *Aida* (1871). By the early 1850s, he was famous throughout Italy. His operas had been premiered and produced in the leading cities and opera houses: Milan, Rome, Venice, and Naples. With *I Vespri Siciliani* he returned to implicitly patriotic themes. The plot was based on an episode of thirteenth-century Sicilian history, in which the patriots of Palermo threw off the French yoke by murdering their overlords. It did not require much sophistication to interpret the plot of the opera as a thin disguise code for the contemporary political situation in Italy. It is notable that *I Vespri Siciliani* was the first of Verdi's operas to be premiered outside Italy (it was first performed in Paris). Other operas of this period include *Simone Boccanegra* (1857), *Un Ballo in Maschera (A Masked Ball)* (1859), *La Forza del Destino (The Force of Destiny)* (1862), and *Don Carlo* (1867). The last two were also written for foreign commissions, in St. Petersburg (Russia) and Paris, respectively. These operas are marked by gradually increasing complexity, both in characterization and in writing for the orchestra. For example, the poignantly comic portrait of Oscar the page in *Un Ballo in Maschera* establishes a tragic dimension for the dénouement in the last act. (Verdi seems to have had no hesitation in following Shakespeare's example in counter-pointing tragedy with hints of comedy). The orchestral writing of *Simone Boccanegra* and *Don Carlo* is richer, darker, and more continuous than in earlier Verdi.

This period of Verdi's work closes with *Aida*, written to celebrate the opening of the Suez Canal and first performed in Cairo in 1871. Here Verdi blended the classic outlines of the melodramatic love plot (passion, jealousy, and betrayal) with exotic musical motifs intended to suggest ancient Egypt. The Ethiopian Princess Aida confronts the dilemma of love versus patriotism; her father Amonasro forces her to betray the Egyptian general Radames, whom she loves. Ultimately she joins Radames in the tomb in which he is buried alive; they both bid farewell to life in one of opera's most famous duets, *O terra, addio (Farewell, oh earth)*. One of the world's most popular operas, *Aida* displays—in its occasion, subject, and style—the true internationalism of Verdi's art.

In 1873, the nationalist poet Alessandro Manzoni died, and Verdi was invited to compose a Requiem. The result is one of the glories of sacred music, ranking with the Mozart Requiem. Verdi's *Requiem* (1874) transcends purely religious faith. It is essentially a dramatic statement, in operatic style, of the universal themes of life and death.

Soon after 1880, the publisher Giulio Ricordi (1840–1912) suggested to Verdi an opera on the theme of Shakespeare's tragedy, *Othello*. Verdi appeared to have put the idea aside. But the canny Ricordi knew that the composer could scarcely resist another adaptation from the works of his most beloved poet, provided that the right librettist was found. In one of the most fortunate collaborations in the history of opera, the right librettist *was* found, in the young Arrigo Boito (1842–1918). Boito had known Verdi for twenty years, and assisted the composer with the revision of *Simone Boccanegra* in 1880–81. In addition, he had the advantage of being a composer in his own right; his opera on the Faust legend, *Mefistofele*, had been produced (with some controversy, followed by popular acclaim) in 1868. Boito had also served as the librettist for Amilcare Ponchielli's opera *La Gioconda* in 1876.

Seldom can there have been a more painstaking transformation of a masterpiece from one medium to another. Boito and Verdi collaborated, argued, negotiated—with the spirit of Shakespeare hovering over them. What emerged was Verdi's greatest opera, *Otello*, first performed in 1887. Entire sections (e.g. all of Act I) and characters in Shakespeare's play were omitted; other parts of the dialogue were faithfully presented (virtually translated by Boito into Italian); still other sections, notably the villainous Iago's soliloquy at the opening of the opera's second act, were created out of whole cloth. Verdi's score ranges in tone from the rapturous love duet of Otello and Desdemona at the end of the first act through the darkly twisted, diminished chords and tremolos of Iago's treachery; from the public grandeur of the third-act embassy to the pathos of Desdemona's willow song and *Ave Maria* in the final act. The orchestra accompanies the action continuously: one may pick out distinct "scenes" and "numbers", but the fluid transitions between them make each act appear seamless. *Otello*, for its faultlessly constructed stage action, its intensity of emotion, and its superb music, is the masterpiece of tragic opera in the nineteenth century.

How could Verdi cap this achievement? Again with Shakespeare, and again with Boito. He had shied away from full-scale comedy in opera for half a century; now Verdi devoted his last years to an adaptation of *The Merry Wives of Windsor* (with elements of the *Henry IV* plays), featuring Shakespeare's greatest comic character, Falstaff. *Falstaff* had its first performance when the composer was nearly eighty. Although it is not produced as frequently as *Aida*, *Otello*, and the operas of the early-middle period, *Falstaff* is to operatic comedy what *Otello* is to tragedy. Not since Mozart's *Così Fan Tutte* (1790) had such a masterful comic work appeared on the operatic stage.

In all the operas of Verdi, we sense a directness, an intense interest in human emotions, which exercise overwhelming appeal. The least theoretical of great composers, Verdi worked with one supreme ambition: to involve his audiences in the human drama being played out on stage. In this, he was not really different from Wagner [see below]. For although Verdi had little interest in mythology, symbolism, and the subconscious mind, and avoided promulgating theories of music-drama in essays and other pronouncements, he believed—like Wagner—that drama and music must co-exist in opera in a highly sophisticated, synergetic relationship. For all the differences in method, style, and subjects between the two giants of opera in the nineteenth century, the aims of Verdi and Wagner were fundamentally similar.

In 1849, Verdi bought a farming estate near the town of his birth; he named the farm Sant' Agata. There he lived for over half a century, leaving only to supervise the premieres of his operas in Italy and abroad. In 1859, he married the singer Giuseppina Strepponi, with whom he had lived for a number of years. As he composed, he took pride in the products of his farm. When his second wife died, in 1897, he directed that the estate be converted into a home for indigent, retired musicians after his own death. At his funeral in 1901, a grieving nation paid its respects. Despite Verdi's wish that no music be played at the simple service, the crowd saluted the composer they had loved by breaking spontaneously into song. What they sang was the chorus from *Nabucco, Va, pensiero*.

Richard Wagner (1813–1883) towers over the later nineteenth century in the way that Beethoven dominates the century's early decades. Wagner's significance derives from three achievements. First, he was able to forge the disparate elements of German Romantic opera into a number of true masterpieces. Second, he vigorously espoused, and finally established beyond question, the concept that opera was music drama, involving a union of poetry, music, and the visual arts. Finally, Wagner's musical originality, and his audacious experiments with the classical rules of tonality, paved the way for a new music; for good or ill, he influenced almost every subsequent composer, down through our own century.

Wagner was born in Leipzig. He became fascinated at an early age by ancient Greek mythology; his other great interests were Shakespeare in literature and Beethoven in music. (It is interesting that the idols of the young Hector Berlioz were the same two artists: see above.) Wagner's cosmopolitan tastes foreshadowed important characteristics of his mature work, much of which was to be based on myth and legend and was to emphasize forcefully the dramatic interplay of characters on stage. Although Wagner became the most important figure in the search for a truly German, national style of opera, the power of his art cannot be explained in purely national terms. Like all great nationalist music, the music of Wagner transcends the narrow limitations of a particular culture and a specific era. Because of his intense dedication to the concept of *Gesamtkunstwerk* (the "total artwork"), he was unique among great opera composers in writing all his own libretti. It is interesting that, of thirteen operas, only one is based on a German historical subject: *Die Meistersinger von Nürnberg (The Mastersingers of Nuremberg)*.

After completing his musical studies at the University of Leipzig, Wagner held a series of minor conducting posts in Germany. In 1839 he traveled to Paris, hoping to establish himself with the aid of the patronage of Giacomo Meyerbeer (1791–1864), the leading opera composer of the time. Meyerbeer, a German who had absorbed both French and Italian influences, wrote grand operas in an essentially derivative but highly popular style. His work *Les Huguenots (The Huguenots)* (1836) had been a great success. Wagner learned considerably from him and was received with good will, but nothing came of his ambitions for a career in the French capital.

Back in Germany in the 1840s, Wagner saw his luck begin to change. Two of his early operas, *Rienzi* and *Der fliegende Holländer (The Flying Dutchman)*, were produced in Dresden. The first was based on an English novel about Rome in the Renaissance and displays some of Meyerbeer's influence on the young composer. *The Flying Dutchman* was more significant: it was Wagner's first excursion into the world of quasi-mystical legend. The story emphasized the theme of redemption through love, an idea that would preoccupy the composer in many of his later operas, from *Tannhäuser* through *Parsifal*.

The success of *Rienzi* and *The Flying Dutchman* brought Wagner a far more important conducting appointment in Dresden. Until 1849 he supervised the orchestra there, worked on his next two operas—*Tannhäuser* and *Lohengrin*—and read widely in Germanic mythology and legends. *Tannhäuser* (1845) was based on a medieval legend of a poet-musician. The hero defies society and Church by professing his love for the pagan goddess Venus, but is finally redeemed through his own penance and the saintly sacrifice of Elizabeth, the woman who loves and pities him. *Lohengrin* (1848) treats an episode of the legend of the knights of the Holy Grail (a story to which Wagner returned in his last opera, *Parsifal*). Lohengrin, a mysterious knight in shining armor, arrives in Brabant to champion the beautiful Elsa against an unjust accusation. They fall in love and are married, but Lohengrin warns Elsa that she must trust him enough to refrain from asking his true identity. She agrees; but Elsa's enemies pretend friendship with her and sow the seeds of suspicion. She yields to her fears and demands to know Lohengrin's identity. He reveals that he is the son of Parsifal and a knight of the Grail, the legendary order of chivalric heroes who guarded the chalice from which Christ drank at the Last Supper. The opera closes as Lohengrin sorrowfully leaves.

Lohengrin marks a turning point in Wagner's operas. It was here that he made the first extensive use of the techniques which he was later to refine in such works as *Tristan und Isolde, Die Meistersinger*, and the group of four operas entitled *Der Ring des Nibelungen (The Ring of the Nibelung)*. First, the symbolism of the libretto should be noted. The story of *Lohengrin* is frankly unrealistic. The character of the hero may represent divine love, or the personified answer to prayer; the heroine suggests innocence that is corrupted by human frailty. Second, Wagner employs (for the first time in his career) a structured system of *leitmotifs*. A *leitmotif* (literally, "leading motive") is a short musical phrase used to represent a person, object, or idea. It is a kind of symbol in music. The *leitmotif* is established at the first appearance of the character or concept it represents. It may then be repeated, varied, or played in combination with other motifs—not only when the person or object associated with it is overtly present, but when the composer wants to suggest the thoughts or emotions of a character on-stage, or to provide a musical foreshadowing of later events.

The *leitmotif* enables the composer of a music-drama to approach the position of an "omniscient narrator" of a short story or novel in literature. For Wagner, it functions as a remarkably flexible technique with which to bind together both the music and the drama. *Leitmotifs* may foreshadow or comment on events; they may probe the hidden thoughts of the characters, and thus reinforce dramatic irony; and a system of repetitions can effectively unify the music of a work, just as a symphony may be unified by the repetition of principal themes. In *Lohengrin*, Wagner initiated the imaginative interplay of musical and dramatic symbolism which lies at the root of the emotional power of his mature works.

In both *Tannhäuser* and *Lohengrin*, Wagner also definitively broke with the traditional pattern for the structure of opera: arias (set numbers for the solo singers), recitative (sung or spoken dialogue), and ensemble (set numbers for chorus). Instead, he directed that the orchestra accompany the action in an unbroken web of sound during each act of the drama. In this departure from traditional practice, Wagner had been preceded to some extent by Gluck [see Chapter 7]—although even in such operas as *Orfeo* the principal singers had been given distinct arias.

During the revolution of 1848 in Dresden, Wagner was involved in political protest, and came dangerously close to being arrested. He was forced to flee the city in 1849. His travels took him first to the court at Weimar, where he visited his friend Franz Liszt; he was later to marry the composer's daughter, Cosima. Liszt was a great admirer of Wagner's music and produced the first performance of *Lohengrin* in 1850. Wagner then moved to Switzerland, where he lived for twelve years in exile. He elaborated his theories of music-drama in a number of essays and books, including *Opera and Drama*, *The Artwork of the Future*, and *Art and Revolution*.

Liszt commissioned from Wagner an opera on the death of the hero Siegfried, a figure of medieval epic legend. Drawing on Scandinavian and German sources—including the great anonymous epic, the *Nibelungenlied* (composed around 1200)—Wagner wrote the libretto of an opera to be named *Siegfrieds Tod (Siegfried's Death)*. But he soon determined that the story was too complex for a single operatic treatment. By 1852, he had worked out a monumental plan for not one opera, but four: a trilogy with a prologue, that was to become *Der Ring des Nibelungen*. Having written the libretti in reverse order, he started to compose the music to the prologue, *Das Rheingold*, in 1852.

The scale of this project had no precedent in the annals of opera, and few equals in the history of art. The composition of the *Ring* occupied more than twenty years. Indeed, from 1857 to 1869, he laid the project aside to compose *Tristan* and *Die Meistersinger*. The four operas of the *Ring*—*Das Rheingold (The Rhinegold)*, *Die Walküre (The Valkyrie)*, *Siegfried*, and *Die Götterdämmerung (The Twilight of the Gods)*—were not finished until 1874, and not performed together as a cycle until 1876. By this time, Wagner had enlisted the support of King Ludwig II of Bavaria, who assisted him in establishing the festival theater at Bayreuth, which was uniquely equipped for the performance of Wagner's works.

In the *Ring*, Wagner's music-drama reaches a culmination. The operas tell a dark story of greed, lust for power, and treachery. The evil dwarf Alberich renounces love, and succeeds in stealing a magical hoard of gold from the bottom of the Rhine. The ring of power, fashioned from the gold by Alberich and his fellow dwarves, the Nibelungs, confers on its possessor the mastery of the universe. Wotan, king of the gods, tricks the Nibelungs; but he in turn is forced to surrender the ring to the giants, Fasolt and Fafner, who have labored to build the gods' new castle in the sky, Valhalla. Wotan belatedly accepts the decree of fate: that the ring must be returned to the Rhine, so that the curse on it may be expiated. He fashions the human hero, Siegfried, to accomplish this task. But Siegfried, who slays Fafner, is in turn corrupted. Betrayed by human enemies, the great hero is slain. Only the self-sacrifice of Brünnhilde, who immolates herself on his funeral pyre, finally breaks the curse's power. At the end of *Die Götterdämmerung*, the old order of the gods is destroyed, as Valhalla collapses in flames; the ring is at last returned to the Rhine and a new age begins, blessed by the redemptive power of human love.

The three principal characters of the *Ring* are Wotan, king of the gods; his daughter Brünnhilde, originally a warrior goddess (a Valkyrie), but then transformed into a mortal woman; and the hero Siegfried. Each is tinged with tragedy: Wotan sorrowfully decrees his own fate, Siegfried's innocence is corrupted, and Brünnhilde must sacrifice her life to expiate the power of the curse on the ring. In that sacrifice, she exemplifies Wagner's essential message: that only human love has the power to triumph over evil in the world.

In the *Ring*, Wagner's system of *leitmotifs* is at its most expansive and complex. The orchestral web is unbroken by specific arias or numbers; and the musical and dramatic unity of the whole work (whose performance time is the equivalent of twenty symphonies) is stunning. Gods, dwarves, dragons, and heroes suspend for us time and space. Dramatic and musical symbolism combine in a powerful re-telling of a myth with universal applications.

Listeners to the *Ring* may notice that the orchestral texture of the work becomes fuller, darker, and more complex beginning with the third act of *Siegfried*. This is the point where Wagner resumed the work in 1869, after an interval of twelve years. In the interim, he wrote the two operas that many regard as his most accessible mature works: the tragedy of love in *Tristan und Isolde* (first performed in 1865) and the comedy of sixteenth-century German bourgeois life,

Die Meistersinger von Nürnberg (1868). *Tristan,* in particular, has exerted enormous musical influence; some critics have dated the beginnings of modern music to its premiere in Munich. Wagner experimented as never before with chromatic harmonies: ascending and descending by half a step in melodies and chords. The prelude to *Tristan und Isolde* clearly announces this approach in its opening measures. The music, like the lovers who will dominate the stage action, seems suspended between keys, with no fixed resting place, or basic tonality. The orchestra constantly seeks after a resolution that is never satisfied. Chromaticism in *Tristan* becomes the perfect musical complement to the opera's dramatic themes of magic and mysticism, physical ecstasy and death. Wagner once remarked that "all music is the art of transition". In *Tristan,* the music is like a constantly developing stream, set free from formal harmonies or set rules.

In contrast to *Tristan, Die Meistersinger* is a sunny, bright celebration of love and the power of song. Its themes include a conflict between artistic innovation and tradition; and Wagner seems concerned about the place of the artist in society. Musically, however, *Die Meistersinger* is more traditional than *Tristan*: it was intended as a popular tribute to German culture, rather than as an audacious experiment. The prelude (theme of the mastersingers), the Bach-like chorale in Act I, the monologue of Hans Sachs, and the hero Walther's prize song in Act III are straightforward and stirrring. In the captious Beckmesser, the "master singer" who nearly spoils Walther's victory, Wagner even incorporated a slyly humorous poke at his contemporary critic, the influential Eduard Hanslick, who had championed the music of Brahms in the controversy of conservatives and progressives [see above, and Chapter 10].

By 1870, Wagner's turbulent and abrasive life had settled down. King Ludwig's patronage removed him from financial troubles and steadily aided the construction of the theater of Wagner's dreams at Bayreuth. The composer regularized his scandalous liaison with Cosima Liszt von Bülow, the daughter of Franz Liszt and the wife of the great conductor Hans von Bülow, who was Wagner's friend. He had resumed composition on the *Ring*. On Christmas Day of 1870 he surprised his new wife Cosima with the *Siegfried Idyll*, a short lyrical piece scored for fifteen musicians who were concealed under the staircase of their house. The piece (later scored for orchestra) incorporated themes from the opera *Siegfried*, from a folk lullaby, and from a string quàrtet written years earlier. Its almost pastoral lyricism has made it Wagner's single most popular non-operatic work.

Wagner's theater at Bayreuth remains today the Mecca for all Wagnerians. It departed radically from theater design at the time. Instead of tiers of seats, as in the great opera houses of Italy, Germany, Paris, and Vienna (and later the Metropolitan Opera House in New York, opened in 1883), Bayreuth featured one, fan-shaped level of seats for the audience. Instead of a proscenium, the stage projected out into the seating area, and the orchestra was completely concealed. Wagner busied himself with endless supervisory duties: he was conductor, designer, impresario, and singing coach. Never before, and seldom since, has a composer been able to control so many aspects of the public performance of his music. To this day, the Bayreuth Festival Theater is directed by the composer's descendants.

After the *Ring* operas received their premiere as a series in 1876, Wagner attempted one last, great project. This was *Parsifal*, the opera on which he had worked from 1877 to 1882. The legend of the Grail had intrigued him since he had conceived *Lohengrin* in the 1840s. In *Parsifal* he universalized the legend in an opera which he called a "stage consecrational play". Wagner was so intensely committed to the proper conditions for its performance that he forbade its production outside Bayreuth; but this restriction lapsed when the copyright expired in 1913. *Parsifal* unites many of the disparate plot themes and musical styles pioneered by the composer. Some listeners have objected to its length (over five hours, uncut); and although some have also objected to what they consider as the religiosity of the plot, Wagner uses the Christian framework to explore universal human traits of innocence and guilt, faith and despair, evil and good. *Parsifal*, because of its length and the difficulties that it imposes on singers and orchestra, is not performed as often as some of Wagner's earlier operas. But its place in the repertory is secure, and its influence on subsequent musicians and composers has been significant.

Wagner died on a visit to Venice the year after *Parsifal* was first performed. There can be few composers who have stirred more controversy, either during their lifetime or for so long a period after their death. The divisions in Germany between the "conservatives" who favored Brahms and the "progressives" who were ardent fans of Wagner's music have continued into our own century. He revolutionized opera—the works of Richard Strauss, and even of Giacomo Puccini, are virtually inconceivable without him. But more importantly, he set in motion an irreversible departure from traditional harmonies and structures in music. Romanticism, in Wagner, was on the brink of Modernism.

Questions for Review

1. With respect to the purpose of their music, what do the four composers of this chapter—Berlioz, Liszt, Verdi, and Wagner—have in common?

2. What key word describes the music of Hector Berlioz?

3. What was the purpose of Berlioz' *Requiem*?

4. Name Berlioz' most celebrated heroic opera. On what epic poem was this opera based?

5. Which figures in music and literature did Berlioz most admire?

6. What was Liszt's conception of the function of music?

7. Why is Liszt significant in the development of the piano as a solo instrument?

8. Why was Franz Liszt so popular in the Paris of the 1830s and 40s?

9. Identify Liszt's relationship (both musical and familial) to Richard Wagner.

10. Characterize the "nationalistic" elements of the music of Liszt.

11. What was the status of opera as an art-form in nineteenth-century Italy?

12. How did Giuseppe Verdi come to be regarded as a national symbol in the Italian struggle for freedom and unity?

13. Summarize briefly the story of Verdi's opera, *Aida*. What conflict faces the heroine in Act 3 of this opera?

14. What was the political "message" implicit in Verdi's chorus, *Va, pensiero (Fly, my thoughts, on golden wings)* from the opera *Nabucco*?

15. Name Verdi's last two operas.

16. Identify Arrigo Boito.

17. Comment on the occasion, style, and effect of Verdi's *Requiem*.

18. Why was Richard Wagner forced to go into exile in 1849?

19. What did Wagner believe about the structure of opera?

20. Briefly summarize the story of Wagner's opera, *Tannhäuser*.

21. Why is the Prelude to *Tristan und Isolde* often called a turning point in the history of Western music? When was this opera first performed?

22. What theme did Wagner deal with in his opera, *Die Meistersinger*?

23. Name the three main characters of Wagner's cycle of operas, *Der Ring des Nibelungen*. In what sense is each of these characters "tragic"?

24. What is a *leitmotif*? How did Wagner use leitmotifs in his music?

25. Identify:
   a) King Ludwig II of Bavaria
   b) Bayreuth
   c) *Siegfried Idyll*

26. Briefly contrast the operatic style and form of Wagner and Verdi.

Answers

1. Berlioz, Liszt, Verdi, and Wagner all used their music to identify with nationalist causes or themes.

2. The music of Berlioz is, above all, *dramatic* (e.g. the autobiographical description of his emotions in the *Symphonie Fantastique*, or the effects of a gigantic orchestra and chorus in the *Requiem*).

3. The purpose of the *Requiem* was to commemorate the patriotic courage of French revolutionary heroes.

4. Berlioz' best-known opera is *Les Troyens (The Trojans)*. It was based on episodes from Virgil's epic poem, *The Aeneid*.

5. Shakespeare and Beethoven.

6. Liszt felt that music should be the vehicle for personal emotion, for patriotic sentiments, and for religious mysticism.

7. Liszt is significant in the development of the piano as a solo instrument because: a) his compositions, intended for virtuoso players like himself, fully exploited the piano's dynamic range; b) he was the first to give "recitals", where his striking looks and virtuoso playing had the effect of turning the pianist into a star performer.

8. Liszt was popular because his looks and personality were those of the showman. A story records that he was the first to turn the piano at right angles to the audience in his recitals, so that the women (who adored him)

could see his handsome profile.

9. Liszt generously supported Wagner's music, which he admired; for example, he undertook to produce *Lohengrin* for the first time in 1850. Later, the two were related by marriage, since Wagner married Liszt's daughter Cosima.

10. The "nationalist" elements in Liszt's music derived more from the composer's imagination than from authentic Hungarian sources. But his *Hungarian Rhapsodies* were eagerly seized on by patriots in Hungary's struggle for liberation from Austria. Liszt became a cultural patron saint.

11. Opera in nineteenth-century Italy was a highly democratic art form. People of all classes attended performances and were often heard to hum the melodies of popular composers in the streets.

12. Verdi's opera *Nabucco* of 1842 (and in particular the choral lament of the Jews in exile, *Va, pensiero*) was interpreted by many Italians as a thinly disguised political statement of protest. Italy was still under the domination of Austria. The struggle for freedom and unity was a cause with which Verdi enthusiastically identified.

13. In *Aida*, the heroine (who is the title character) is faced with a conflict of love vs. national duty. In love with Radames, the Egyptian general, Aida is forced by her father (the King of Ethiopia) to betray her lover. When Radames is condemned in disgrace to be buried alive, Aida joins him in death.

14. The political message of Verdi's music was a veiled protest in behalf of Italy, which was then under Austrian domination. *Nabucco* presented a chorus of Jewish captives under Nebuchadnezzar, King of Babylon; the chorus was widely understood by Italians as referring to their own countrymen, ruled by the Austrian Empire in the 1840s.

15. *Otello* and *Falstaff*.

16. Boito served as Verdi's librettist for *Otello* and *Falstaff*; earlier, he had composed a successful opera on the Faust legend, entitled *Mefistofele*.

17. Verdi's *Requiem* (1874) was composed to commemorate the Italian nationalist poet Alessandro Manzoni, who had died in 1873. Operatic in style, the work transcends purely religious faith and deals with universal issues of life and death.

18. Wagner was forced to go into exile because he had participated in political protests during the Revolution of 1848.

19. Wagner believed that the structure of opera should be a single, continuous unity of drama and music. In his operas, therefore, he radically departed from the traditional pattern of arias, recitative, and ensemble.

20. In *Tannhäuser*, the hero is torn by the conflict of sacred and profane love. Although Elizabeth is devoted to him, and ultimately sacrifices herself for Tannhäuser's redemption, he recklessly abandons himself to rapturous love with the goddess Venus. Tannhäuser belatedly repents his sin, and is saved by invoking the name of Elizabeth before he dies.

21. *Tristan und Isolde* was first performed in 1865. Its prelude is often called

a turning point in Western music because the chromatic harmonies and the lack of any basic, fixed tonality mark a decisive break with traditional technique. The prelude to *Tristan* announces some of the fundamental approaches of modern music.

22. In *Die Meistersinger* Wagner dealt with the theme of the artist's relationship to society and with the conflict of innovation and tradition in art.

23. The three main characters of the *Ring* are Wotan, Siegfried, and Brünnhilde. Wotan, king of the gods, decrees his own downfall. Siegfried, the young hero, is corrupted by greed, and is treacherously slain. Brünnhilde, Wotan's daughter, is transformed from a warrior goddess into a mortal woman; she sacrifices her life on Siegfried's funeral pyre in order to redeem the world through love.

24. A *leitmotif* is a brief musical phrase used to represent a person, object, or idea. Wagner used an elaborate system of *leitmotifs* in his mature operas; they enabled the orchestra to "comment" on the stage action, to recall or foreshadow events in the drama, and to suggest the hidden thoughts or emotions of characters.

25. a) Ludwig II of Bavaria was Richard Wagner's patron; his financial support enabled Wagner to carry out the project of his dreams: the construction of the theater at Bayreuth.

b) Bayreuth was the name of the special, festival theater that Wagner designed for the production of his operas. Innovative in its plan, it remains one of the most important European focal points for Wagnerian production.

c) *Siegfried Idyll* is the short orchestral piece which Wagner wrote for his wife Cosima. It was originally performed in 1870, by a small group of musicians who were concealed under the staircase in Wagner's home.

26. Verdi's operas do not depart as radically as Wagner's from the traditional pattern of aria and ensemble. He makes far less extensive use of *leitmotifs* in the orchestra than does Wagner; instead, his strength derives from his direct appeal to human emotions and his infinitely varied, striking melodies. Wagner's operas are longer, and their orchestration tends toward density and complexity. Most of Wagner's operas are based on myth or legend, and they rely more heavily than Verdi's on symbolism and an appeal to the human subconscious mind. But both composers may be said to have had the same end objective: to involve their audiences in the drama being played out on stage.

Chapter 12

Land of Our Fathers

Land of Our Fathers

In the later nineteenth century and the first half of the twentieth, nationalist movements arose in a number of countries where music had not enjoyed a continuous tradition of formal composition and performance. These countries included Czechoslovakia, Hungary, Spain, Norway, Finland, England, and America. Some of the nations, like Czechoslovakia and Hungary, were under the political domination of a foreign power—in their case, the Austro-Hungarian Empire. Other lands, such as Spain, Norway, and Finland, possessed rich folk traditions but had remained outside the mainstream of European music. America looked to Europe for music of quality, and had ignored the cultural resources of a sprawling continent; American music, by native composers on native subjects, started comparatively late, as did Russian music [see Chapter 13].

But the yearnings for national identity and political freedom that characterized Italy in Giuseppe Verdi's time [see Chapter 11] were simultaneously being felt in a number of other countries. The growth of nationalism only culminated after the end of World War I in 1918; thus, nationalism contributed to the creative energies of musicians and composers well into our own century. Such composers as Bedřich Smetana and Antonín Dvořák in Czechoslovakia, Zoltán Kodály in Hungary, and Manuel de Falla in Spain were largely inspired by native folk songs and dance rhythms. In Scandinavia, Edvard Grieg of Norway and Jean Sibelius of Finland developed distinctive styles intended to celebrate their countries' heritage; they literally put their nations on the cultural map of Europe. In England, which had not produced a major composer since the death of Henry Purcell in 1695 (though it had played host to such giants as Handel and Haydn), Ralph Vaughan Williams fused folk music, sacred music, and programmatic motifs into an English "music of the community". And in America, which had had no continuous tradition of native "serious music", the eccentric genius, Charles Ives, blazed a new trail.

None of these composers is today considered to have the stature of Bach, Mozart, or Beethoven. Yet we should recall that each of those earlier figures, however brilliantly original, benefited by inheriting a tradition of highly developed musical forms. As we study the national composers, we should remember that their primary aim was to create music with a distinctive sense of place. They could not help but remain conscious of their great predecessors in Europe, especially Beethoven, Brahms, and Wagner. But they succeeded to a remarkable degree in conveying a picture of lands and peoples in sound. In Grieg we can hear the majestic scenery of sky and fjord in Norway; in Sibelius we can sense the wintry bleakness of the Finnish landscape. De Falla's music speaks of the exotic, bitter-sweet passion of Southern Spain; in Ives, we seem to see the small village greens of New England towns.

Bedřich Smetana (1824–1884) never totally turned his back on Western European styles. Smetana was a native of Bohemia, which had for centuries been a possession of the Austrian Empire. Like his fellow Czechs, he was in intimate contact with the mainstream of musical tradition; like most of the middle and upper class, he grew up speaking German, not Czech. Smetana was especially influenced by Franz Liszt, whom he visited in Weimar and who became a close friend. Liszt's invention, the symphonic poem [see Chapter 11], especially appealed to Smetana. He was to exploit the new form in *Má Vlast (My Country)*, a series of six programmatic tone poems for orchestra, each describing a feature of Czech life. The gracefully melodic poem *Vltava*, for example, pictures the course of the river Vltava, which flows by the city of Prague.

Smetana incorporated enough nationalist motifs into his works to be regarded as the founder of Czech music. After travels in Europe he returned to Prague, where he enjoyed considerable success with two operas, *The Brandenburgers in Bohemia* (1863) and *The Bartered Bride* (1864); the latter has a small place in the standard repertory today. In addition to his operas and symphonic works, Smetana composed a variety of chamber music, short pieces for piano, and works for solo voice and chorus. He was working on an operatic adaptation of Shakespeare's *Twelfth Night* when he died in an asylum at the age of sixty.

Although much of Smetana's music is charmingly melodic, he is overshadowed in importance by his follower, **Antonín Dvořák** (1841–1904). The chief influences on the young Dvořák were Wagner and Brahms; the latter took an active interest in furthering his career.

Dvořák showed talent on the violin as a child and was sent to Prague to study. There he obtained a place as a violist in the national symphony, then directed by Smetana. Dvořák's credentials for writing a truly nationalist music were far better than those of Smetana: Czech was his mother tongue, and he grew up accompanying dances and folksongs in a village band. In his *String Quartet in E-flat* (Opus 51), as well as in a variety of his other chamber works, one may hear the *dumka*, a Slavonic dance with a distinctive alternation of very swift rhythm with slow, melancholy lament.

Dvořák's music was not known or appreciated until the composer was well past thirty. His greatest early success was a series of *Slavonic Dances*, composed originally for two pianos and later scored for orchestra. Light, tuneful, and rhythmically inventive, these have remained some of his most popular pieces. There followed the *Stabat Mater* (1876), a work for chorus that Dvořák conducted with great success on the first of his many trips to England. Growing international fame brought Dvořák financial security, an honorary doctorate from Cambridge University, and (in the early 1890s) an invitation to work in America, where he was to write some of his best-known music.

In 1892, Dvořák left Prague to become the director of a new musical conservatory in New York. He remained in New York for three years, traveling for summer holidays to the Czech immigrant community of Spillville, Iowa. In this period, Dvořák wrote his *Concerto for Cello and Orchestra* (one of the most celebrated works in the literature for that solo instrument), and his most often heard Symphony, No. 9, entitled *From the New World*. There is a great affinity between Dvořák and Brahms, particularly with respect to rich orchestration and treatment of the principal themes; but Dvořák's work differs strikingly in its use of native Czech elements. In the case of the *Symphony from the New World*, we have an intriguing mixture of Czech and American elements. Nostalgia for his homeland is mingled with fascination for Negro spirituals and the folk songs of composers like Stephen Foster. Dvořák was so taken by America that he even composed a cantata on the flag, and offered to write a new national anthem for the United States.

In 1895, Dvořák returned to Prague and resumed his post as director of the music conservatory. His last years were filled with compositions on national themes: symphonic tone poems on a number of old Bohemian legends, and a charming opera entitled *Rusalka (The Water Sprite)*, which was first produced in 1900. By the time of his death, he was regarded as Czechoslovakia's most important composer. The attractive, tuneful quality of his work and an increased appreciation of its structural subtlety have steadily increased critical recognition of Dvořák in our own time.

Leoš Janáček (1854–1928), in contrast to Smetana and Dvořák, is usually regarded as a composer of the twentieth century. His music came to public attention when he was older even than Dvořák. Until the turn of the century, he worked as music master of a small provincial training college in Brno. While there, he devoted many years to harmonizing and arranging the folk songs of Moravia. In 1904, when he was nearing fifty, his opera *Jenufa* was performed in Brno. Despite its success, personality disputes between Janáček and the director of the Prague Opera delayed the work's performance there until 1916. *Jenufa* displayed a markedly new style in opera: Janáček's music, for both orchestra and voice, combined short melodic bursts with a complex sense of underlying rhythm. Like Mussorgsky in *Boris Godunov* [see Chapter 13], Janáček's goal was to emulate the patterns of natural speech as closely as possible in the vocal lines he composed. Orchestrally, his music is marked by sudden changes in tonality and dynamics.

Despite his departures from the late-Romantic style of Dvořák, Janáček was acclaimed in Prague when *Jenufa* was premiered. His success with this opera inspired a remarkably rich period of composition during the last ten years of his life. Among his notable later works are the operas *Kátya Kabanová* (1921) and *The Cunning Little Vixen* (1923). In *Kátya Kabanová*, Janáček looked to Russia for inspiration; he regarded his work not only as Czech but as pan-Slavonic. Based on a Russian play, the opera told the bleak story of a woman who was unfaithful to her husband, confessed her guilt to her family and community, and then drowned herself. Janáček's last period also includes some excellent chamber works, and the *Glagolitic Mass* (1924): its title refers to the text of the mass in the Old Slavonic vernacular of medieval times. The important part given to the organ in the *Mass* probably reflects Janáček's experience as the founding director of an organ conservatory in Brno.

Zoltán Kodály (1882–1967) emerged as the leading representative of Hungarian nationalist music in the period immediately after

World War I. Trained at the Franz Liszt Academy of Music in Budapest, he became a great friend of another significant Hungarian composer, **Béla Bartók** (1881–1945). Kodály and Bartók traveled the Hungarian countryside together, collecting and recording folk music. Kodály won fame with his choral work, *Psalmus Hungaricus*, a specifically nationalist work which was composed to celebrate the fiftieth anniversary of Budapest as the capital in 1923. Kodály was determined to create a place for Hungarian music in the operatic repertory. He never composed a conventional opera but his musical drama, *Háry János* (1926), was warmly received as an operatic adaptation of folklore motifs. The opera was re-scored by Kodály as an orchestral suite in 1927.

In the United States, little serious music by native composers existed before the end of the nineteenth century. Of course, folk music had always existed: folk songs, spirituals, patriotic marches, and church hymns. But for serious concert music, America (like Russia before about 1850) largely looked to Western Europe. **Edward MacDowell** (1861–1908) had attempted to write American music, like his *New England Idylls* for piano (1902). But MacDowell, who studied in Europe, was still heavily influenced by nineteenth-century composers such as Edvard Grieg [see below].

Charles Ives (1874–1954) is now generally regarded as the founder of a vital, modern American tradition in music. Ives was a remarkable individualist who (like his fellow Yale graduate, the poet Wallace Stevens) for many years pursued his art as an avocation. His main profession was as the successful founder and manager of an insurance agency. In his youth, he was fascinated with the sounds, even more than the sights, of small New England villages. His father had been a bandmaster. Such sounds as the different tunes of two bands at a parade, mingling with each other and yet separate, intrigued Ives: he began to experiment with many of the techniques that would later dominate modern music (e.g. polytonality, atonality, tone clusters, chromaticism [see Chapters 15 and 16]. Ives' *Three Places in New England*, a set of orchestral tone poems composed between 1903 and 1914, is the first major symphonic work of a distinctively American stamp. The last movement, subtitled *The Housatonic at Stockbridge*, presents an impressionistic picture of sights and sounds along the river: the rustling of the trees, the rippling of the current, the distant singing in church which is half-heard from a path across the stream.

Other notable works by Ives include the Piano Sonata No. 2 (called the *Concord Sonata*, since each movement is named for one of the group of nineteenth-century writers who gathered in Concord, Massachusetts: Ralph Waldo Emerson, Nathaniel Hawthorne, the Alcotts, and Henry David Thoreau); the symphonic *New England Holidays*; and a work for chamber orchestra entitled *Central Park in the Dark*. Ives composed little after 1917, when a serious illness forced him to curtail both his business activities and his work in music. Few of his important works were performed before the 1930s; but they have continued to gain in critical recognition, and have served as rich sources of influence for younger American composers.

In Scandinavia, two nationalist composers of the late nineteenth century are especially noteworthy; in contrast to Leoš Janáček of Czechoslovakia and Charles Ives of the United States, the music of both is far less Modernist in sound—it recalls, rather, the nineteenth century, late Romantic tradition of Dvořák.

The first is **Edvard Grieg** of Norway (1843–1907). Grieg's most famous work is doubtless the *Piano Concerto in A Minor* (1869), with its famous descending chords on the piano announcing the introductory theme. A staple of the concert repertory, the concerto is a good index to the style of Grieg, in which the Romanticism of Liszt and Mendelssohn is combined with unmistakable references to Norway. Norwegian songs and dances, with their highly chromatic harmonies, lowered seventh chords, and alternating triads between the major and minor, shaped much of Grieg's work, especially in the short piano pieces and songs. Many of the latter were written for the composer's wife, who was a concert singer. Particularly important for Grieg's development was his meeting with the great Realist playwright, Henrik Ibsen (1828–1906) in Rome in 1866. The dramatist whose plays of nineteenth-century bourgeois life were to take world drama in a completely new direction invited Grieg to compose program music for one of his early plays, *Peer Gynt* (1874). Grieg's orchestral suite for the play is still one of his most popular compositions. Grieg's music retains its freshness and a delicately poetic lyricism. He was essentially a miniaturist who avoided the larger forms of opera, symphony, and longer piano works. (His single piano concerto is a conspicuous exception.)

The Finnish composer **Jean Sibelius** (1865–1957) attempted more ambitious music, and is now one of the most popular late Romantic composers in the standard repertory. Just as the Finnish language is virtually isolated in Europe (Hungarian is the only tongue even distantly related), the genius of Sibelius seems mysterious. Highly original, he steered his own course, avoiding the marked influence of any other foreign composer. It was the rich heritage of Finnish folklore and myth that inspired Sibelius, together with the stark landscape of his native country and the patriotic struggle of the Finns to be free from their Russian overlords.

Before the nineteenth century, Finland had had no musical tradition—a fact which makes one of Sibelius' best-known works, the symphonic poem *Finlandia* (1900), all the more remarkable. Sibelius composed this work as a hymn to his fatherland. Grand, bleak, and majestic, the ominous chords and pulsating rhythm suggest a landscape of harsh winds and great, open skies. The charming fjords and peasant dances of Grieg's Norway could not be further removed from the spirit of Sibelius' music, where brass, strings, and woodwinds encompass a great symphonic landscape. Also distinctive are Sibelius' fragmented themes, which gradually coalesce in the course of a work, and ominous, dynamic climaxes in the orchestra.

Unlike Grieg, Smetana, and Kodály, Sibelius does not often quote folk melodies; his music is not "nationalist" in the narrowly programmatic sense. His important works—the seven symphonies, *Finlandia*, and the tone poems on Finnish legend, *The Swan of Tuonela* (1898), *Pohjola's Daughter* (1906), and *Tapiola* (1925)—were all written by his sixtieth year; after 1925, he composed only small pieces. Sibelius' isolation from the musical experiments of his contemporaries—radical composers like Arnold Schoenberg, Alban Berg, and Igor Stravinsky (to name just three of the seminal figures of twentieth-century music)—caused him to be neglected and undervalued for some time. But he is now recognized as a truly international composer whose use of nationalist themes transcends local geography.

In Spain, **Manuel de Falla** (1876–1946) played a role similar to that of Charles Ives in American music. De Falla had been preceded by Isaac Albéniz (1860–1909), in the way that Ives' effort to create a truly American music had been foreshadowed by Edward MacDowell [see above]. Albéniz was a pupil of Liszt, and his twelve piano compositions entitled *Iberia* (published 1906–1909) were significantly indebted to Liszt's brilliant piano style. The young de Falla was determined to forge a truly Spanish style. While living in the Southern city of Cádiz, he was greatly impressed by the assertively national character of Edvard Grieg's music, which he heard performed at concerts. After studies in Madrid, de Falla spent some years in Paris, beginning in 1907—a sojourn that was crucial for his composing career, since he met and became friendly with three important composers: Claude Debussy (1862–1918), Maurice Ravel (1875–1937), and Igor Stravinsky (1882–1971). He was particularly struck by the innovations of Debussy—experiments with modal harmonies, the wholetone scale, and delicate "impressionistic" effects of color for both orchestra and piano. De Falla's *Homage to Claude Debussy*, written for guitar and later arranged for both piano and orchestra, attests to the crucial importance of Debussy for de Falla, even as it succeeds in evoking unmistakably Spanish sights and sounds. De Falla was able to translate the typically Impressionist techniques of Debussy and Ravel (which conveyed impressions rather than direct statements) to a different cultural heritage, and to work with these techniques for both the guitar and the piano with equal effectiveness. This was a priceless asset for a Spanish composer who hoped to create a nationalist style, since the guitar had long been the most distinctive national instrument, employed by both the nobility and the peasantry for musical entertainment.

De Falla's best-known compositions are the *Fantasia for Piano and Orchestra, Nights in the Gardens of Spain* (1916), and the ballet *The Three-Cornered Hat* (1919), which was produced in London by Diaghilev's celebrated dance company. Some of the most brilliant and influential pianists of this century (e.g. Arthur Rubinstein and Wanda Landowska) befriended de Falla and helped to make his work known by including it in their concert programs. De Falla is also remembered as the piano teacher of the great Spanish poet and playwright, Federico García Lorca (1898–1936).

In England, no native composer had established a secure place in the musical repertory since the death of Henry Purcell in 1695. In the latter years of the nineteenth century, this gap began to be filled by Sir Edward Elgar (1857–1924) and Gustav Holst (1874–1934). But to **Ralph Vaughan Williams** (1872–1958) belongs the credit for reviving the English musical tradition, and for bringing it firmly into the twentieth century. Uncommonly prolific, Vaughan Williams composed in almost every musical form, from operas and symphonies to chamber music and short works for piano and voice. His musical style is reflective and evocative; a Vaughan Williams composition has something of the delicate Impressionism of Claude Debussy [see Chapter 14], something of the modernist boldness of Charles Ives [see above]. Two streams of influence inspired Vaughan Williams: the British tradition of folksongs and hymns (which he spent many years in editing and arranging), and a selection of European masters, particularly Bach and Handel from the Baroque period, and Debussy and Ravel from the late nineteenth and early twentieth century in France.

Vaughan Williams' music was thus colored by unusually disparate influences. It unites directness of purpose, an intense awareness of form, and a delicate suggestiveness of orchestral color that borders on symbolism. He was equally imaginative in handling pastoral and urban motifs. For example, his *Norfolk Rhapsody*, an orchestral tone poem composed in 1909, manages to capture the flavor of the English countryside: it is based on three folksongs from the region of Norfolk in Eastern England. The *London Symphony* of 1914 reflects the bustle and confusion of the great city, and focuses on a symphonic picture of the heart of the city: the river Thames. Here, Vaughan Williams' impressionistic technique is strongly reminiscent of the play of light and color on the river in the works of such painters as Claude Monet (1840–1928) and James McNeill Whistler (1834–1903).

Vaughan Williams' important compositions also include the romance for violin and orchestra entitled *The Lark Ascending* (1920) and the Fantasia on the old English tune *Greensleeves* (1934). He strove to create a truly national music whose art would be "an expression of the whole life of the community." To that end, he created a variety of untraditional pieces in addition to his formal works, e.g. music for films (as in *Scott of the Antarctic*, which was adapted into the *Sinfonia Antarctica* of 1952), and music for amateur performers, including the *Household Music* of 1941. Although Edward Elgar has a permanent place in British musical history (his *Pomp and Circumstance March* No. 1 has become virtually a second national anthem), Vaughan Williams—Elgar's successor—is widely acknowledged as the most original and influential British composer of the last 250 years.

Questions for Review

1. Identify Bedřich Smetana's *Má Vlast*. What was the purpose of this group of symphonic tone poems?

2. Why did Antonín Dvořák possess better credentials than Smetana for creating a Czech national music?

3. Identify and comment on:
   a) the *dumka* and its relationship to the music of Dvořák
   b) the circumstances of composition and the character of Dvořák's *Symphony from the New World*.

4. What is the significance of Charles Ives in the development of American music? Name one of Ives' major compositions.

5. How did Leos Janáček continue the search of Smetana and Dvořák for a Czech national music?

6. How did Edvard Grieg "put his country on the map"?

7. Identify Henrik Ibsen, and comment on Ibsen's significance in the career of Grieg.

8. What was the importance of France in the career of Manuel de Falla?

9. Which great twentieth-century Spanish poet was a piano student of de Falla in Granada?

10. Comment on de Falla's use of the guitar as a solo instrument.

11. What were some of the major influences on the music of Ralph Vaughan Williams?

12. In what respects can we compare the style of Vaughan Williams' *London Symphony* to that of such painters as Claude Monet and James McNeill Whistler?

13. How did Zoltán Kodály secure a place for Hungarian music?

14. Characterize the music of Jean Sibelius.

15. What nationalist feelings does Sibelius express in his famous symphonic work, *Finlandia*?

Answers

1. Smetana's *Má Vlast (My Country)* was a group of symphonic tone poems, composed 1874–79, whose purpose was to describe various prominent features of Czech national life.

2. Dvořák possessed better credentials than Smetana for creating Czech national music because he spoke Czech (as opposed to German) and grew up accompanying native folksongs and dances in the village band. He was influenced by Wagner and Brahms, but Dvořák's acquaintance with folk motifs was clearly reflected in his music.

3. a) The *dumka* is a Slavonic dance-form alternating very fast rhythms with a slow, melancholy lament. Dvořák incorporated the *dumka* in his *String Quartet in E-Flat*, as well as a number of other chamber works.

b) Dvořák composed his Symphony No. 9, *From the New World*, during his sojourn in New York as the director of a new musical conservatory. The symphony combines nostalgia for his Czech homeland with the excitement of American pioneers, free to explore a sprawling new continent.

4. Charles Ives is credited with the beginnings of a truly American style in serious music. His major compositions include *Three Places in New England*, the *Concord Sonata*, *Central Park in the Dark*, and the symphonic *New England Holidays*.

5. Janáček continued the search for a Czech national music by bringing his country's musical idiom into the twentieth century. This is especially marked in the operas *Jenufa* and *Kátya Kabanová*, where the vocal lines resemble the rhythms of actual speech and the orchestral score combines short melodic bursts with sudden changes in tonality and dynamics.

6. Grieg put his country, Norway, on the map through his power (especially in short piano pieces and songs) to suggest distinctively Norwegian landscapes and folk motifs.

7. Henrik Ibsen (1828–1906) was Norway's leading playwright and a pioneer of the Realist school of drama; his plays had a leading role in shaping new directions for modern drama in Europe and America. Grieg met Ibsen in Rome in 1866; eight years later, Ibsen invited the composer to furnish an orchestral suite as incidental music for the play *Peer Gynt* (based on a folk-hero of Norwegian legend).

8. Manuel de Falla's visit to France, where he met the composers Debussy, Ravel, and Stravinsky, was crucial in the development of a Spanish national style in music. The Impressionist techniques and harmonic experiments of these composers furnished de Falla with a musical framework with which to depict the sights and sounds of his native Andalusia, in music for piano, orchestra, and guitar.

9. Federico García Lorca (1898–1936).

10. De Falla's use of the guitar as a solo instrument (in such works as his *Homage to Claude Debussy*) is especially significant in the development of a Spanish national style, since the guitar was the favored instrument for both peasant

folk music and for aristocratic entertainment in Spain.

11. Vaughan Williams was influenced by English folk melodies and hymns; he also studied the music of Bach and Handel, and was affected by the Impressionist experiments of Claude Debussy and Maurice Ravel.

12. Vaughan Williams' *London Symphony* (1914) focuses on a picture in music of the Thames River. The music suggests, rather than states, the blurred interplay of light and color on the river, in much the same manner as the Impressionist paintings of Monet and Whistler.

13. Zoltán Kodály (together with his friend, the composer Béla Bartók) spent many years collecting and arranging Hungarian folk songs. The melodies, rhythms, and subjects of such songs were consciously incorporated by Kodály into his formal compositions, especially the nationalist musical play *Háry János* (1926).

14. Sibelius' music is marked by bleakness, breadth, and symphonic grandeur. His use of the orchestra manages to suggest the vast harshness of the Finnish landscape, the myths and legends of antiquity, and the Finnish yearning to be free from the domination of Russia. His symphonies and tone poems make extensive use of fragmented themes, which gradually come together in great, sustained climaxes.

15. *Finlandia* is a symphonic anthem proclaiming the majesty of the Finnish landscape and specifically commemorating the Finnish struggle for liberation from Russian overlords.

Chapter 13

The Mighty Fistful

The Mighty Fistful

There are always two kinds of music: the music of the people (for example, folk songs and religious hymns) and the formal music of the court and the concert hall. In the Russia of the Tsars up until the second half of the nineteenth century, the people and their music were despised, and true culture was thought to originate only in Western Europe. That is why Russian music was an imitation of French, German, and Italian music. Mozart or Haydn might use native children's songs as themes; but Russian composers considered everything Russian and non-European as inferior and barbarian. The court of the Tsars looked to the West for composers and performers. Italy was especially popular, and Italian musicians were regularly lured to the court at St. Petersburg (now Leningrad). Promising native composers were sent to Italy for study, on the theory that only in Europe could a musician learn his craft and polish an acceptable style.

This situation, however, began to change as a result of the philosophical tenets of Romanticism and nationalism. Russia was rich in native musical traditions: folk songs, music for native dances, the chants and other sacred music of the Orthodox Church, and music improvised for distinctive native instruments, such as the balalaika. Such material had been largely ignored prior to 1850. The development of a Russian style in music was linked with the systematic exploitation of these resources by a formally associated group of composers who consciously set out to write music with a "Russian sound". They called themselves the "Mighty Fistful"; sometimes they are referred to as the "Russian Five", or merely "The Five". These composers—Mily Balakirev, Modest Mussorgsky, Alexander Borodin, Nikolai Rimsky-Korsakov, and César Cui—were inspired by the founder of the musical nationalist movement in Russia, Mikhail Glinka. Their music explores the vast landscape of the mother country, the diverse folkways of the people, and the rhythms of Russian life itself. It is often inspired by Russian history and literature; and it exploits effects from native instruments such as the balalaika (a triangularly shaped, 3-string guitar with a distinctive resonant quality). It is paradoxical that, of the Mighty Fistful, only the founder of the group, Balakirev, was a professional musician. Mussorgsky was a soldier and minor civil servant, Borodin a distinguished chemist, and Rimsky-Korsakov a naval officer. Perhaps the very range in the backgrounds and careers of these composers aided them in their ambition to express uniquely Russian emotion and experience in their music.

Related to the Mighty Fistful, although not formally a member of their group, was Peter Ilyich Tchaikovsky. Composer of some of the world's most enduringly popular music, Tchaikovsky carried the movement a step further. He combined European and Western elements in his music, as in his personal style of life. Although some of his best-known melodies were written for the French-dominated ballet theater at St. Petersburg, he protested that he was "Russian, Russian, Russian" to the core of his soul. When we listen to the melancholy expressiveness of his last symphony, the *Pathétique*, we can hardly doubt him. Tchaikovsky's cosmopolitan taste and international success paved the way for acceptance of Russian music all over Europe. Fittingly, he was buried alongside three members of the Mighty Five (Mussorgsky, Borodin, and Rimsky-Korsakov) in St. Petersburg.

After Tchaikovsky, two composers foreshadowed new directions in the twentieth century, each in a different way. Alexander Scriabin believed in the possibility of music as a totally spiritual expression. Fascinated by mysticism, he aimed to translate soul into music in a way that had never been done before. For his tone poem *Prometheus*, first performed in 1910, Scriabin designed a light-board to accompany the instruments: flashing colors were intended to suggest or augment the listener's emotions and moods.

Igor Stravinsky, ten years younger than Scriabin, finally assured the complete integration of Russian music into the Western mainstream and the standard repertory. The first performance of Stravinsky's *Sacre du Printemps (The Rite of Spring)* in Paris in 1910 was a turning point in the development of twentieth-century music. The nationalist movement which had begun with Glinka some eighty years before became international with Stravinsky. Russia had not only succeeded in freeing herself from the domination of foreign musical styles; Russian music now became an international influence in its own right.

The first important composer in the development of Russian nationalist music is **Mikhail Glinka** (1804–1857). The son of a wealthy landowner, Glinka studied piano, violin, and harmony in St. Petersburg. He traveled abroad to pursue his musical studies, visiting such centers as Milan, Vienna, and Berlin in the 1830s. To this point, he was following the usual pattern for Russians who aspired to compose and perform. But Glinka remained Russian. He longed to create a truly national opera company, and returned to St. Petersburg after a relatively short period abroad. In 1836, he composed an opera which, although it is now rarely performed outside Slavic countries, is an important milestone in musical history, for it marked Glinka as the "father of Russian opera". Called *A Life for the Tsar*, this work is Russian through and through, in story, language, and music. The story recounts how the Poles, in 1613, plotted to capture the Russian Tsar, who was saved by the heroism of Ivan Sussanin. In his music, Glinka incorporated Russian folk tunes; he anticipated Richard Wagner's use of the *leitmotif* (a musical phrase repeatedly employed to suggest a specific character, object, or emotion [see Chapter 11]; and his harmony lent a new, richer color to the orchestra.

Six years later, Glinka's opera *Russlan and Ludmilla* (1842) had its first performance. The story was based on a tale of the poet Alexander Pushkin (1799–1837), who exerted a major influence on several Russian composers of the later nineteenth century. The plot, almost a fairy tale, deals with a beautiful woman, Ludmilla, who is rescued by the hero, Russlan, from an evil dwarf. The music features what is possibly the first use in the West of the whole-tone scale (C, D, E, F-sharp, G-sharp, A-sharp, C); other exotic elements included melodies from Persia.

Glinka's two operas were successful with the public; more important than their immediate success was the example he bequeathed to a slightly younger generation of composers, who were able to fashion from these beginnings a national style in a variety of musical forms.

Mily Balakirev (1837–1910) first met Glinka in St. Petersburg when Balakirev was eighteen. Drawn to music from an early age, Balakirev became the actual founder of the Mighty Fistful. Perhaps more important as a driving inspirational force than as a composer in his own right, Balakirev founded the Free School of Music in St. Petersburg in 1862. The concerts of the school featured the compositions of his friends Borodin, Mussorgsky, and Rimsky-Korsakov. Balakirev himself wrote two symphonies, a number of orchestral overtures, and various pieces for piano, including the virtuoso Oriental fantasy, *Islamey* (1869).

César Cui (1835–1918), like Balakirev, was more important to the Russian Five as a catalyst and critic than as a profoundly original composer. He wrote a number of operas, three string quartets, and various songs, piano pieces, and choral works. By profession he was an army engineer, not a musician. In 1917 Cui produced a completed version of Mussorgsky's unfinished opera, *Sorochintsy Fair*.

Without question, the most important member of the Mighty Fistful was **Modest Mussorgsky** (1839–1881). Mussorgsky met Balakirev in 1857, studied with him, and was a member of the Russian Five from the group's inception in 1861. Two of his compositions are staples of the repertory today: the opera *Boris Godunov* (1874) and the series of character pieces for piano entitled *Pictures at an Exhibition* (1874).

Pictures at an Exhibition consists of ten short pieces intended to suggest in music the actual pictures of a museum exhibition which Mussorgsky had seen in 1873; the show was a memorial exhibition for the Russian artist Victor Hartmann. Each piece has a title, ranging from the homely to the grand: examples are *The Gnome, The Old Castle, Baba Yaga,* and *The Great Gate at Kiev*. Most of the sketches are quintessentially Russian in their themes. They are linked by a haunting, stately melody (called *Promenade*) that recurs to represent the listener walking from picture to picture, as in a gallery. In addition to its original form as a solo work for piano, *Pictures at an Exhibition* has been arranged for orchestra several times—the most frequently heard orchestration is by the French composer Maurice Ravel.

Boris Godunov is now recognized as a unique masterpiece of the operatic repertory, even though when it was first produced its reception was disappointing. Its Russian qualities include the subject (which Mussorgsky adapted from Russian sources, including a verse play by Pushkin, for his own libretto); the melodies, especially those for the chorus, which assumes a major role in the opera; and the bold new harmonies. Mussorgsky, like Glinka, was influenced by the peculiar characteristics of Russian folk songs, the melodies of which tend toward an irregular repetition, in syncopated rhythm, of the same phrases. In *Boris*, Mussorgsky attempted to reproduce the rhythms of natural speech in the opera's vocal music, so there are few set pieces, or arias [see Chapter 12 on Janáček].

The story of *Boris Godunov* is based on the historical reign of the Tsar of that name in the early seventeenth century. Though controversy still surrounds the historical guilt or innocence of Boris, the opera assumes for dramatic purposes that Godunov had indeed ordered the murder of the young Dimitri, the rightful heir to the throne. In Act I, Boris is crowned Tsar, even though his agents give out that he is reluctant to assume power. In the "Coronation Scene", as the chorus cries *slava* ("glory"), Boris' quiet monologue betrays the onset of the guilt that will lead to fits of insanity, and eventually to his death. Grigori, a young monk, learns from the old chronicler, Pimen, a rumor of the Tsar's crime, and resolves to impersonate the young Dimitri and lead a rebellion against Boris' rule. Grigori gains crucial assistance from the cynical Marina, a Polish princess who allies her forces with his.

Meanwhile Boris Godunov, although he rules his people justly and compassionately, increasingly suffers the tortures of a guilty conscience. His agony is portrayed in the famous "Clock Scene" of Act II, where—in a hallucination—he thinks he sees the ghost of the murdered child among the small figurines of an ornamental clock. In a remarkable orchestral passage in this scene, Mussorgsky suggests both the striking of the clock and the throbbing terror within the mind of Boris. At the end of the opera, as the councillors gather, the Tsar bequeathes the kingdom to his young son Feodor, and collapses from a fatal attack. In a revised version of the work, a final scene is appended, in which a simpleton, meant to represent the common man, sings a mournful lament for Mother Russia as the rebellion against Boris' rule reaches its height.

Even though Boris only appears three times, for relatively short periods, in a long four-act opera, his personality completely dominates the drama. Much of the opera's dramatic power derives from Mussorgsky's skill in presenting Boris as a sympathetic character, despite his crime; surrounded by hypocrites and schemers, Boris meets a fate that may be deserved, but is simultaneously ironic. The other major "character" in the opera is the Russian people: one of the chief glories of *Boris Godunov* is its choral singing. Mussorgsky asserted that whenever he composed, his imagination was dominated by the vast panorama of the Russian people. But here too, in *Boris*, there is irony; for all his sympathy with the common people, Mussorgsky sees them as fickle and cruel, perhaps condemned always to suffer bitter cycles of repressive rule. The psychological tension of *Boris* is especially apparent in the "Coronation Scene", where the piercing dissonant chords of the orchestra, the giant notes of the cathedral bells, and the ebullient choral song are all pointedly contrasted with the quiet, haunted lyricism of Boris' monologue.

Boris Godunov is almost completely independent of the other great European operas of the nineteenth century. It was only in Russia, perhaps, that Mussorgsky could have escaped the influence of Richard Wagner in Germany, Charles Gounod and Georges Bizet in France, and the great Italian composers Gioacchino Rossini and Giuseppe Verdi. The musical achievement of *Boris* is even more impressive when we recall that Mussorgsky was not extensively trained in harmony and orchestration. In fact, the original orchestration of the opera was considered so unsatisfactory that it was revised several times: first by Mussorgsky himself, and then by such composers as Nikolai Rimsky-Korsakov and Dimitri Shostakovitch. The Rimsky-Korsakov version of the opera was the one most frequently performed until 1975, when a corrected edition of Mussorgsky's original music was published.

Alexander Borodin (1833–1887) accomplished for Russian chamber music what Mussorgsky had achieved in the grander form of opera. A brilliant scientist, Borodin was persuaded by Mily Balakirev (whom he met in 1862) to devote his leisure hours to musical study and composition. Borodin's two string quartets import a decidedly Russian, oriental atmosphere into chamber music. The occasion of the second was highly personal; it was written to celebrate the twenty-fifth anniversary of the composer's engagement to his wife. In addition to the quartets, Borodin is remembered for his symphonic tone poem, *In the Steppes of Central Asia*; the very title indicates some of the exotic flavor of the music. He also composed an opera, *Prince Igor*, on a uniquely Russian subject; but he did not live to complete it. As with many composers of the nationalist school, Borodin favored Russian folk melodies and dance rhythms in much of his work.

Nikolai Rimsky-Korsakov undertook to complete *Prince Igor* after

Borodin's death, and the opera was first performed in St. Petersburg in 1890. It has fallen out of the standard repertory of the world's leading opera houses, but is still occasionally revived.

Nikolai Rimsky-Korsakov (1844–1908) was in many ways the most versatile of the Mighty Fistful. He wrote 15 operas, the form of composition in which he was most prolific. Almost completely self-taught in music, Rimsky-Korsakov wrote the first notable Russian symphony (1865). Although he knew little of harmony and counterpoint, he was named a professor of composition at the St. Petersburg Conservatory. He rose to the post, educating himself from books, from wide exposure to the music of others (especially Richard Wagner), and in the most practical way he could: by composition. His talent for rich and thrilling orchestration appears in the colorful pieces, *Capriccio espagnol*(1887), *Sheherazade*(1888), and the *Russian Easter Overture*(1888). One of his best-known short works is the virtuosic sketch, *The Flight of the Bumble Bee*.

Like the other composers of the Mighty Fistful, Rimsky-Korsakov was strongly influenced by Russian folk tunes; and, as in the music of Alexander Borodin, his harmonies are often colored by non-traditional, dissonant chords. His most famous pupil was Igor Stravinsky [see below]; the influence of his music is perceptible in Stravinsky's early period of composition. Rimsky-Korsakov's operas include: *Snow Maiden* (1881), *Sadko* (1886), *A Bride for the Tsar* (1898), and *Le Coq d'Or (The Golden Cockerel)* (1907). *A Bride for the Tsar* is especially notable for its grand Italian scale, combined with uniquely Russian feeling. The plot concerns the love of Tsar Ivan the Terrible for a beautiful girl, Marfa. Marfa, in turn, loves Lykov, and is herself pursued by Gryanznoy. The latter attempts to win Marfa's affections by means of a love potion; but Gryanznoy's jealous mistress substitutes poison for the magic drink. Marfa falls fatally ill, and goes mad when she hears that Lykov has been wrongly executed by the Tsar for the crime.

There is probably no nineteenth-century composer whose music is more popular (in its direct appeal to large numbers of listeners) than **Peter Ilyich Tchaikovsky** (1840–1893). Tchaikovsky's most famous compositions include his six symphonies (especially the last, in B minor, called the *Pathétique*), the *1812 Overture*, the overture to *Romeo and Juliet*, the first piano concerto in B-flat minor, the violin concerto, and three ballets: *Swan Lake*, *The Sleeping Beauty*, and *The*

Nutcracker. Almost any random sampling of Tchaikovsky's music reveals its tunefulness, its rich orchestration, and its powerful expressiveness. Tchaikovsky is an arch-Romantic: he writes for the heart, rather than for the head. He appeals directly to the listener's feelings—although the notion that his work is carelessly structured and purely emotive, current for some years, is now dismissed by music scholars.

There is doubtless much of Tchaikovsky's tempestuous life in his music. After studying law, he went to Moscow in 1866, where he became acquainted with the nationalist group of composers. While he admired their efforts to create music that was truly Russian, he never became a formal member of the Mighty Fistful. His sympathies and interests were too broadly cosmopolitan for him to restrict himself to a single tradition. Like his personal tastes in art, books, and style of dress, his music is a fusion of West and East; among European composers, he especially admired Mozart and the Frenchman, Georges Bizet (1838–1875).

Tchaikovsky became a professor of harmony at the Moscow Conservatory in the late 1860s, but his personal life turned tragic after a disastrous marriage to one of his pupils. For a time, he enjoyed the patronage of a wealthy widow, Mme. von Meck, but in 1890 she withdrew her support and his fits of melancholy grew ever stronger. He died four days after the first performance of the *Pathétique* Symphony in 1893—possibly from cholera, although recently discovered evidence suggests that he poisoned himself.

Although Tchaikovsky was criticized by some of his contemporaries for being too "Western", he always maintained an image of himself as Russian to the core of his soul. *Eugene Onegin* (1879), considered his best opera, is based on a Russian subject: a poem by Alexander Pushkin about the tragic love of an older man for a young girl. The *1812 Overture* commemorates the historic defeat of the Emperor Napoleon when he attempted to invade Russia. And although Tchaikovsky composed for the ballet theaters in Moscow (the Bolshoi) and St. Petersburg (later the Kirov Ballet), which were dominated by French influences at the time, it is impossible to ignore the Russian flavor in the music of *Swan Lake* or *The Nutcracker*.

Many regard the Symphony No. 6 (*Pathétique*) as Tchaikovsky's masterpiece. The title was suggested by the composer's brother, and means "full of passion" or emotion, rather than "pathetic" in the usual sense of that word. The first movement opens solemnly and slowly, with the theme sung by the bassoon. In the second movement, Tchaikovsky uses a modified waltz tempo (5/4 rather than 3/4 rhythm) for a spirited effect; but this movement closes as the first began, in a contemplative, almost melancholy fashion. The third movement, a scherzo, is the loudest and most brilliant in the symphony. It strongly contrasts with the mournful, fatalistic tone of the last movement, where the finale is almost a lamentation.

The most idiosyncratic of the Russian composers was **Alexander Scriabin** (1872–1915). He can hardly be called a nationalist; and he is as much a forerunner of Modernist music as a Romantic. A brilliant pianist (who was the classmate of Sergei Rachmaninoff at the Moscow Conservatory), Scriabin began by composing short works for the piano, very much in the manner of Frédéric Chopin and Franz Liszt. But he soon found his Romantic models inadequate for the expression of his ultimate ideal in music: a direct expression of man's innermost soul. He turned to more and more dissonant harmonies, to strange and unexpected chord progressions, and to utterly untraditional rhythms. Instead of the usual short piano forms—Mazurkas, Études, and Nocturnes—Scriabin wrote tone-poems for piano with such titles as *Desire, Satanic Poem,* and *Toward the Flame*. His pieces made unprecedented technical demands on the soloist; one of Scriabin's foremost champions in recent decades was Vladimir Horowitz, whose mastery of piano technique make him one of the few performers equal to the task of playing the works of Scriabin.

Scriabin's mysticism led him to dream of a perfect union of the arts, in which sight and sound would reinforce the same, ultimate revelations of spiritual being. (Compare, in some respects, Richard Wagner's theory of a *Gesamtkunstwerk*, or "total work of art" in opera [see Chapter 11]. Scriabin designed a lightboard for the first performance of his tone poem *Prometheus* (1910); certain colors were to be flashed electrically in the concert hall at various points in the score. At his death, he was hoping to compose a mystical drama for a cast of two thousand, in which color, perfumes, poetry, and music would all play a role. Although he did not live to complete this project, Scriabin's piano works have established him as one of the visionary forerunners of a Modernist idiom in music.

The development of Russian music begun by Glinka comes to an ironic culmination in the work of **Igor Stravinsky** (1882–1971). The irony lies in the fact that, although Stravinsky was the only Russian composer whose work itself influenced (rather than was influenced by) the mainstream of European composition, Stravinsky himself had been forced to flee his homeland by the Communist Revolution of 1917.

Stravinsky was born into a musical family (his father was a singer in the Imperial Opera) and became a pupil of Rimsky-Korsakov at the St. Petersburg Conservatory. His earliest works—including the ballet *The Firebird* (1910)—are characterized by exotic melodic and harmonic content, and especially by brilliant orchestral writing. As a very young man, Stravinsky became associated with the ballet impressario Serge Diaghilev whose troupe, the *Ballets Russes* (Russian Ballet), drew together the finest dancers, choreographers, scenic designers, and composers of the early twentieth century. So successful was *The Firebird* that Diaghilev commissioned another work—*Petrushka*— from Stravinsky the following year. In this ballet, although Stravinsky relinquished nothing of the Russian sound inherited from Rimsky-Korsakov, there is a disturbing dissonant quality that is in keeping with the fantastic plot, which concerns a love triangle among a troupe of Punch and Judy puppets that have been mysteriously brought to life. This dissonance was to find its full expression in Stravinsky's third major work, *Le Sacre du printemps (The Rite of Spring)*, first performed in Paris in 1913.

The disjunctions of modern life and new fashions in modern thought had created an interest in man's tribal prehistory, and Stravinsky seized on this as the central topic of *Le Sacre*. The ballet is divided into two sections. In the first, a number of springtime rituals are depicted: games between rival cities, athletic contests among adolescents, Maypole dances. In the second section, a sacrificial maiden dances herself to death. The music draws on every available resource: untraditional scales, extreme dissonance, violent rhythms, all bound together by perhaps the most virtuosic orchestral writing achieved to that point. Combined with modernistic sets and eccentric choreography by the danced Vaslav Nijinsky, the work induced a riot at its premiere and launched Stravinskly firmly into the avant garde.

Today the work is often cited as the composition which inaugurated modern music, though certain basic elements were already in place nearly fifty years before in Wagner's *Tristan und Isolde* [see

225

Chapter 11] and in the works of Claude Debussy [see Chapter 14]. One has only to compare *The Rite of Spring* with Tchaikovsky's *Sleeping Beauty*, first produced only twenty years before in 1890, to see how far Stravinsky had taken the basic elements of music: harmony, rhythm, and melody. It is perhaps no accident that *The Rite of Spring* was written and performed in Paris, for Paris was the center of Modernism in the arts; among Stravinsky's acquaintances at this time were the painter Pablo Picasso (1881–1973) and the surrealist playwright Jean Cocteau (1891–1963).

Stravinsky enjoyed a long and productive life, creating a body of music which will surely place him among the musical masters of all time. He composed in a broad variety of forms: symphonies, ballets, chamber music, songs, and operas. Like Johann Sebastian Bach—whose music he revered—Stravinsky modified every form in which he worked, making it uniquely his own. Like his contemporary, Picasso, he experimented relentlessly with different styles, and a number of "periods" can be distinguished in his music. We have already noted the influence the Russian nationalistic influence of his teacher Rimsky-Korsakov, which culminated in the three ballets already mentioned. After the extremes of *The Rite of Spring*, Stravinsky turned to a more simple, starkly severe style which has been called "Neo-classicism", in which he invoked the spirit of the eighteenth and nineteenth centuries, combining their elegance and grace with piquant twentieth-century harmony and rhythm. Subsequently, he became interested in the "Serialism" of Arnold Schoenberg [see Chapter 14], although he practiced this technique in his own way and the musical results are unmistakably Stravinsky. Like his idol, Tchaikovsky, he was an eclectic, never attaching himself to a specific school. He was as interested in sacred music as in American jazz, as attracted to Russian folk music as to the most cerebral compositional theories of the avant-garde.

The latter portion of his life was spent in New York and Southern California, yet he remained quintessentially Russian. Classical myth, folk tunes, circus dances, and nonsense verse all formed part of his inspiration, but—despite his use of many sources and his extraordinary knowledge of the music of the past—his work is never derivative or in direct imitation. On the contrary, Stravinsky managed to draw from the resources of a vast variety of forms, periods, and models to create a personal, distinctively modern idiom.

Questions for Review

1. Why was Russia so late in developing a national style in music?

2. Name some of the major musical traditions in Russia which were largely ignored until the second half of the nineteenth century.

3. What was the importance of Mikhail Glinka? Name one of Glinka's operas.

4. Identify the group of nineteenth-century Russian composers who were nicknamed the "Mighty Fistful".

5. What did Modest Mussorgsky say about the relationship of the Russian people to all his musical compositions? How is this statement specifically borne out in his opera, *Boris Godunov*?

6. Was *Boris Godunov* successful when it was first presented? Who undertook to revise the opera?

7. Why is the title character in Mussorgsky's opera plagued by guilt?

8. What was the relationship of Russian literature to the nineteenth-century "nationalist" composers? Which poet was especially significant to them?

9. Who was the founder of the Mighty Fistful?

10. How did Tchaikovsky successfully bring together the styles of East and West?

11. Describe Tchaikovsky's importance as a composer for ballet. Name two of his works in this form.

12. What was Tchaikovsky's relationship to the "Russian Five"?

13. Why is Tchaikovsky's music so popular?

14. What was Alexander Scriabin's primary objective in his music? Describe the innovations of his tone-poem, *Prometheus*.

15. What is ironic about the culmination of Russian national music with the work of Igor Stravinsky?

16. When and where did the premiere of Igor Stravinsky's *The Rite of Spring* take place? Why was this event such an important turning point in the development of Russian music?

Answers

1. Russia lagged behind other European countries in developing a national style because, until the middle of the nineteenth century and the advent of the Mighty Fistful, Russian music deliberately imitated the styles of the West (especially the Italian styles).

2. Some of the major traditions in Russia which were largely ignored include Russian sacred music (e.g. chants of the Eastern Orthodox Church), folk songs, dance tunes, and native instruments (such as the balalaika).

3. Mikhail Glinka was the founder of the Russian nationalist movement in music. Although he traveled widely in Europe for musical training, he remained Russian. His operas (e.g. *A Life for the Tsar* and *Russlan and Ludmilla*) treated distinctively Russian subjects, and their musical style was influenced by folk melodies, Russian dance rhythms, and the harmonies of popular music.

4. The Mighty Fistful consisted of the following five composers: Mily Balakirev, Modest Mussorgsky, Alexander Borodin, Nikolai Rimsky-Korsakov, and César Cui.

5. Mussorgsky asserted that whenever he wrote music, the vast panorama of the Russian people dominated his imagination. In *Boris Godunov*, with its many crowd scenes and important role for the chorus, we possess ample illustrations of the truth of his assertion.

6. *Boris Godunov* was not successful when it was first presented. (In fact, even after the revision of 1874, the opera was withdrawn after just 25 performances.) The most influential revision after Mussorgsky's death was that of Nikolai Rimsky-Korsakov, whose version was first presented in 1896.

7. Boris is plagued by guilt because of his responsibility for the murder of young Dimitri, the rightful heir to the throne.

8. Russian literature (by which is meant both formal literature and folkloric materials) inspired the nationalist school with specifically Russian subjects for their work. Especially important was the early nineteenth-century poet and playwright Alexander Pushkin (1799–1837), whose works furnished the basis for Mussorgsky's *Boris Godunov* and for Tchaikovsky's *Eugene Onegin*.

9. The founder of the Mighty Fistful was Mily Balakirev, who was the only professional musician of the group.

10. Tchaikovsky successfully united the styles of East and West by combining distinctively Russian feeling and melody with a wide range of influences from the mainstream of Western music down to his day. Among Western composers, he especially admired Mozart and Bizet.

11. Tchaikovsky composed for two notable ballet theaters: the Bolshoi in Moscow and the Imperial Ballet Theater (later the Kirov Ballet) in St. Petersburg (now Leningrad). The exquisite fantasy of his plots, the lyric grace of his music, and his tuneful expressiveness have made Tchaikovsky's ballets some of the most popular in the repertory of dance. Works such as *Swan Lake*, *The Sleeping Beauty*, and *The Nutcracker* are staples of modern ballet

companies all over the world.

12. Tchaikovsky admired the nationalist aspirations of the Russian Five but was never formally associated with the group. They, in turn, came to regard Tchaikovsky's music as insufficiently "Russian".

13. Tchaikovsky's music is popular for a variety of reasons. His melodies speak directly to human emotions. The powerful sense of fate that is evoked in works such as the *Pathétique* Symphony unfailingly moves listeners. Tchaikovsky's orchestration is brilliant and colorful (listen, for example, to the *1812 Overture*). And the Romantic sweep and grandeur of his music are often irresistible, as in the opening theme of the *First Piano Concerto* in B-Flat Minor.

14. Scriabin's primary objective in his music was to translate his very soul into sound. In his tone poem *Prometheus* he employed non-traditional means, such as his famous "light-board" to reinforce emotions and moods.

15. The irony is that the culmination of Russian national music was reached in the compositions of a man who was in self-imposed exile from Russia because of the Communist Revolution of 1917.

16. Stravinsky's *Rite of Spring* had its first performance in Paris in 1913. The work provoked a riot which launched Stravinsky into the avant garde as one of the foremost of twentieth-century composers.

Chapter 14

The Turn of the Century

The Turn of the Century

By 1900, the rich vein of Romanticism in music seemed played out to many. Wagner and Brahms had explored the tradition stretching back to Beethoven—Brahms its more conservative elements and Wagner the most radical ones. Several generations of nationalistic composers had expressed the spirit of their countries in the Romantic idiom.

Just as the early Romantic composers, a century before, had been determined to liberate music from what they considered the constraints of Classicism, so the composers of the early twentieth century sought to escape the limitations of Romanticism itself. Though the music of the past eighty years has evidenced a broader diversity of styles and techniques than at any previous time in the history of music, the composers of the twentieth century are united in their quest for an unknown objective.

Two manifestations of this quest are apparent. The first (and shorter-lived) was outward in its direction. For the first time in Western music, composers became seriously interested in the arts of the Orient. Railways and steamships had opened the Far East to Europeans and Americans in the second half of the nineteenth century; the painting and poetry of China and Japan became known and even fashionable in European capitals. Where music had been written to celebrate the familiarity of the composer's own nationality, it now reached outward to embrace the exotic elements of far-distant places.

The second manifestation was inward: the reflection of a neo-humanism perhaps best expressed in the philosophy of Friedrich Nietzsche and the psychology of Sigmund Freud. This direction had its roots in Romantic self-expression, though music reflected the more general concern with the darker side of human nature.

The Italian **Giacomo Puccini** (1858–1924), perhaps the greatest successor of Giuseppe Verdi [see Chapter 11], created operas which exemplify both of these new directions. Like Verdi, Puccini possessed a remarkable gift for creating memorable, singable melodies. At the same time, he had little taste for Verdi's princes, courtesans, and Shakespearean figures. Nor was he interested in Wagner's gods and mythic heroes. Rather, he chose stories concerned with everyday events, realistic settings, and believable characters. This style of opera is known as *verismo* (literally, "truthfulness"), and is a musical manifestation of the Realist movement in late nineteenth-century literature.

Puccini's first genuine masterpiece, *La Bohème (The Bohemian)*, met mixed reviews when it was first produced in 1896, although it has since become one of the most popular works in the entire repertory. The libretto was adapted from the French Realist novel, *Scènes de la vie de Bohème (Scenes from Bohemian Life)* by Henri Murger, one of a group of novelists of the 1840s and 50s who explored the darker side of Parisian life: the poor, the crippled, the criminal. The plot recounts the unhappy love affair between Rodolfo, a struggling artist, and Mimi, an impoverished and consumptive seamstress. Set against the background of Paris on Christmas Eve—which allows a particularly festive scene at a rowdy café—the work tugs at the audience's emotions with frankly melodramatic intent. The popularity of the opera rests, not on subtlety, but rather on the vocal and dramatic displays which it permits to its cast.

Following *La Bohème*, Puccini turned to more exotic settings—in particular, two plays by the American theatrical entrepreneur David Belasco. These became the operas *Madama Butterfly* (1904) and *La Fanciulla del West (The Girl of the Golden West)* (1910). The latter work features the sheriffs, outlaws, and saloons of frontier America—an "exotic" scene to early twentieth-century Italians.

Madama Butterfly is one of two Puccini operas set in an Oriental locale; the other is his unfinished last work, *Turandot*, set in ancient China. Again a tragedy, *Madama Butterfly* recounts the story of Cio-Cio-San, a beautiful geisha girl living in Japan soon after Commodore Perry's landing which opened that country to the West in the nineteenth century. She rejects tradition, family, and religion in order to marry the American naval officer Pinkerton. Shortly afterwards, he is required to leave for America but promises to return to her. Three years pass; Cio-Cio-San bears Pinkerton's child and awaits his return with unwavering faith. In the opera's last act, the American fleet returns (symbolized musically by strains of *The Star-Spangled Banner*). Cio-Cio-San is ecstatic, but not for long. Word reaches her that Pinkerton has indeed returned—with his American wife. Cio-Cio-San realizes that she has been betrayed, that Pinkerton has thought of her as little more than a butterfly—a charming exotic creature suitable for a brief dalliance, but not to be brought back to his homeland. The American wife asks Butterfly for the child. She agrees; but when Pinkerton arrives in person, she commits suicide, redeeming her honor in the traditional way of her own nation.

Madama Butterfly, like *La Bohème*, draws on Puccini's greatest compositional strengths: an inexhaustible fountain of melody, a flair for the melodramatic, a sure hand at harmonic and orchestral color. From late Verdi (and also Wagner), Puccini learned the value of continuous stage action and a seamless orchestral web. From his predecessors, too, he learned how to use the orchestra to comment—ironically or sympathetically—on the stage action.

Like Claude Debussy [see below], Puccini explored new techniques of harmonic progression and orchestral color. He was especially adept at including exotic effects which were appropriate to the far-away settings of some of his operas. Thus, in *Madama Butterfly* and *Turandot*, we hear distinctively Oriental rhythms and melodies; the orchestral sound is often colored by percussion instruments (e.g. gong and chimes). Finally, Puccini wrote with remarkable economy: a few phrases of dialogue (generally quite close to the rhythms of actual speech) and a few notes in the orchestra suffice to establish the mood of an entire scene. He was not afraid to experiment with untraditional effects: e.g. the beautiful humming chorus at the end of Act II of *Madama Butterfly*, which so pathetically evokes Cio-Cio-San's loyalty as she watches through the night until sunrise for the return of Pinkerton's ship to the harbor of Nagasaki.

Other Puccini operas which are staples of the international repertory today include *Manon Lescaut* (1893), *Tosca* (1900), and the comic one-act opera *Gianni Schicchi* (1919).

One of the most original figures in the history of music was the Frenchman **Claude Debussy** (1862–1918), important not only for his own compositions but for the vast influence which he exercised on other composers. He studied piano at the Paris Conservatory in the 1870s and, in the summer of 1880, journeyed to Russia as the pianist in a trio employed by Tchaikovsky's patron, Mme. von Meck [see Chapter 13]. His acquaintance with Russian music was deepened by a detailed study of the score of Mussorgsky's opera *Boris Godunov*. Debussy was especially impressed by the close correlation between the rhythms of Mussorgsky's vocal lines and those of everyday speech. On a later visit to Rome, Debussy came under the influence of Franz Liszt; the music of Richard Wagner also had a profound impact on him. All of these disparate influences were surpassed by the impact of the Far East. At the Paris Exposition of 1889, Debussy first encountered Oriental visual art as well as the music of the Indonesian *gamelan*, an instrumental ensemble consisting predominantly of tuned percussion instruments [see Chapter 1] such as gongs, xylophones of different sizes, as well as drums. Combined with the influence of Impressionist painting and Symbolist poetry of the 1880s and 90s, the culture of the East revealed to Debussy the artistic possibilities of indirect suggestion rather than direct statement. In addition, the strange harmonies of the gamelan, not tuned to any Western scale, suggested the potential of music based on hitherto unexplored harmonic principles.

One of Debussy's first significant orchestral works was the *Prélude à l'Après-midi d'un faune (The Afternoon of a Faun)*, based on a poem by the Symbolist Stéphane Mallarmé. The work is evocative rather than powerful, its melodies and harmonies shimmer in an indistinct haze rather than move directly and forcefully. The musical structure of the work is closely linked to the structure of the poem, which led many critics to scorn it initially because of its untraditional form.

Debussy had turned away from Romanticism. Although he himself did not appreciate the analogy, it became traditional to refer to Debussy's music by a term borrowed from art history: Impressionist. For the grandeur of Wagner's orchestration, Debussy substituted delicate, sensuous sonorities. Though his orchestras were as large as Wagner's, he employed the forces in an entirely different way. In place of the harmonic system that had dominated music since the time of Bach, Debussy experimented with effects based on the medieval modes, as well as a number of special scales which he made up himself under the influence of Oriental music. His music often floats between keys, much as the waterlilies in the paintings of Claude Monet are suspended in a shimmer of light.

From 1892 to 1902, Debussy devoted most of his energies to a single work: the opera *Pelléas et Mélisande*, based on a drama of the contemporary playwright Maurice Maeterlinck. The opera was given its first performance in Paris at the Opéra-Comique in 1902; although the story has a medieval setting, the music announces the twentieth century in opera more clearly than does any work of Puccini. Short scenes, which are better described as tableaux, are linked by a continuous orchestral web of sound. Both dramatic action and musical accompaniment are supremely economical, and the orchestral effects are tightly integrated with the vocal line, which manages to simulate actual speech even as it maintains a supreme lyricism.

In 1905, Debussy's orchestral tone poem, *La Mer (The Sea)*, had its first performance. It is probably his best-known work. *La Mer* is a remarkably evocative picture of the sea in all its moods; at times, the orchestra suggests brilliantly sparkling reflections of light and color on a calm ocean, and at other times the regular rhythmic swells and angry waves. Debussy was undoubtedly influenced in the form of the work by Franz Liszt, who had invented the symphonic poem; but the harmonies and rhythmic structure were totally his own.

Debussy's predilection for program music is apparent not only in the *Prélude à l'Après-midi d'un faune* and *La Mer*, but also in his piano works, which served to open a new era in the music of this solo instrument. Especially significant are the two books of *Préludes* (1910 and 1913), each bearing a title (e.g. *The Wind in the Plain, What the West Wind Saw, The Interrupted Serenade,* and *The Submerged Cathedral*). The titles of the preludes, which often reflect the mingling of senses popular in symbolist imagery (e.g. *Sounds and Perfumes Mix in the Evening Air*), are some indication of the delicately exotic tone of the pieces themselves. Deliberately untraditional chords (ascending and descending in block-like intervals of sevenths and ninths) are combined with highly syncopated rhythms in Debussy's piano music. Just as Beethoven and Schumann inaugurated Romantic music for the piano, Debussy's subtle artistry opened new possibilities for the instrument in our century.

Arnold Schoenberg (1874–1951) is the most revolutionary of this group of composers. Born in Vienna, Schoenberg studied the violin and the cello in youth; he was not formally trained in harmony, but received some lessons in counterpoint from the conductor Alexander von Zemlinsky. Schoenberg, like most German-speaking musicians in the late nineteenth century, had to reckon with Richard Wagner's powerful influence. Early in his composing career, he showed signs of breaking away from Wagner's ultra-Romantic style. Ironically, the means to this end was one that Wagner himself had provided: the break with classical harmony exemplified in such works as *Tristan* and *Parsifal*.

Whereas Claude Debussy cultivated a distinctively French style—impressionistic, mysterious, and ultimately graceful—Schoenberg looked inward, to explore new intensities and complexities of emotion in music. If Debussy may be compared to the Impressionists in painting, who sought to suggest (rather than directly state) the external world, Schoenberg is closer to the school of Expressionist painters and playwrights: artists whose goal was to plumb the depths of inner reality and to express the most profound emotions, using whatever means were appropriate, no matter how untraditional. Expressionism is an even more drastically subjective style in the arts than Impressionism: the artist purposefully imposes his own vision of psychological truth, and intentionally distorts external reality to conform to that personal view. (Notable exponents of expressionism include the dramatists Luigi Pirandello and August Strindberg, the painters Edvard Munch and Oskar Kokoschka, and the sculptor Ernst Barlach. It is significant that one of the most fertile grounds for the growth of Expressionism in the arts was the Vienna of the young Arnold Schoenberg. In 1903, Schoenberg's first major full-length work (*Verklärte Nacht*, or *Transfigured Night*) clearly showed that he had embraced the new movement. Composed for a string sextet (two violins, two violas, and two cellos), the piece portrayed the nightmare of a tortured mind, unable to rest because of a tormented love affair.

Schoenberg became a noted teacher in Berlin and Vienna, and his experiments in harmony (both in his own works and with his students) led to far-reaching consequences. Encouraged by both Richard Strauss and Gustav Mahler [see below], both of whom professed not to understand his new style, he contemplated a total break with the classical harmonic rules that had dominated Western music since the early seventeenth century. Schoenberg is generally regarded as the father of modern atonality (meaning, literally, "without tonality"): music that exhibits no fixed key on which harmonies were traditionally erected.

The first major work of Schoenberg to display distinctively atonal style was *Pierrot Lunaire (Moonstruck Pierrot)* (1912), a mini-drama or cycle of songs for contralto with a chamber ensemble of eight instruments played by five players (violin interchanging with viola, cello, flute interchanging with piccolo, clarinet interchanging with bass clarinet, and piano). In 1911, Schoenberg published a textbook on harmony, *Harmonielehre*; and in 1912, he extended his theories in the *Five Orchestral Pieces*. Because of the hostility which these works encountered when they were first performed, Schoenberg founded with his students a society for private musical performances, which excluded the critics. After World War I, Schoenberg developed a new system for the organization of atonal music, a theory first exemplified in the *Five Piano Pieces* (Opus 23) and the chamber work *Serenade* (Opus 24); both works were first performed in 1923. They were organized through a method known as serialism: all twelve notes of the chromatic scale were introduced in a specific order, or series, which then governed every harmonic and melodic aspect of the works. Variations of the series were permitted: the order of notes could be turned upside down (inversion), or appear backwards (retrograde form), or in a combination of both (retrograde inversion). Although the system may sound complex and artificial, it is scarcely more arbitrary than the classical rules of harmony. Schoenberg employed it in a variety of later works, although he disconcerted his followers periodically by abandoning serialist music and atonality for more traditional, tonal harmonies. Perhaps the culmination of his work was the opera *Moses und Aron (Moses and Aaron)*, first conceived in 1930, and revised until the composer's death in 1951. Schoenberg lived to complete only two of the opera's three acts, which were composed to his own libretto.

Schoenberg's influence in twentieth-century music is not only due to his own works. He also exercised a powerful sway over a number of disciples; because of their master's initial rejection by the musical establishment, his pupils maintained an almost fanatical devotion to him. The most important followers of Schoenberg were the composers **Alban Berg** (1885–1935) and **Anton Webern** (1883–1945). Berg began private lessons with Schoenberg in 1904; his commitment to the atonal technique in composition was evident as early as the String Quartet (Opus 3) of 1910. Although Berg was not a prolific composer, his influence on twentieth-century music was profound: especially significant were his two operas, *Wozzeck* (1925), which was based on the pioneering Expressionist play of the same name by Georg Büchner (1813–1837), and *Lulu* (1935), adapted from two plays of Franz Wedekind (1864–1918). Both works were Naturalistic in that they dealt with the sordid realities of everyday life; they also employed markedly Expressionistic techniques, since the music conveyed the tortured, inner souls of the chief characters in decidedly untraditional fashion.

Anton Webern, two years older than Berg, came to study with Schoenberg in the same year, 1904. He became a conductor of operettas in various cities in Germany in the World War I period; after the war, he was active as a conductor in Vienna. In the years before World War II, he maintained an important contact with England, and was regularly invited by the British Broadcasting Corporation as a conductor in the late 1920s and early 1930s. His music (like that of Kurt Weill [see Chapter 15] was proscribed as subversive by the Nazis after 1933, and he was forced to work as a publisher's proof-reader during World War II. At the end of the war, he was accidentally shot by an American sentry. Webern's compositions, which have influenced an entire generation of leading modern composers [see Chapter 16], are marked by their strict atonality and extreme brevity. A great admirer of the medieval composers, Webern resembles—in some of the mathematical complexity of his work—such masters as Johannes Ockeghem [see Chapter 3]. Webern's principal works include the *Concerto for Nine Instruments*, two cantatas, *Five Canons* for voice and instrumental accompaniment, the *Symphony for Chamber Orchestra*, Opus 21 (1928), and the choral composition, *Das Augenlicht (Light of the Eyes)* (1935).

Not all composers in this period were as radical as Schoenberg, Berg, and Webern. Perhaps the most conservative major musician of the 1890s was **Richard Strauss** (1864–1949). Strauss made his mark early as a conductor; a child prodigy who was born into a musical family, he was that rare phenomenon among musicians, a legend in his own time. Early in his composing career, he adopted the form of the symphonic tone poem, which had been invented by Franz Liszt. Strauss' success was such that many lovers of late Romantic music associate the form exclusively with him. His symphonic poems became established in the international repertory almost immediately after their first performances. The composer was hailed as the successor of Johannes Brahms and Richard Wagner. Strauss' leading tone poems of this period are *Aus Italien (From Italy)* (1886), *Macbeth* (1888), *Don Juan* (1889), *Tod und Verklärung (Death and Transfiguration)* (1890), *Till Eugenspiegel* (1895), *Also sprach Zarathustra (Thus Spake Zoroaster)* (1896), *Don Quixote* (1898), and *Ein Heldenleben (A*

Hero's Life) (1899). The tone poems were inspired by a broad variety of sources. Strauss' own tour of Italy led to *Aus Italien; Macbeth* and *Don Quixote* were responses to Shakespeare's tragedy and Cervantes' novel; *Also sprach Zarathustra* (used as the theme music for the popular film, *2001*) was inspired by a prose-poem of the contemporary German philosopher, Friedrich Nietzsche (1844–1900). In *Till Eugenspiegel,* Strauss playfully explored aspects of a medieval German legend; in the tone poem, the horn represents the mischievous hero, Till.

After the turn of the century, however, Strauss reversed himself. After his fundamentally conservative orchestral works, he pioneered a new style in opera: sensuous, lushly post-Romantic, and sensational, both in its dissonance and in its subject matter. Opera offered Strauss the chance to display his remarkable gift for orchestration in a longer, more ambitious form. However, Strauss established his operatic fame with two "shockers", both one-act works. These were *Salome* (1905) and *Elektra* (1909). *Salome* was based on Oscar Wilde's play of the same name; first performed in Dresden, the opera reeked of decadence and caused a furor. Many denounced the work as obscene, although it was an adaptation of the Biblical narrative of Salome's attempted seduction of John the Baptist, imprisoned by her father, King Herod the Great.

Elektra, which inaugurated Strauss' remarkably productive collaboration with the poet Hugo von Hofmannsthal, was just as offensive to many critics. Based on Sophocles' ancient Greek tragedy, the plot recounts Elektra's obsession with avenging her murdered father, Agamemnon. Both works were uncompromising in their presentation of sensual lust and bloodthirsty vengeance; both featured shocking finales—the repulsive fondling of John the Baptist's severed head by Salome, and the triumphal dance of death by Elektra after her brother has slain their mother. In both works, Strauss employed an enormous orchestra of over a hundred players; his uncanny ability to suggest through the orchestra the bizarre and perverse turns of plot is evident from listening even to short extracts.

Just as abruptly as he had changed his style in 1905 with *Salome,* Strauss now proceeded to a totally different subject: a romantic comedy of manners, set in eighteenth-century Vienna. This was *Der Rosenkavalier (The Cavalier of the Rose)* (1911). Delicate and lyrical, the opera captures perfectly the social mores of an entire era in its plot;

its music epitomizes the style and grace of Europe's most musical city. *Der Rosenkavalier* entered the international operatic repertory immediately after its premiere; although Strauss was to compose ten more operas over a period of thirty years, none has rivaled *Der Rosenkavalier* in popularity.

Strauss never became allied with the Schoenberg school of atonality and serialism: the closest approach he made to this style was in *Elektra*. His music descends from the German tradition of Mozart (whom he greatly admired), Mendelssohn, and Wagner. In his later operas, the vocal line tends more and more to the conversational; and his remarkable gifts in composing for voice were employed in a series of first-rate *Lieder*. He may be seen as the last composer in a certain tradition of music: magnificently imaginative and rich in his technical invention, yet looking basically toward the past, rather than the future. His best-known later operas include: *Ariadne auf Naxos*(1912), *Die Frau ohne Schatten (The Woman Without a Shadow)* (1919), *Intermezzo* (1924), *Arabella* (1933), and *Capriccio* (1942).

Strauss' dual reputation as composer and conductor is paralleled by the career of his contemporary and friend, **Gustav Mahler** (1860–1911). Mahler, like Claude Debussy, was also attracted in his youth to Oriental themes and Eastern art: a selection of poems from the ancient T'ang dynasty in China became the basis for his great symphony for orchestra and voice, *Das Lied von der Erde (The Song of the Earth)* (1909). Mahler studied at the Vienna Conservatory and then held a succession of conducting posts in Prague, Budapest, and Hamburg. He conducted the premiere of his own First Symphony in 1889; in 1897, he achieved major success in the musical world of Vienna by being named director of the Court Opera, a post he retained until 1907. During this period, he continued to compose symphonies, song cycles, and a cantata entitled *Das klagende Lied (The Song of Sorrow)*, which was first performed in 1901.

Despite his professional success as a conductor and the friendship of Richard Strauss and Anton Bruckner, Mahler was ill at ease. His conducting duties left him little time to compose; as a Jew in turn-of-the-century Vienna, he felt himself an outsider, both socially and culturally. At a deeper level, this introspective artist was profoundly disturbed by the psychoanalytical theories of Sigmund Freud, which came to prominence around 1900. Mahler experienced alienation, a morbid and inexplicable sense of dread, and conflicting emotions that he poured into his music: his ten symphonies constitute a sustained, psychological self-portrait. The Adagio, or slow movement from the Tenth Symphony in F-Sharp Major, which Mahler left unfinished when he died, furnishes a good illustration of the anguish that tormented the composer.

The typical Mahler symphony contains almost a mirror of the composer's disquieted soul. Deeply attracted to nature, Mahler juxtaposes simple, almost child-like passages with complex polyphony; he uses unconventional forms, involving vocal parts in a number of the symphonies; and some of his music anticipates Schoenberg's atonality in its extreme chromaticism. Many have felt that the contrasts in style and mood of Mahler's symphonic works typify the period itself: an era of contradictions and conflicting tendencies in music, when there was little certainty except the inevitability of change. Mahler seems to look both forward and backward simultaneously: his symphonies nostagically evoke the Romantic era even as they face the more complex realities of a new century. Anton Bruckner, whom Mahler admired, had erected his enormous symphonic structures on the sure foundation of religious faith. Mahler's music, which rivaled that of Bruckner in its scale, was at the other end of the spectrum, in that it grew from a prolonged scrutiny of modern man's spiritual crisis. Events were to prove Mahler closer to the mainstream of twentieth-century music.

Questions for Review

1. Give two specific examples of the ways in which European fascination with the Orient is reflected in music at the turn of the twentieth century.

2. What were Giacomo Puccini's objectives in opera?

3. Name two of Puccini's operas.

4. Briefly summarize the plot of Puccini's *Madama Butterfly*.

5. Define Impressionism in the arts. How does Impressionism differ from Romanticism?

6. Which contemporary French poet's works were especially significant for the young Claude Debussy?

7. Name two of Debussy's most influential works.

8. How was "outward exploration" complemented by "inward exploration" in music of this period?

9. Describe some of the specific ways in which Arnold Schoenberg revolutionized music.

10. Name two of Arnold Schoenberg's most influential disciples.

11. Identify briefly:

    a) atonality

    b) serialism

    c) *Till Eugenspiegel*

12. What was Schoenberg's objective in his early piece, *Verklärte Nacht*? What is the meaning of the title?

13. Why may the early works of Richard Strauss be called conservative? Which two composers of the nineteenth century did Strauss seem to be following in his early works?

14. What musical form did Strauss favor in his early compositions?

15. Name two of Strauss' best-known operas.

16. Why did Gustav Mahler feel himself to be an outsider in turn-of-the-century Vienna?

17. How do the symphonies of Mahler simultaneously look backward and forward in time?

Answers

1. Two examples of composers' fascination with the Orient around the turn of the century: Debussy's interest in Oriental visual arts and the Indonesian gamelan at the Paris Exposition of 1889; Gustav Mahler's interest in ancient Chinese poetry, which served as the basis for his symphonic poem, *Das Lied von der Erde* (1909). One may also add Puccini's operas, two of which are set in the Orient: *Madama Butterfly* and *Turandot*.

2. Puccini's objectives in opera were to present realistic stories of everyday life (as in *La Bohème*) and to explore exotic locales (as in *Madama Butterfly*, *Turandot*, and *La Fanciulla del West*).

3. Puccini's operas include: *Manon Lescaut*, *La Bohème*, *Tosca*, *Madama Butterfly*, *La Fanciulla del West*, *Gianni Schicchi*, and *Turandot*.

4. In *Madama Butterfly*, the American naval Lieutenant Pinkerton marries the beautiful Japanese geisha, Cio-Cio-San. He calls her Madame Butterfly and their life together seems at first to be blissfully happy. But Pinkerton deserts Butterfly (who bears his child) to return to America, saying only that he will one day come back to Japan to claim her and his child. Three years pass.

When Pinkerton returns, he brings with him an American wife; it is evident that he has considered his relationship with Butterfly as nothing but a brief dalliance. The humiliated heroine agrees to surrender their child, and then commits suicide.

5. Impressionism in the arts (poetry, painting, and music) refers to a style of suggestion, rather than direct statement. The external world makes an impression on the artist's mind, and he then renders that impression (which may include some distortion and/or symbolism) in his art. Impressionism differs from Romanticism in that the chief aim of the latter style is the authentic statement of personal emotion; Impressionism is a generally cooler, more detached style.

6. The French poet who was especially significant for the young Claude Debussy was the Symbolist Stéphane Mallarmé. Debussy composed an orchestral tone-poem based on Mallarmé's work, "L'Après-midi d'un faune".

7. Debussy's influential works include: the two books of piano *Préludes*, the symphonic poem *La Mer*, and the opera *Pelléas et Mélisande*.

8. "Outward exploration" in the music of this period refers to the interest of many composers (e.g. Puccini, Mahler, and Debussy) in foreign musical traditions and settings; "inward exploration" refers to the tendency to plumb the depths of the human unconscious mind. Such a psychoanalytic approach was encouraged by the theories of Sigmund Freud; we have hints of this approach in the music of Mahler, Richard Strauss, and Arnold Schoenberg.

9. Schoenberg revolutionized music by radically departing from the traditional harmonic system, which was designed on the major and minor keys. He experimented with atonal music (compositions in no fixed key); later in his career, he imposed a logical system on atonality, i.e. serial composition, in which each note of the twelve-tone scale appeared in a fixed order in any given work. Schoenberg also borrowed some of the techniques of Expressionist painting: his music used all available means to express the inner soul of the composer—often distorting external reality in order to impose the artist's vision upon it.

10. Two of Schoenberg's most influential disciples: Anton Webern and Alban Berg.

11. a) atonality: the technique of composing music in no fixed key (or tonic system).

b) serialism: a compositional technique invented by Arnold Schoenberg in which all twelve tones of the chromatic scale are regularly employed in a predetermined order.

c) *Till Eugenspiegel*: popular symphonic tone poem by Richard Strauss, which he composed in 1895. It was based on a medieval German legend about a mischievous hero (represented in Richard Strauss' work by the French horn).

12. *Verklärte Nacht (Transfigured Night)* was a musical description of a tormented love affair.

13. The early works of Richard Strauss may be called conservative because their harmonies and orchestration seemed to be following the example of Johannes Brahms and Richard Wagner.

14. Strauss favored the form of the symphonic tone poem in his early works.

15. Strauss' best-known operas include: *Salome* (1905), *Elektra* (1909), *Der Rosenkavalier* (1911), *Ariadne auf Naxos* (1912), and *Die Frau ohne Schatten (The Woman Without a Shadow)* (1919).

16. Mahler felt himself socially ostracized as a Jew in turn-of-the-century Vienna. Because of his conducting duties, he had little time to devote to composing. And the psychoanalytical theories of Freud, when combined with the composer's instrospective nature, led to a series of morbid conflicts and anxieties in Mahler, many of which seem reflected in his music.

17. Mahler's symphonies look back to the Romantic era in their lyricism; but their unconventional form and psychological insight seem to adumbrate many typical motifs of twentieth-century art, literature, and music.

Chapter 15

War and Peace

War and Peace

Artistic expression develops in relation to contemporaneous events and ideas: sometimes it is a result of these events and ideas, at other times a reaction against them. As we approach our own time and become more familiar with the facts and the emotions, we can evaluate this relationship between creative art and historical event more closely. Thus, we can trace the effect of the two World Wars (1914–1918 and 1939–1945), not only in political and social ways, but musically as well.

Long before the outbreak of World War I, many poets, painters, and musicians were convinced that the Romantic idiom in art was inadequate for the realities of modern, urban man. Claude Debussy and Arnold Schoenberg revolutionized harmony in music; writers like T.S. Eliot (1888–1965) employed a new language for poetry; Pablo Picasso (1881–1973) and the Cubists radically altered form in painting. Impressionism in the arts yielded to Expressionism: the use of all available means to express the inner, psychological realities of the human spirit.

On the eve of World War I, the determination of artists to probe beneath the surface of ostensibly civilized society was exemplified in Igor Stravinsky's iconoclastic ballet, *The Rite of Spring* (1913); untraditional harmonies, pulsating rhythms, and a plot based on a pagan ritual of human sacrifice made the ballet so controversial that a riot broke out at the premiere in Paris. Stravinsky's music seemed to possess no relation to what had gone before; like Debussy and Schoenberg, many of whose works provoked public confusion and scorn, Stravinsky was one of the founders of the avant-garde in music—although now, with the benefit of historical perspective, we may compare him to Beethoven in his dynamic attempt to create a new musical language, one more in keeping with the world of his time.

If Stravinsky's *Rite of Spring* seemed to anticipate the first barrage of guns trained on an old order, the music of the 1920s displays a heady relief that World War I was over. Ten million people had perished, the political map of Europe was redrawn, and a cultural and artistic world had been swept away. In 1919, Edward Elgar (1857–1934) dedicated his last major work, the *Cello Concerto in E Minor*, as a Requiem for all those who had died in the conflict. The work furnishes a superb illustration of the elegiac power of the cello as a solo instrument. Elgar's music seems to look backward in time; it is a last, nostalgic farewell to the nineteenth century. In the 1920s, however, a new generation of composers was determined to take music forward—either in the atonal style pioneered by Arnold Schoenberg and his disciples Alban Berg and Anton Webern, or in new styles of tonal music. One of the principal influences on the tonal music of the period was jazz, a form of popular music that profoundly affected the works of some of this century's outstanding composers: Erik Satie, Scott Joplin, Paul Hindemith, Darius Milhaud, George Gershwin, and Maurice Ravel.

The derivation of the word "jazz" itself is obscure: it may be connected with the Creole patois of Southern America (especially New Orleans), where jazz first emerged around the turn of the century. Jazz flourished prominently (although not exclusively) among Black musicians; it combined West African rhythms, traditional European harmonies, and some features of American Protestant religious music (especially Gospel-singing). Known also as ragtime, jazz first flourished as an improvisatory style; its origins were in instrumental music, with the piano as the most popular instrument. Gradually, the highly syncopated instrumental solos (often called rags) began to be written down; and jazz paralleled (and sometimes mingled with) another genre, the "blues". Blues music was influenced by Negro spirituals of the nineteenth century; invariably containing melancholy themes and harmonies, blues as a vocal form made the transition from oral folk tradition to the printed page more swiftly, once the form took hold. One of the most famous combinations of jazz and blues in this period was the *St. Louis Blues* of the Black composer, W. C. Handy (1873–1958).

In America, the popularity of jazz soon led to the development of diverse sub-forms: the instrumental "Dixieland" style (featuring trumpet, piano, saxophone, trombone, and drums, or a combination of these instruments); the big jazz bands of the 1920s, which added strings; the "swing" music of the 1930s (dominated by virtuoso instrumentalists such as Benny Goodman on the clarinet); and the improvisational compositions of one of the greatest exponents of the form, Duke Ellington (1899–1972).

One of the most significant early jazz composers was the Black pianist, **Scott Joplin** (1868–1917). Joplin's piano "rags" have lately enjoyed a revival; but at the time they were composed, the majority of listeners did not associate them with "serious" music. Joplin improvised on the piano in St. Louis and Chicago bars in the 1890s; around the turn of the century, he came to New York and settled there, hoping that his music could secure a more respectful (and respectable) audience. His leading works include the *Maple Leaf Rag*, *The Entertainer*, and the *Wall Street Rag*, as well as the first jazz opera, *Treemonisha* (1911). Joplin's music was neglected, however: *Treemonisha* received only a single performance (without scenery) in 1915, and the composer's disappointment at its failure led to his own early death.

The "jazz craze" quickly spread to the large cities of America, and thence to Europe, where it was especially prominent in Paris after World War I. Although Joplin did not know it, he had worked in a vein that was to become highly significant for modern composers. In 1919, Igor Stravinsky celebrated the end of World War I with a work called *Piano Rag-Music*. Remarkably, Stravinsky had heard very little American jazz at the time; but he was intrigued by the possibilities of combining its earthiness and rhythmic vitality with more traditional classical forms. Stravinsky was not alone: the 1920s witnessed a stream of diverse, jazz-inspired works.

Erik Satie (1866–1925) was one of the first French composers to be attracted by the flamboyant, humorous aspects of jazz. In his one-act ballet, *Parade*, he employed jazz rhythms; the work was first produced in Paris in 1917, in collaboration with the playwright Jean Cocteau (1891–1963) and Pablo Picasso, who designed and executed the stage set. Satie's approach to music was similar to that of Claude Debussy, whom he had met in 1890; both composers sought a new style in French music, sparer and more economical than the lush expansiveness of Romanticism.

But whereas Debussy is clearly an Impressionist composer, Satie's playful, drily humorous music resembles the approach of the Surrealists in painting: Salvador Dalí, Paul Klee, and Joan Miró. In Surrealism, which is an extreme form of Expressionism, the world is turned inside out and upside down; the proportions and outlines of objects are often radically distorted; and whimsical juxtapositions illustrate the irrationality and absurdity of life. Thus, Satie playfully included the sounds of a typewriter and a steamship whistle in the instrumentation of *Parade*; his piano pieces were often accompanied by bizarre commentaries, as in the *Three Waltzes of the Fastidious Dandy*; some pieces have absurdist titles (as in *Three Pear-Shaped Pieces* of 1903, which actually contains six works for piano). He often wrote chords that lacked harmonic resolution; and in some of his pieces, the bar-lines (basic in the musical notation of rhythm) were totally omitted.

In 1922, the French composer **Darius Milhaud** (1892–1974) journeyed from Paris to New York to play his own piano works in concert. Milhaud was associated with Erik Satie and Jean Cocteau in the group of artists known as "Les Six" ("The Six"); in 1920, he based a ballet on Cocteau's early surrealist play, *The Wedding on the Eiffel Tower*. Milhaud's New York trip brought him into contact with jazz; he visited Harlem at the height of the so-called Harlem Renaissance. Upon his return to France, he composed a jazz-inspired ballet, *La Création du monde (The Creation of the World)*, which was produced in 1923 with set designs by the avant-garde painter, Fernand Léger.

Six years after Milhaud crossed the Atlantic, the young American composer **George Gershwin** (1898–1937) visited Paris. Gershwin spent his youth as a song-writer and composer of popular musicals for Broadway. Like many other composers of the period, he was intrigued by the challenge of bridging popular and concert styles; he admired Igor Stravinsky as much as he loved jazz. His early work, *Rhapsody in Blue* (1924), might be described as a new type of piano concerto: in a work of substantial length, Gershwin combined soaring melody, jazz rhythms and harmonies, and classical form.

In Paris, Gershwin hoped to learn more of European musical styles. The visit of 1928 inspired his "rhapsodic ballet" again for piano and orchestra, entitled *An American in Paris*, in which Gershwin described in music the wonder and excitement of a visiting tourist, whose "blues" are dispelled when he leaves a small café in Paris to look around the great city. This work, together with *Rhapsody in Blue*, is now one of the staples of the concert repertory.

Gershwin's premature death, at the age of 39, is one of the tragedies of American music. Besides his best-known orchestral works, he composed one of the few American operas which is regularly performed: *Porgy and Bess* (1935). He was also the author of hundreds of popular songs (*I Got Rhythm*, *Embraceable You*, *Fascinating Rhythm*, and *Swanee*), as well as some of the best shows of the musical theater in the 1920s: *Strike Up the Band*, *Show Girl*, *Girl Crazy*, etc. Scott Joplin's ambition to be regarded as a serious composer was fulfilled in the career of Gershwin; but both men would have undoubtedly accomplished much more, had they lived longer.

Also in Paris in the 1920s was the Russian composer **Serge Prokofiev** (1891–1953). Prokofiev's early work centered on opera and ballet; his *Love for Three Oranges* was commissioned by the Chicago Opera (first performed in 1921), and the great impresario of the dance, Serge Diaghilev, offered him commissions for a number of ballets. (Diaghilev's associations with the leading composers and artists of the time are a fascinating sidelight in this period; the list includes Matisse, Picasso, Utrillo among the painters, and the composers Milhaud, Satie, Debussy, Falla, Stravinsky, Prokofiev, Poulenc, Richard Strauss, and Ravel.)

Prokofiev was popular in Paris for the same reason that a number of other avant-garde artists flourished; his music—dry, dissonant, and humorous—sounded almost insolent. It was designed to shock. Dissonant chords alternated with puckish melodies; listen, for example, to the famous march from *Love for Three Oranges*. Although Prokofiev, like Stravinsky, seemed to break entirely with tradition in his music, we can now see him in the direct line of the nineteenth-century Russian nationalists [see Chapter 13], adapting a lyrical style to the bleak realities of modern life, with a dash of pungently satirical wit. His greatest works include the opera *War and Peace* (1942), which was based on Tolstoy's novel; the Symphony No. 5 (1945); the ballet *Romeo and Juliet* (1935); and the endearing suite for narrator and orchestra, *Peter and the Wolf* (1936). The latter remains one of the most entertaining and instructive guides to the instruments of the orchestra.

Maurice Ravel (1875–1937), like a number of the composers of this period, was profoundly affected by World War I, in which he served as a stretcher-bearer. Ravel's music was inspired by a variety of sources (Debussy, Mussorgsky, Orientalism, jazz); but he managed to forge a cool, personal style, in which his facility at orchestration and technical mastery are the outstanding features. Stravinsky called him a "Swiss clock-maker"; but if we listen to the *Piano Con-*

certo in G (1931), the lyrical melodies which seem to long for order, calm, and peace make the criticism seem somewhat unfair. Ravel is perhaps best known for the tour-de-force *Boléro* (1928). Originally a ballet score, it is often performed by the orchestra without sets or choreography. *Boléro* consists of a sequence of repetitions of only one melody: each repetition is in the same key (C Major) and in constant rhythm. Although the piece is often dismissed as a "war-horse" of the repertory, it serves as an index to Ravel's skill in exploiting effects of orchestral color and dynamics. Other notable works by Ravel include: the ballet *Daphnis and Chloe* (1911), the symphonic poem *La Valse (The Waltz)* (1920) (originally a ballet score), the *Rhapsodie espagnole (Spanish Rhapsody)* for orchestra (1907), and the opera *L'Enfant et les sortilèges (The Child and the Spells)* (1925).

The explosion of jazz in America and Europe of the 1920s thus involved experimentation in "serious music" on both sides of the Atlantic. In Germany, jazz became the vehicle for social satire in the hands of **Kurt Weill** (1900–1950), who incorporated the genre in a new style of popular opera in Berlin of the 1920s. A period of moral decadence and economic crisis did not encourage in Germany the optimism of a Gershwin or the cool detachment of a Ravel. Weill collaborated with the renowned playwright Bertolt Brecht (1898–1956) and the popular singer Lotte Lenya (who became Weill's wife) in *The Rise and Fall of the City of Mahagonny* (1929) and in *Die Dreigroschen Oper (The Threepenny Opera)* (1928); the latter was an updated version of John Gay's popular *Beggar's Opera* [see Chapter 6]. Just as Gay's work satirically presented the London underworld of thieves and prostitutes in the early eighteenth century, Weill and Brecht presented an acerbic picture of Berlin cabaret life between the World Wars [compare the satirical art of the German-born painter George Grosz (1893–1959)]. Both Brecht and Weill were condemned by the Nazis when Adolf Hitler came to power in 1933; both fled Germany, eventually for the United States. *The Threepenny Opera* was successfully produced in New York in 1954, with an English libretto by Marc Blitzstein; the song *Mac the Knife* became its remarkably popular trademark.

Another German, **Paul Hindemith** (1895–1963) spent his early career in Frankfurt as a member of a string quartet, and as the first violinist of the city's opera orchestra. He quickly established a reputation as a controversial, avant-garde composer of chamber music and one-act operas. His *Suite for Piano (1922)* combines superficially jaunty elements from jazz with sinister tones that recall the horrors of World War I. Hindemith is often associated with the Bauhaus school of functional architecture, founded in Germany by Walter Gropius (1883–1969); this school swiftly became known for its adaptations of modern technology to design and construction. The musical equivalent of this utilitarian approach is known as *Gebrauchsmusik* ("utility music"). Hindemith, for example, wrote sonatas for almost every orchestral instrument; he composed *Sing- und Spiel Musik (Music to Sing and Play)* to combine teaching and entertainment; and he wrote operatic and choral works for children. Hindemith's most frequently-performed work is the opera *Mathis der Maler (Matthias the Painter)* (1935); the first performance took place in Switzerland in 1938, since Hindemith's music had been banned as subversive in Nazi Germany (as had that of Mendelssohn, which was deemed unfit for Nazi ears because Mendelssohn's grandfather was Jewish).

Hindemith became an American citizen in 1945; during a prolonged sojourn in the United States, one of his pupils was the American conductor and composer, Leonard Bernstein. Hindemith's conception of "functional" music, freely borrowed from popular genres like jazz, and accessible to the whole community, may be compared to the ideals of the English composer, Ralph Vaughan Williams [see Chapter 12].

Like Hindemith, Brecht, and Weill, the Hungarian composer **Béla Bartók** (1881–1945) was forced into exile by the Second World War; he, too, took refuge in the United States. Bartók may properly be considered a nationalist composer, since he made the ethnic music (folk songs, dances, etc.) of Hungary his life study, as did his compatriot Zoltán Kodály [see Chapter 12]. But Bartók's significance transcends nationalism; there are those who rank him as the fourth "B", after Bach, Beethoven, and Brahms. Like Debussy, Ravel, and other composers of the first half of the century, Bartók opened up new possibilities for the piano as a solo instrument. His music treated the piano as essentially a percussion instrument, rather than as the expressive vehicle for lush Romantic composition. Listen, for example, to Bartók's *Sonata for Two Pianos and Percussion* (1937), which includes xylophone, cymbals, and drums in what amounts to a work of percussion chamber music. It was in chamber music and piano solo works that Bartók felt most at home; his *Mikrokosmos* (153 "progressive pieces for piano") has become a staple of the teaching repertory on the piano, while his six string quartets unite a Classical sense of form with innovative harmonic and structural procedures.

The greatest symphonic composer of the World War II period was the Russian **Dmitri Shostakovich** (1906–1975). Shostakovich had a conventional conservatory training in Petrograd; he was encouraged by Alexander Glazounov, the composer who had been a friend of Liszt and the pupil of Rimsky-Korsakov. In 1926, he offered his First Symphony as his diploma-composition at the conservatory; performed in Leningrad and Moscow, it earned world fame for the young composer. Shostakovich's career illustrates the ambiguities and difficulties of the musician in a modern, totalitarian society; he professed an unwavering dedication to socialism, but because of quirks in Soviet ideology, his loyalty to the state was subjected at several points to ruthless attack. Memoirs attributed to him (though doubt has been cast on their authenticity) were published in 1976. They suggest that Shostakovich became privately disillusioned with Soviet life, and that his mature works reflect the inner misery of.a man condemned to live a lie.

What is indisputable, however, is the extraordinary power of Shostakovich's music. He composed fifteen symphonies, fifteen string quartets, two piano concerti (the first also features the trumpet as a solo instrument), several operas and ballets, a variety of works for chorus and solo voice, and (like his countryman Serge Prokofiev) a string of successful film scores. Some critics have argued that the quality, range, and variety of Shostakovich's music justify the accolade of his being called this century's greatest composer. Nearly all his music is distinguished by great emotional tension. In the symphonies, he is best considered as a successor to Gustav Mahler, since he juxtaposes apparently simple, childlike passages with the complex, the intense, and the technically difficult. Like the symphonies of Anton Bruckner, those of Shostakovich are massive edifices of sound: many are over an hour in length. Themes are continually fragmented, only to coalesce again in great climaxes. The mood of the orchestra ranges from tragic sublimity to mordant sarcasm. Shostakovich often indulges in musical quotation, borrowing of specific themes from his own works or those of other composers for a particular effect. Solo instruments (e.g. trumpet, violin, or clarinet) emerge from the web of sound in a totally individual fashion; they are often deliberately employed at the extremes of their ranges (high or low), in tensely evocative passages.

Perhaps Shostakovich's most famous work is his Symphony No. 7 in C Major, the *Leningrad*, specifically written as a response to the siege of that Russian city by the Germans in 1941–42. Shostakovich served as a fire-fighter in the conflict, in which a quarter of a million people perished. Driving rhythms combine with menacing passages for percussion and brass to suggest the horrors of World War II. Shostakovich's work was immediately accepted as an artistic summation of that dark time, not only in Russia, but in England and the United States as well.

In 1958, and again in 1974, Shostakovich paid visits to England, where he became a close friend and admirer of the composer **Benjamin Britten** (1913–1976). During World War II, Britten was an outspoken pacifist; he dedicated his great *War Requiem* (1962) to the memory of all who were killed in the World War, and to the universal hope for the end to all wars. The work was first performed at the opening of the new Anglican Cathedral in Coventry, a city in the English Midlands which had been severely damaged by German bombing raids during the war. A deliberate reminder of humanity's power to destroy, the civic and ecclesiastical authorities left standing the bombed shell of the old Cathedral, directly across from the new structure. Britten's *War Requiem*, considered by many critics to be his masterpiece, similarly juxtaposed the old and the new: the traditional Latin text of the Requiem Mass alternates with nine poems by Wilfred Owen (1893–1918), the gifted British poet whose career was tragically cut short in the trenches of World War I.

Britten's works have secured his reputation as the most significant British composer of this century, after Ralph Vaughan Williams [see Chapter 12], and as one of the few twentieth-century composers who have forged an effective style in opera. He was primarily gifted as a composer for voice, and his operas, song cycles, and choral works have been firmly established in the international repertory. Many were composed with specific artists in mind: notably Britten's friend, the English tenor Peter Pears, and the German baritone Dietrich Fischer-Dieskau. Britten deeply admired Alban Berg, the leading exponent of atonal music in the early 1930s, and was influenced by Berg's operas, *Wozzeck* and *Lulu*. Despite this admiration, his own music is not strictly atonal: he employs conventional harmonic structures, as well as hints of *polytonality* (writing in several keys). Britten has been of incalculable importance in modern British music, both by virtue of his works and through the Aldeburgh Festival in Suffolk, which he founded in 1948. His principal works include the operas *Peter Grimes* (1945), *Billy Budd* (1951), *The Turn of the Screw* (1954) based on the short novel of Henry James, *A Midsummer Night's Dream* (1960), and *Death in Venice* (1973) based on the novella of Thomas Mann; the choral *Spring Symphony* (1949); *A Ceremony of Carols* (1942) for boys' voices and harp; and the symphonic song-cycle *Our Hunting Fathers* (1936), based on a text by the poet W. H. Auden.

Questions for Review

1. What continuing theme may be discerned in the musical works of many composers between 1918 and 1945?

2. Identify Igor Stravinsky's *The Rite of Spring*. What was the subject of this work? When was it first performed? Why did audiences find it so disturbing?

3. To whom was Edward Elgar's Cello Concerto of 1919 dedicated?

4. What were some of the sources of jazz music? When and where did jazz first emerge as a popular genre?

5. Name at least one noted American composer of jazz.

6. List some of the European and American composers of "serious" music on whom jazz had a marked influence.

7. Define Surrealism. Explain the connection between the Surrealist movement and the French composer Erik Satie.

8. Identify briefly the following:

    a) *Treemonisha*

    b) *Suite for Piano (1922)*

    c) Wilfred Owen

    d) "Swing" music

9. From what musical source did Béla Bartók derive much of his inspiration? What was Bartók's approach to the sound of the piano?

10. Identify briefly the following:

    a) Darius Milhaud

    b) *Leningrad* Symphony

c) Serge Diaghilev

11. What is remarkable about the form of Maurice Ravel's work, *Boléro*?

12. Name one of the satirical operas of Kurt Weill and Bertolt Brecht.

13. What is the form of Benjamin Britten's *War Requiem*? What were the circumstances of this work's first performance?

14. Name one of Britten's operas.

Answers

1. The response to war (especially the two World Wars of 1914–1918 and 1939–1945) has been a continuing theme in the works of twentieth-century composers, just as it has dominated much of modern literature and painting.

2. *The Rite of Spring* is the title of Stravinsky's ballet, first produced in Paris in 1913. The untraditional harmonies, syncopated rhythms, and peculiar plot of the work (it simulated a primitive ritual of human sacrifice) so shocked the audience at the premiere that a riot broke out.

3. Elgar's Cello Concerto of 1919 (his last major work) was dedicated as a Requiem to all those who perished in World War I; it is a valedictory to an old order, which was destroyed forever by the Great War.

4. The sources of jazz music include: West African rhythms, traditional European harmonies, and features of American Gospel-singing. Jazz first emerged as a popular genre around the turn of the century in cities of the American South, especially New Orleans.

5. Noted composers of American jazz include W. C. Handy, Scott Joplin, Duke Ellington, and George Gershwin.

6. Some European composers who were notably influenced by jazz include: Erik Satie, Paul Hindemith, Igor Stravinsky, Darius Milhaud, and Maurice Ravel.

7. Surrealism (which André Breton founded in 1924) is an extreme form of Expressionism in the arts. It literally means "beyond the real"; images, sounds, and words are distorted to transcend reality, in an effort to convey an accurate impression of the interior state of the artist. Some of the techniques of Surrealism later became popular among the "absurdist" school of writers and artists. Prominent Surrealist painters include Salvador Dalí, Paul Klee, and Joan Miró. Erik Satie was connected to the Surrealist movement by virtue of the fanciful titles for his works (e.g. his *Three Pear-Shaped Pieces* and *Three Waltzes of the Fastidious Dandy*), the dry, economical humor of his musical style, and his collaboration with the noted Surrealist playwright, Jean Cocteau. Just as Cocteau introduced machines as characters in some of his plays (e.g. *The Wedding on the Eiffel Tower*), Satie provided for machine-like noises in the scores of his works (e.g. the ballet *Parade*).

8. a) *Treemonisha*: the first jazz opera, composed by Scott Joplin in 1911, but neglected during the composer's lifetime.

b) *Suite for Piano (1922)*: an early work of the German composer Paul Hindemith, heavily influenced by jazz, which combined superficial jauntiness with sinister undercurrents that evoked the horror of World War I.

c) Wilfred Owen: the British poet (1893–1918) killed in World War I whose remarkably moving works on trench-warfare were employed as texts by Benjamin Britten in his *War Requiem* (1962).

d) "Swing" music: the term applied to the music of American big bands in the 1930s, which often featured solo virtuosi (e.g. Benny Goodman on clarinet).

9. Bartók derived much of his inspiration from Hungarian national folk songs and native dances. His approach to the piano was essentially as a composer for a percussion instrument (as in the Sonata for Two Pianos and Percussion of 1937).

10. a) Darius Milhaud: French composer whose visit to Harlem in New York (1922) inspired the jazz style of his ballet, *La Création du monde* (1923).

b) *Leningradt21* Symphony: the nickname of Dmitri Shostakovich's Symphony No. 7 in C Major, specifically written as a response to the siege of Leningrad by the Germans in 1941–42. The composer served as a fire-fighter in the conflict, in which a quarter of a million people were killed.

c) Serge Diaghilev: the Russian ballet impresario, whose productions at the Ballets Russes in Paris transformed the world of dance between 1909 and 1929. Diaghilev enlisted the talents of a remarkable number of front-rank artists, dancers, and composers during this period, e.g. Nijinsky, Balanchine, Picasso, Matisse, Ravel, Stravinsky, Falla, Prokofiev, Satie, Milhaud, and many others.

11. Ravel's *Boléro* consists of a series of repetitions of a single theme, in strict, unvarying rhythm. Composed as a one-act ballet score in 1928, it made its composer world famous.

12. The satirical operas of Bertolt Brecht and Kurt Weill are *Die Dreigroschenoper (Threepenny Opera)* (1928) and *The Rise and Fall of the City of Mahagonny* (1929).

13. Benjamin Britten's *War Requiem* (1962) alternates the texts of the Latin Mass with the poems of the British writer Wilfred Owen, who was killed in World War I.

14. Britten's operas include: *Peter Grimes* (1945), *Billy Budd* (1951), *The Turn of the Screw* (1954), *A Midsummer Night's Dream* (1960), and *Death in Venice* (1973).

Chapter 16

Today and Tomorrow

Today and Tomorrow

The Age of Technology has affected music profoundly in terms of its mood, its pace, its sense of alienation and depersonalization, and in the uses of technology itself. The purposes, techniques, and circumstances of performance have changed. Audio and video have given music a far wider public than ever before, and recording tape, synthesizers, and computers have radically influenced the ways in which music is composed. Popular music has become ever more popular—the English rock group, the Beatles, made more money and reached a wider audience than any other musicians in history. And the interpenetration of "pop" and "serious" music which began with the Jazz Age [see Chapter 15] has continued.

It is difficult to gain perspective on the diverse and sometimes contradictory tendencies of art in one's own time. This chapter will summarize the principal developments in music since World War II, and will suggest a framework for considering the various combinations by modern composers of the old and the new. One of the few certainties is that the music of tomorrow will be influenced at least in part by some of these contemporary tendencies—although no one can predict the exact character of the music of the future.

In contemporary music, melody, harmony, and rhythm—the three fundamental elements of music—have been stretched to their apparent limits. Many composers have pioneered a new approach, insisting that melody and harmony can no longer be taken for granted. In the cacophonous twentieth century, the timbre and the texture of sound itself (and the presence of silence) have become musical values. The avant-garde composer **Edgar Varèse** (1883–1965) was one of the first musicians to direct attention to sound as a "living material". Varèse was born in France and studied at the Paris Conservatory and in the Italian city of Turin. He conducted in Berlin in the years before World War I and in 1915 traveled to America, where he founded a society for the performance of contemporary music in New York. In 1926, Varèse became an American citizen; he combined his composing and conducting duties with teaching at a number of universities. Both in his teaching and in his own works, he was a strong advocate of experimentation with unusual sounds. As early as 1933, he scandalized New York audiences with his piece, *Ionisation*, scored for a large group of percussion instruments exclusively. He is reported to have once remarked, "The century of the airplane deserves its own music." In 1953, he began to incorporate tape recordings of actual sounds into his works; these were sometimes electronically altered, sometimes not.

The direction of Varèse in music was prophetic; a number of modern composers have proceeded to take music even further into the electronic age, advancing far beyond Schoenberg's atonality and serialism. These composers might be called the philosophers, dreamers, and theorists of a new music; they have cared little about reaching large audiences. They are balanced by a group of Modernists who may be called entertainers—serious composers who have always insured that their music contains elements appealing to the public. The entertainers' chief aim has been to communicate to an audience. This group includes Igor Stravinsky [see Chapter 13], Aaron Copland, and Michael Tippett. The theorists have been largely influenced by two seminal composers of this century: Schoenberg's disciple Anton Webern and the French organist Olivier Messiaen. This group includes Karlheinz Stockhausen, Pierre Boulez, György Ligeti, Hans Werner Henze, and the Italians Luciano Berio and Luigi Nono.

Stravinsky [see Chapter 13] announced the advent of Modernist style with his ballets *Petrushka* and *The Rite of Spring*, first performed in Paris in the years just before World War I. By 1917, he was an international figure. He turned away from Romanticism and from the folk sources of the Russian nationalists to seek a new, more economical style in music: Neo-classicism. This was an adaptation of Classical forms to the new currents in music provided by jazz, by the innovations of Debussy and Schoenberg, and by Stravinsky's research in primitive ritual. Almost everything Stravinsky composed is distinguished by powerful, sophisticated rhythms and marked by a theatrical instinct; his music, in a wide variety of forms, is never far from the dance, in which he achieved his greatest early success. The *Symphony in C* (1940) furnishes a good illustration of Stravinsky's combination of theatrical elements, twentieth-century dissonance, Classical form, and provocative rhythms.

Aaron Copland (1900–   ), who has been regarded for some years as the dean of modern American composers, was born in Brooklyn, New York. He studied in Paris with the celebrated teacher of composition, Nadia Boulanger, and inaugurated his composing career in Europe. The lukewarm reception of his early works convinced Copland that his music was too theoretical and he made a conscious decision to incorporate more popular elements. Thus, he borrowed from jazz and from regional music like the folk songs of Appalachia and popular Mexican tunes. He turned to American history and literature for inspiration—for example, his songs based on *Twelve Poems of Emily Dickinson* (1950), his suite of film music for Thornton Wilder's play, *Our Town* (1940), and the famous *Lincoln Portrait* (1942), composed for narrator and orchestra.

Copland's most popular compositions are suites arranged from his ballets; they include *El salón México* (1936)—based on folk melodies that Copland heard during a visit to Mexico City—*Billy the Kid* (1938), *Fanfare for the Common Man* (1942), *Rodeo* (1943), and *Appalachian Spring* (1945). Although Copland also experimented with Schoenberg's atonality—as in his *Short Symphony* of 1933—none of the works written in this style has become established in the concert repertory. Like George Gershwin [see Chapter 15], Copland's greatest achievement was to narrow the gap between "popular" and "serious" music by incorporating elements of both in a series of accessible, attractively melodic works.

The English composer **Michael Tippett** (1905–   ) has pursued much the same course. Tippett studied at the Royal College of Music in London, and served for some time as the music director of Morley College. His music is in the tradition of the English pastoral style, developed by Ralph Vaughan Williams in the early twentieth century [see Chapter 12]. Like Vaughan Williams, Tippett has drawn on Purcell, the early English madrigalists, and popular native folk songs for inspiration. He did not achieve substantial recognition for his music until he was past thirty; but since 1935 he has continued to produce ambitious works in a variety of major forms: oratorio, opera, symphony, concerto, and choral anthem. Essentially a lyrical composer, Tippett has retained melody and harmony as fundamental constituents of music, and nearly all his works possess a melodic impulse that have made them attractive and accessible to audiences. Among his leading compositions are: *Concerto for Double String Or-*

chestra (1939), the oratorio *A Child of Our Time* (1944), four symphonies, and the operas *The Midsummer Marriage* (1955) and *King Priam* (1962). *A Child of Our Time* is especially representative. Based on Tippett's own libretto, its theme is the Nazi persecution of the Jews in the 1930s; in form, it directly recalls Bach's Passions, since Tippett employs Negro spirituals periodically throughout the work, in the same fashion that Bach used chorales.

The philosophical group of composers in this century, in contrast to such figures as Copland and Tippett, has withdrawn from the marketplace. Anton Webern, one of Arnold Schoenberg's most important disciples, and Olivier Messiaen have been the most important influences on this group. Webern's sophisticated experiments with the note-row of serial music, and the extreme brevity of some of his works (one piece, in the collection entitled *6 Pieces* (1910) has only six bars), have emphasized timbre (tone quality), rhythm, and silence over melody and harmony, and have made unprecedented demands on the listener. Especially significant for Webern's followers have been his experiments with apportioning an individual theme among several instruments, thus introducing complex contrasts of timbre. This technique has been called *Klangfarbenmelodie* (literally, "sound-color melody").

Perhaps more accessible to the average audience has been the music of the French organist, **Olivier Messiaen** (1908–   ). Messiaen's works first came to public attention in 1931, the year he was appointed organist at L'Église de la Trinité in Paris (a post he has retained ever since). Although he acknowledges that melody is a necessary element of all music, Messiaen has continually experimented with combining exotic elements from a broad spectrum of sources: ancient Indian ragas, modal harmonies, the gamelan of Indonesia [see Chapter 14], the chromatic chords of Claude Debussy, and many others. He has incorporated the irregular, quantitative rhythms of ancient Greek poetry in his music, and has attempted to assimilate birdsong as a major element in some of his works, having notated and classified the sounds of a large number of birds in France. All of Messiaen's music has been inspired by his deep religious faith and his love of nature; one suspects that his preoccupation with untraditional elements has grown from a conviction that all space and time should be united by music in praise of God. Messiaen's major works include the following: *L'Ascension (The Ascen-*

sion) (1933), the orchestral suite *Oiseaux exotiques (Exotic Birds)* (1956), and the *Messe de la Pentecôte (Pentecostal Mass)* for organ (1950).

At the end of World War II in 1945, composers from the occupied countries of Europe were finally afforded the chance to catch up with new developments in modern music. Especially significant was the international summer school founded at Darmstadt in Germany. The next three composers we will discuss all studied at Darmstadt at crucial turning points in their careers: Karlheinz Stockhausen, Pierre Boulez, and Luciano Berio.

Karlheinz Stockhausen (1928–   ) is perhaps the most audacious composer of the electronic avant-garde. After the war, he studied the music of Schoenberg, Berg, and Webern intensively; he became a pupil of Olivier Messiaen at Darmstadt in 1951. In the 1950s, the advent of more sophisticated technology offered Stockhausen the chance to extend Webern's methods of serialism to the engineering of sound itself. As a professor at Darmstadt and Cologne, Stockhausen has evolved a theory of "dimensions" or "parameters" of sound: these include pitch, intensity, duration, and timbre. His more complex version of serialism involves not only a specific order for the note-row, but all the other sound parameters as well. With his pupils, Stockhausen has electronically transformed melody to micro-melody consisting of one, sustained note. And he has employed technology to transform the duration of sound, into what he calls "moments".

Especially important in the music of Stockhausen (and in a number of other contemporary composers) has been the element of chance (sometimes referred to as a principle of indeterminacy, or as the "aleatory" element, from Latin *alea* for "dice"). Aleatory music has emerged from the self-evident fact that no two performances of a musical work are ever exactly the same. Stockhausen and his followers have therefore left many decisions, traditionally made by the composer, to the discretion of the performer. Thus, in a work called *Zyklus* (1959) for solo percussion, the performer is free to begin on any page of the score, and to continue until a complete cycle is finished. (The performer may also execute the piece by turning over the score and reading the notes from right to left!) Stockhausen has also experimented with the way in which tones can be altered in space (by placing microphones, speakers, and other devices at different locations), and he has introduced electronic feedback, echo-effects, and filters to alter the timbre of his music. Such experiments explicitly acknowledge acoustics in the ultimate quality of sound for an audience at a specific point in time and space.

Much of Stockhausen's music departs so radically from traditional, instrumental composition that it requires a conscious effort from us to suspend our preconceptions. But it is emphatically "serious" music, in that it is constructed, for the most part, on logical systems. Even the principle of indeterminacy has a parallel in the "uncertainty principle" of the observation of tiny particles in modern physics. Stockhausen has enjoyed a considerable public, despite the theoretical tendencies of his music, because he has not hesitated to explore the musical potential of new media. His leading works to date include: *Gruppen* for three orchestras (1957); *Momente* (1964), composed for solo soprano, four choruses, and thirteen instrumentalists; *Prozession* (1967), for tam-tam, piano and electronic sounds; *Gesang der Jünglinge (Song of the Young Boys)* (1956), in which one boy's voice is multiplied on tape so that it produces the sound of a whole chorus; and *Stimmung (Tuning)*, a composition for six unaccompanied singers who vocalize without words.

Similar to Stockhausen in his effort to explore electronic and computer techniques in music has been the French composer and conductor, **Pierre Boulez** (1925–). Boulez also studied with Messiaen at the Darmstadt summer school; like Stockhausen, who became his close friend, Boulez made an intensive study of Webern's serialism. In 1946, his early works—the Piano Sonata No. 1 and the *Sonatine* for flute and piano—established him as a promising composer. They were followed by *Le Marteau sans maître (The Hammer without a Master)* (1955), an unorthodox work for contralto, flute, viola, guitar, vibraphone, and percussion instruments. About this time Boulez started to experiment with electronic sounds and with "concrete music"—the term coined in 1948 by the composer Pierre Schaeffer to differentiate the music of concrete sound objects (natural or manmade) from "artificial" notated music. Boulez was also attracted by the indeterminacy principle: in his Third Piano Sonata of 1957, the five movements of the work can be played in any order, except that the third movement must always occupy the central position. In 1971–74, Boulez served as the principal conductor of the New York Philharmonic Orchestra; he has played a major role in introducing European contemporary music to American audiences. In 1977, he became the director of the French government research institute known as I.R.C.A.M. (Institut de Récherche et de Co-ordination Acoustique/Musique), a central laboratory in Paris for the exploration of new techniques in acoustics and composition.

Although Stockhausen and Boulez have both composed works for voice, the leading vocal composer of their generation is the Italian **Luciano Berio** (1925–   ). Berio has transformed the Italian heritage of operatic music through the use of electronic sound, and also through what he has named the "collage" technique: the use of extensive quotations, by both singers and orchestra, of texts and themes from world literature and from the music of previous composers. An example is his work *A-Ronne* (1974), which he has called a "documentary" for human voices; besides the intelligible, textual elements, the eight singers produce indeterminate sounds, e.g. smacking of the lips, moans, sighs, and whistles. In *Laborintus II* (1965), for voices, instruments, reciter, and tape, street cries combine with disparate elements from jazz and madrigals. Perhaps Berio's most conventional composition is his *Sinfonia* (1968), scored for voices and ordinary instruments: in this work, Berio has compiled an accessible and ingenious collage of themes from the music of Mahler, Wagner, Ravel, and Richard Strauss.

Luigi Nono (1924–   ), one year older than Berio, has also experimented with untraditional works for voice. Nono's work is dominated by his political commitment to socialism: such compositions as his *Epitaffio per García Lorca* (1953), which commemorates the great Spanish poet and playwright (1898–1936) who was executed in the Civil War, display the music of social protest. Nono often obscures the social message of his works, however, through fragmenting their texts: just as melodies, harmonies, and rhythms have been "atomized" by modern composers into tiny, constituent parts, Nono's words are often presented as syllables, letters, and vocalized sounds.

In contrast to Nono, the German composer **Hans Werner Henze** (1926–   ) delivers clear political statements in his works. Henze's early compositions display the influence of Arnold Schoenberg and Anton Webern; later he developed a highly individual, eclectic style, incorporating elements of Stravinsky, Wagner, and Debussy in his music. Fundamentally a dramatist, Henze has used the forms of opera, ballet, solo recital, and choral music to convey his extreme,

Leftist political views. A representative example is his work for baritone, flute, guitar, and percussion instruments entitled *El Cimarrón* (1970), in which the narrator presents a frightening picture (based on a true story) of the life of a runaway Cuban slave. Henze's operas include *Boulevard Solitude* (1951), *König Hirsch (King Stag)* (1955), and *The Bassarids* (1965) (with a libretto by the poet W. H. Auden, based on Euripides' ancient tragedy, *The Bacchae*).

In contrast to many of the most radical modern composers (Stockhausen, Boulez, Berio, and Nono), the Hungarian composer **György Ligeti** (1923–) has refused to employ electronic means since the late 1950s, preferring to write for live performers. Ligeti left Hungary at the time of the Soviet invasion in 1956 and moved to Cologne, where he worked with Stockhausen. Subsequently he settled in Vienna and has produced a stream of richly attractive works in the last quarter of a century. Ligeti derived from Webern the concept of "micropolyphony"—a system involving harmonies of micro-intervals (intervals smaller than those of the twelve-tone scale). His works are lyrical and provocative in their intricate sound textures; among his major compositions are the orchestral *Atmosphères* (1961) and *Melodien* (1971), the *San Francisco Polyphony* (1974), an opera entitled *Le Grand Macabre (The Great Macabre)* (1978), and the Double Concerto for Flute and Oboe (1972). Ligeti has also written a variety of choral works.

Perhaps the most visionary composer of our time is the American **John Cage** (1912–). Cage has combined composing talent with a career as a pianist and writer. His unfettered enjoyment of, and receptivity to, sounds of every sort serves as a touchstone for the music of our age—and also, very likely, for the music of the future. Automobiles, airplanes, electronic noises, birds, and the sound of splashing water are all legitimate musical components for Cage; he has himself declared that he does not deal in musical "purposes" (contrast Nono and Henze), but only in sounds. "Music is continuous," as he said, "it is only we who turn away."

In his music, Cage has attempted to unite the most disparate cultural elements: Oriental philosophies, electronic and visual techniques of the West, environmental noises, silence, etc. His complete abandonment of conventional, formal structures is complemented by an idealistic vision that music—in his broad sense of the term—of all times and places may be unified. Although he studied with Arnold Schoenberg in the 1930s, he rapidly rejected the rigid forms of serialist music: one of his indeterminate compositions, entitled *Music of Changes* (1951), involves the tossing of a coin, while another, called simply *O' O''* (1962) can be performed in any way by anyone. He has used tapes, radios, and gramophone turntables in his scores; and he was the inventor of the "prepared piano", in which objects such as rubberbands and hatpins were inserted between the strings to create new timbral effects. Cage's imaginative richness and his gentle awareness of the potential for beauty in every sound have provoked considerable incomprehension and hostility among conservative critics.

If history is any guide, these composers who in their own time are considered daring and shocking, will in time become accepted, uneventful, and after a time outdated. We can not guess which of today's composers will "last" or which of those whose works are ignored today will be judged by posterity to have been the true giants. Nor can we guess what tomorrow's music, or that of the next century, will be like. We can, however, take it fundamentally for granted that the music of the future will continue to combine the old and the new; and that music—in whatever form and by whatever means—will continue to move people in all places and of all ages. For as long as men and women continue to love and suffer and worship and dance, music will remain the great unifying language, the one that speaks directly to the soul of each of us.

Questions for Review

1. Name two ways in which twentieth-century technology has affected the purposes, techniques, and circumstances of performance of contemporary music.

2. Why was the approach of the composer Edgar Varèse prophetic for much of the music of our time?

3. We may make a rough division of contemporary composers into two groups: the "entertainers" and the "philosophers" or "theorists". How do the objectives of these groups differ? Name at least two prominent representatives of each group.

4. What were some of Aaron Copland's sources of musical inspiration? Name one of Copland's popular symphonic suites.

5. Identify the theme and form of Michael Tippett's oratorio, *A Child of Our Time*.

6. How does Tippett's musical style resemble that of Ralph Vaughan Williams?

7. Identify briefly the following:

   a) *Klangfarbenmelodie*

   b) micropolyphony

   c) indeterminacy principle

   d) Luigi Nono

   e) *The Bassarids*

8. What is the primary motivation of Olivier Messiaen's music?

9. How did Karlheinz Stockhausen extend the "serialist" theory of Anton Webern?

10. How does Pierre Boulez' Third Piano Sonata (1957) illustrate the indeterminacy principle of much contemporary music?

11. Explain the "collage" technique of the Italian composer, Luciano Berio. Name one of Berio's works which illustrates this technique.

12. What is John Cage's vision of the nature and purposes of music? How does his concept contrast with that of such composers as Luigi Nono and Hans Werner Henze?

13. "Modern" music has often turned to the remote past, or to distant lands, for some of its sources and techniques. Select two of the composers discussed in this chapter, and show how their works illustrate the truth of this statement.

Answers

1. Twentieth-century technology (phonographs, tapes, radio, television, etc.) has made music accessible to a far wider audience than ever before. Tape, electronic synthesizers, and computers have also affected techniques of composition; many composers have used them to split the fundamental components of music (melody, harmony, and rhythm) into ever smaller units of time and pitch.

2. Edgar Varèse (1883–1965) experimented with tape and electronic music in the early 1950s; this direction was followed by a number of leading contemporary composers. But, as early as 1933, Varèse had experimented with unusual sounds, e.g. in his piece *Ionisation*, scored for percussion instruments. Varèse's insistence that timbre and texture in music were more im-

portant than traditional melody and harmony was echoed by such composers as Webern, Messiaen, and Stockhausen.

3. The contemporary group of "entertainers" consists of composers like Igor Stravinsky, Aaron Copland, and Michael Tippett. Their objective is to communicate with audiences, and they have always insured that their works contain accessible and attractive elements. The "philosophers" (or "theorists") have largely withdrawn from the marketplace and have not sought large audiences for their compositions; the objective of this group, rather, has been to pioneer new approaches to musical sound and to the fundamental elements of music. This group includes Olivier Messiaen, Karlheinz Stockhausen, Pierre Boulez, Luciano Berio, Luigi Nono, Hans Werner Henze, and John Cage.

4. Copland's sources have included jazz, regional folk-music, and American history and literature. His popular symphonic tone poems and suites are: *El salón México*(1936), *Billy the Kid* (1938), *Fanfare for the Common Man*(1942), *A Lincoln Portrait* (1942), *Rodeo* (1943), and *Appalachian Spring* (1945).

5. Michael Tippett's oratorio *A Child of Our Time* (1944) is a meditation on the theme of the Nazi persecution of European Jews in the years prior to and during World War II. In form, the work recalls the Passions of Johann Sebastian Bach [see Chapter 5], since Tippett employs Negro spirituals throughout the work, in much the same way that Bach used chorales.

6. Tippett's style resembles that of Ralph Vaughan Williams in that both composers were inspired by some of the same sources: e.g. the music of Henry Purcell (1659–1695) and the Elizabethan madrigals. Both Tippett and Vaughan Williams have composed superbly evocative program music in a "pastoral" vein—describing the rural regions of England—and both have been active contributors to Anglican Church music.

7. a) *Klangfarbenmelodie*: literally, "sound-color melody": referring to the complex contrasts in timbre of Anton Webern and his followers—contrasts which were often achieved by fragmenting a melody and sharing it among different instruments.

b) micropolyphony: a system involving harmonies of micro-intervals (smaller than the intervals of the twelve-note scale), associated with the music of a number of modern composers, especially the Hungarian György Ligeti.

c) indeterminacy principle: the element of chance which has been deliberately introduced into music by many modern composers, on the theory that no two performances (even of more traditional works) are ever exactly alike.

d) Luigi Nono: Italian composer who has used his vocal works as political statements for his own socialist views; a prominent example is the *Epitaffio per García Lorca* (1953), which commemorates the Spanish poet and playwright shot by the Fascists in the Civil War.

e) *The Bassarids*: opera by Hans Werner Henze, first performed in 1965, to a libretto by the poet W. H. Auden (based on Euripides' tragedy, *The Bacchae*).

8. The primary motivation of Olivier Messiaen's music has been his profound religious faith. Since 1931, he has served as the organist of the Église de la Trinité in Paris; in his works, he has attempted to incorporate a univer-

sal celebration of God by suggesting sounds from all nature (especially bird-song).

9. Stockhausen extended the "serialist" theory of Anton Webern by applying the technique of the serial note-row to all the other parameters, or dimensions, of music: pitch, intensity, duration, and timbre.

10. Boulez's Third Piano Sonata illustrates the indeterminacy principle because the composer has left the order of playing the five movements almost entirely to the discretion of the pianist: the only requirement is that the third movement of the score occupy the central position in performance.

11. Berio's "collage" technique involves the use of extensive quotations (vocal and orchestral) of texts and themes from world literature and from the music of previous composers. Two works which illustrate the technique are the documentary *A-Ronne* (1974) and the *Sinfonia* of 1968. In the latter, Berio quotes extensively from such composers as Mahler, Ravel, Wagner, and Richard Strauss.

12. John Cage's vision of the nature of music is that it should unite the potential of sounds from every medium and cultural environment, past and present. Thus, Cage has not hesitated to use the noise of radios, turntables, automobiles, and other machines in his music; he combines such sounds with "concrete" music from the world of nature (e.g. birdsong); and he would argue as well that silence is properly considered a musical "sound" in a cacophonous, post-industrial age. As he has said: "Music is continuous; it is only we who turn away." Cage is interested solely in the beauty of sounds; he has refused to declare a "purpose" for his music. He is thus a representative of absolute music (as opposed to program music) in our time; and his concept differs markedly from that of Luigi Nono and Hans Werner Henze, who have regarded music as a vehicle of political and social protest.

13. Some of the ways in which modern music has turned to remote traditions, either chronological or geographical:

a) Olivier Messiaen's use of Indian ragas, ancient Greek rhythms, the medieval modes, and the timbre of the Indonesian gamelan.

b) Igor Stravinsky's combination of jazz and primitive ritual motifs with classical forms, in his "Neo-classical" compositions.

c) Michael Tippett's use of folk song, madrigals, and Baroque techniques in his anthems and oratorios.

d) Luciano Berio's "collage" technique, involving extensive musical and textual quotations from a wide variety of composers and authors in world literature.

Glossary

absolute music. Music which has no literary "program". [See "tone-poem".]

antiphonal. A style of music in which two choirs (or groups of instruments) sing (or play) separate musical phrases in alternation with each other. The term is particularly used to denote such a performance of Gregorian chant.

aria. A highly developed form of song, usually for solo voice, characteristic of Baroque opera and cantata (see "da capo"). The term continued to be used into the Classic and Romantic eras, where it acquired a more general meaning.

atonal. In twentieth century music (and particularly in the music of Arnold Schoenberg and his disciples), a style of composition that is distinguished by the absence of a clearly defined key-center.

canon. A polyphonic composition in which each part sings or plays the same melody beginning at a different time specified by a rule, or "canon". The folk-tune Frere Jacques is a particular kind of canon known as a "round".

chamber music. Music composed for a small ensemble of instruments (such as the string quartet or piano trio) intended for performance as diversionary music for the entertainment of a patron, or for the enjoyment of the performers.

chord. The simultaneous sounding of two or more musical pitches.

chromaticism. A style of composition in which most or all of the twelve notes of the chromatic scale are freely employed.

da capo. Literally, "from the top" (Italian). A type of solo vocal composition (aria) widely employed in Baroque opera and cantata whose musical structure consists of an opening section in the home key, a middle section which contrasts in key and often in mood, followed by a return to the opening section played either in its entirety or in an abbreviated form. The name derives from the fact that instead of writing the opening section out twice, the composer indicated its repeated performance merely by writing "da capo" in the score.

dynamic range. The technical term which refers to the loudness or softness of music. A composition which exhibits a wide divergence of extremes is said to have a wide dynamic range.

form. In its general sense, the overall structure of a musical composition. In a more specific sense, form denotes certain commonly encountered types of compositions, such as "sonata form", or "concerto form". [See Introduction for a discussion of the more important genres.]

formes fixes. The standardized forms of medieval French poetry: ballade, rondeau, and virelai [see Chapter 2].

incidental music. Music composed to be performed in conjunction with the performance of a stage play to set the mood and highlight events; the nineteenth-century equivalent of a movie soundtrack.

interval. The vertical distance between two musical pitches.

libretto. Literally, "little book" (Italian). The term given to the entire text of a large-scale vocal composition of the Baroque period such as a cantata, opera, passion, etc.

lute. A plucked stringed instrument with frets and six or more pairs of strings called "courses". The lute was extensively used in the Middle Ages, Renaissance, and Baroque periods, though it was subsequently superceded by the guitar as the most popular such instrument.

Mass. The central act of worship in the Roman Catholic Church. The Mass commemorates Christ's Last Supper and Sacrifice on the Cross. The text of the Mass consists of certain invariable portions called the Ordinary (Kyrie, Gloria, Credo, Sanctus, Agnus Dei), and certain portions called the Proper which change in accordance with the ecclesiastical calendar. The sections of the Ordinary are those most commonly set to music.

melisma. A musical pattern in which many notes are set to a single syllable of text.

meter. The organization of the rhythmic pulse of music into regular patterns of accented and unaccented notes. Duple meter consists of a pattern of two pulses every other one of which receives an accent: ONE-two ONE-two. Triple meter organizes patterns of three pulses in this way: ONE-two-three ONE-two-three. Quadruple meter: ONE-two-three-four ONE-two-three-four.

mode. In its most general sense, "mode" refers to a systematic organization of pitches which functions as a background basis for the creation of melodic patterns. The most familiar modes are the modern Major and Minor modes. Note that a "mode" differs from a "key": the term "mode" denotes the general class of which a particular "key" is an example. In its historical sense, "the modes" refers to a system of eight such background structures which formed the theoretical basis of Gregorian chant and polyphonic music until nearly the seventeenth century.

notation. The familiar system of lines, notes, and symbols by which music is written down. Modern musical notation evolved only very slowly since the Middle Ages; the history of the writing of music runs parallel to the history of music itself.

plainsong. A kind of liturgical chant consisting of a single vocal line sung in unison by a choir of religious. The term is commonly used as a synonym for Gregorian chant.

polytonality. In twentieth-century music, a harmonic style in which music in more than one key is played simultaneously.

ragas. The Indian system of musical modes. [See "modes".]

recitative. A style of narrative vocal composition in which the words take precedence over melodic considerations. Originally employed in Baroque opera and cantata, elements of the recitative style continued to be employed in the Classic and Romantic eras. In operas as late as those composed by Mozart, recitative is often accompanied solely by the harpsichord ("recitativo secco" literally, "dry recitative"). Another style, called "accompanied recitative", continued to be employed in the operas of Verdi, though in his mature works the lines of distinction between recitative and aria become somewhat blurred.

Requiem. The Roman Catholic Mass for the Dead. The "German Requiem" by Johannes Brahms is set to biblical passages chosen by the composer (a Protestant) rather than to the traditional texts. It is called "Requiem" because it was composed upon the death of Brahms's mother.

responsorial. A style of performing Gregorian chant in which a single soloist, or cantor, intones the initial phrase of text which is then taken up by the entire choir.

scale. An organizational pattern which distributes musical pitches in an orderly fashion through an octave. There are many different kinds of scales; the most familiar is the "diatonic major scale" which distributes the pitches in the following way: W-W-H-W-W-W-H. (W represents a Whole-step; H represents a Half-step.) [See Introduction for further discussion.]

serialism. A technique of composition invented by Arnold Schoenberg (1874-1851) in which all twelve pitches of the chromatic scale are organized in a pattern known as a "tone row". This row or series then is employed to govern the compositional procedure.

tempo. The rate at which the rhythmic pulses of a composition move. Tempo is said to be quick if the pulses move rapidly; it is said to be slow if they move at a more moderate rate of speed.

texture. The specific quality of musical composition or a portion of it. Texture may be described by certain technical terms such as monophonic, homophonic, or polyphonic [see Introduction]. It may also be spoken of in qualitative terms such as "thin", "thick", "heavy", or "light".

timbre. Tone-color. That is, the specific quality of sound that differentiates the tone of a violin, say, from that of a flute.

tone cluster. A twentieth-century sonority in which a number of adjacent pitches are sounded simultaneously.

tone poem. A composition which seeks to express or represent in music a specific theme, place or event. Such music is called "program" music, because it depends upon an external literary text (program) for its structure, rather than strictly upon internal musical form.

viols. A family of bowed stringed instruments widely used in the Renaissance, the precursors of the violin family. They differ from the latter in having much deeper bodies, fretted finger-boards, and six (rather than four) strings.

virginals. A plucked-string keyboard instrument similar to the harpsichord, popular in Elizabethan England.

word-painting. A musical technique in which the meaning of a text is mirrored in the musical gesture to which it is set, e.g., a rising melody set to words referring to the rising sun.

Index

275